Old Testament Cosmology and Divine Accommodation

Old Testament Cosmology and Divine Accommodation

A Relevance Theory Approach

John W. Hilber

CASCADE *Books* • Eugene, Oregon

OLD TESTAMENT COSMOLOGY AND DIVINE ACCOMMODATION
A Relevance Theory Approach

Copyright © 2020 John W. Hilber. All rights reserved. Except for brief quotations in critical publications or reviews, no part of this book may be reproduced in any manner without prior written permission from the publisher. Write: Permissions, Wipf and Stock Publishers, 199 W. 8th Ave., Suite 3, Eugene, OR 97401.

Cascade Books
An Imprint of Wipf and Stock Publishers
199 W. 8th Ave., Suite 3
Eugene, OR 97401

www.wipfandstock.com

PAPERBACK ISBN: 978-1-5326-7621-5
HARDCOVER ISBN: 978-1-5326-7622-2
EBOOK ISBN: 978-1-5326-7623-9

Cataloging-in-Publication data:

Names: Hilber, John W., author.

Title: Old Testament cosmology and divine accommodation : a relevance theory approach / John W. Hilber.

Description: Eugene, OR: Cascade Books, 2020. | Includes bibliographical references and index.

Identifiers: ISBN: 978-1-5326-7621-5 (PAPERBACK). | ISBN: 978-1-5326-7622-2 (HARDCOVER). | ISBN: 978-1-5326-7623-9 (EBOOK).

Subjects: LCSH: Biblical cosmology. | Relevance theory. | Bible. OT—Criticism, interpretation, etc. | Bible. Genesis—Criticism, interpretation, etc.

Classification: BS651 P37 2020 (print). | BS651 (epub).

Manufactured in the U.S.A.

Scripture quotations marked (ESV) are taken from The Holy Bible, English Standard Version® (ESV®) Copyright © 2001 by Crossway, a publishing ministry of Good News Publishers. All rights reserved. ESV Text Edition: 2016.

Scripture quotations marked (NIV) are taken from the Holy Bible, New International Version®, NIV®. Copyright © 1973, 1978, 1984, 2011 by Biblica, Inc.™ Used by permission of Zondervan. All rights reserved worldwide. www.zondervan.com The "NIV" and "New International Version" are trademarks registered in the United States Patent and Trademark Office by Biblica, Inc.™

Scripture quotations marked (NJPS) are taken from the TANAKH: The Holy Scriptures: the new JPS translation according to the traditional Hebrew text, copyright © 1985. Used by permission. All rights reserved.

Scripture quotations marked (NRSV) are taken from the New Revised Standard Version Bible, copyright © 1989 National Council of the Churches of Christ in the United States of America. Used by permission. All rights reserved worldwide.

Unless indicated otherwise, translations from the Bible are my own.

For our daughters
Janice Elaine
and
Adrienne Jean†

Contents

List of Figures | x

Preface | xi

Acknowledgments | xiii

Abbreviations | xv

Introduction | 1

1. Reading with Relevance Theory | 5

2. Assessing the Ancient Cognitive Environment | 43

3. Divine Accommodation in Historical Perspective | 84

4. Accommodation and Relevance | 127

5. Validation of Relevance and Theological Implications | 153

Bibliography | 185

Ancient Texts Index | 203

Author Index | 211

Figures

Figure 1: Ancient Cosmic Geography | 45

Figure 2: Egyptian Creation | 62

Figure 3: Babylonian Sun-God Tablet | 64

Figure 4: Babylonian World Map | 66

Figure 5: Inferred Interpretation | 133

Preface

Since my days as a geology major at the University of Washington, I have wrestled with understanding the nature of cosmological language in the Old Testament in the light of science. There have been many helpful discussions on this subject across the centuries. In one form or another, they incorporate the notion that God accommodated himself to the limitations of human language in Scripture. As valuable as these contributions have been, I never found them fully satisfying. It remains to be seen how satisfying this book will be, which incorporates a relatively recent model of communication called *relevance theory*. Hopefully, it advances the conversation.

My research on this began as a paper I delivered in 2011 to a small group of Old Testament colleagues in which I applied relevance theory as a means of evaluating different reading strategies for Gen 1. This small symposium, sponsored by the John Templeton Foundation, gave rise to a slightly larger, interdisciplinary symposium in 2013; and the momentum of those two gatherings eventuated in the Creation Project, undertaken by the Henry Center at Trinity Evangelical Divinity School and funded by the Templeton Religion Trust. It was in this context that the bulk of my work took place. At the time of this writing, the Creation Project is completing its third year and about to embark on another three-year iteration. Anyone who has been involved in the project can attest to the fruitfulness of this multidisciplinary conversation. In discussions concerning the advancement of Christian doctrine, we often forget that it has always been, historically, a very slow process; and rightly so. Matters of Christian faith and practice involve questions of eternal significance.

Of course, the topic of divine accommodation is meaningful only if God has spoken in Scripture. Readers who do not share this presupposition will only find this book to be an interesting experiment in linguistic theory. Those who take Scripture as in some sense divinely inspired will perhaps be challenged to think in new ways about what dual authorship entails. It is the particular strength of relevance theory to evaluate how language engages the broader context of ideas and assumptions in the cognitive environment of speakers and listeners, or authors and readers. This leads to the heart of how the language of the Old Testament relates to the cosmological ideas of ancient Israel. Not only are there implications for the doctrine of Scripture, but significant theological ideas can also be considered in different light by the application of relevance theory.

If readers attend to anything beyond this preface, may it be my acknowledgement of the people and organizations who have helped me on my way in this project. But if they wish to venture beyond this, chapter 1 is most essential, as it lays out the basic groundwork and application of relevance theory. Next in importance are the technical discussions in chapter 4, which address accommodation directly. I have intentionally left unwritten a concluding chapter, for fear that some would simply read the conclusion and make a judgment without having understood the theory underlying it.

John W. Hilber
Lent 2019

Acknowledgments

During my 2016–2017 sabbatical, I enjoyed the great fortune of participating as a Senior Research Fellow on the Creation Project at the Henry Center, Trinity Evangelical Divinity School. My wife and I recall fondly the warm hospitality of staff and faculty. Of course the entire project would not exist were it not for the generous funding by the Templeton Religion Trust, whose only expectation on me was that I do my best work. I also wish to thank my home institution, Grand Rapids Theological Seminary, for releasing me for an extended, full-year sabbatical—a high price paid by my colleagues in a small institution!

Many individuals contributed to the joy and fruitfulness of my time there. Geoffrey Fulkerson and Joel Chopp not only managed daily affairs but offered their warm friendship, as did codirectors Dick Averbeck and Tom McCall. Dick Averbeck was a valued dialogue partner on ancient Near Eastern backgrounds, as was Jim Hoffmeier on things Egyptological. Other Henry Fellows included Jack Collins, Hans Madueme, Clinton Ohlers, and Todd Patterson, whose daily conversation I enjoyed on many matters beyond the formal topic at hand. The fingerprints of these wonderful colleagues are all over this work; of course they are not responsible for any smudges!

Numerous other scholars made substantial contribution to my work. In addition to those mentioned in the "Special Acknowledgement" below, Lawson Younger and Kevin Vanhoozer sharpened my understanding of ancient cosmology and hermeneutics. I thank Brad Gundlach and Mickey Mattox, historical theologians, for carefully reading my chapter on the history of thought and commenting extensively. Help on historical matters also arose from Paul Fields and Karin Maag at Calvin College's Meeter Center and from Todd VandenBerg on anthropology. Jeffrey Stevenson offered his general linguistic sensibilities, and Vern Poythress gave helpful critical reflection. His recent book, *Interpreting Eden: A Guide to Faithfully Reading and Understanding Genesis 1–3*, did not appear in time for integration into this book; however, I have interacted with numerous of his articles that underlie *Interpreting Eden*. Jeremy Funk, copy editor for Wipf and Stock, has my gratitude for cleaning up my style in many places. There are no doubt others whose names I've overlooked. Please forgive my failed memory.

My wife, Charlotte, deserves recognition for leaving behind her cozy cottage in Grand Rapids to live once again in student housing for the third time in our married life! If she had not already understood basic contours of relevance theory based on her own grasp of contextual communication in family systems, I would surely have broken her long-suffering patience. Thank you, dear, for enduring my endless chatter on this subject.

Special Acknowledgment

I want to thank my former colleague Joe Fantin for introducing me to the basic concepts of relevance theory. It was this fruitful interaction that led me to begin thinking about creation texts and accommodation in relevance theoretic terms over a decade ago. I am not formally trained in linguistics, and had it not been for the considerable help of Gene Green and Christoph Unger, my arguments would have been a mess. Any remaining weaknesses are not attributable to my tutors in relevance theory, to be sure. Joe provided constant encouragement throughout the project that my application had promise in advancing the discussion. Gene Green came alongside early on with considerable help in the crucial chapters 1 and 4. Then Christoph Unger undertook a laborious reading of the whole manuscript, chapter 4 twice (!) and commented in generous detail. My debt to them cannot be repaid.

Abbreviations

ABS	Archaeology and Biblical Studies
ACCS	Ancient Christian Commentary on Scripture
AfO	*Archiv für Orientforschung*
AnBib	Analecta Biblica
ANET	*Ancient Near Eastern Texts*. Edited by James B. Pritchard. 3rd ed. Princeton: Princeton University Press, 1969
AOAT	Alter Orient und Altes Testament
BA	*Biblical Archaeologist*
BBR	*Bulletin for Biblical Research*
BBRSup	*Bulletin for Biblical Research Supplements*
BK	*Bibel und Kirche*
BSac	*Bibliotheca Sacra*
BZAW	Beihefte zur Zeitschrift für die alttestamentliche Wissenschaft
BWA(N)T	Beiträge zur Wissenschaft vom Alten (und Neuen) Testament
CAD	*The Assyrian Dictionary*. 20 vols. Edited by Ignace J. Gelb et al. Chicago: University of Chicago Press, 1956–2010
CAT	*Cuneiform Alphabetic Texts from Ugarit, Ras Ibn Hani and Other Places*, M. Dietrich et al., Münster: Ugarit-Verlag, 1997; see Simon B. Parker, *Ugaritic Narrative Poetry*

CHANE	Culture and History of the Ancient Near East
COS	*The Context of Scripture*, ed. 4 vols. William W. Hallo and K. Lawson Younger Jr. Leiden: Brill, 1997–2017
CM	Cuneiform Monographs
CT	Coffin Text
CTJ	*Calvin Theological Journal*
EA	El-amarna tablets
EM	Egyptian Museum, Cairo
FAT	Forschungen zum Alten Testament
GKC	E. Kautzsch, *Gesenius' Hebrew Grammar*. 2nd ed. Translated by A. E. Cowley. Oxford: Clarendon, 1910
GMTR	Guides to the Mesopotamian Textual Record
HTS	Harvard Theological Studies
JANES	*Journal of the Ancient Near Eastern Society*
JBL	*Journal of Biblical Literature*
JCS	*Journal of Cuneiform Studies*
JETS	*Journal of the Evangelical Theological Society*
JSJSup	Journal for the Study of Judaism Supplements
JNES	*Journal of Near Eastern Studies*
JNSL	*Journal of Northwest Semitic Languages*
JSOTSup	Journal for the Study of the Old Testament Supplement Series
KTU	*Die keilalphabetishe Texte aus Ugarit*, M. Dietrich et al., Neukirchen-Vluyn, 1976; see Simon B. Parker, *Ugaritic Narrative Poetry*
NICOT	New International Commentary on the Old Testament
OtSt	*Oudtestamentische studiën*
PAe	Probleme der Ägyptologie

PT	Pyramid Texts
RBS	Resources for Biblical Study
RS	Ugaritic texts from Ras Shamra
SAA	State Archives of Assyria
SAACT	State Archives of Assyria Cuneiform Texts
SBL	Society of Biblical Literature
SHANE	Studies in the History of the Ancient Near East
SNTSMS	Society for New Testament Studies Monograph Series
SSN	Studia Semitica Neerlandica
SymS	Symposium Series
TBN	Themes in Biblical Narrative
TynBul	*Tyndale Bulletin*
UET	Ur excavation texts
UF	*Ugarit-Forschungen*
VT	*Vetus Testamentum*
WAW	Writings from the Ancient World
WAWSup	Writings from the Ancient World Supplement Series
WMANT	Wissenschaftliche Monographien zum Alten und Neuen Testament
WTJ	*Westminster Theological Journal*
ZÄS	*Zeitschrift für ägyptische Sprache und Altertumskunde*

Introduction

Reading Contextually

A friend and colleague of mine once said, "Linguistics has a way of taking simple ideas and making them complicated." There is a measure of truth in this. But linguistics can also bring a much-needed level of precision into discussions that involve complicated questions. How we read ancient texts, and biblical creation texts in particular, is one of those complicated questions. It is complicated first by the languages in which ancient Near Eastern literature is written. All of these—classical Hebrew, Akkadian, Hittite, Ugaritic, Egyptian—ceased to be spoken long ago, making it impossible to consult native speakers, who had intuitive instincts about the use of these languages. Moreover, since languages do not function in a cultural vacuum, even a modern reader with competence in basic word meanings and grammar still faces the challenge of cultural literacy.

When we commit ourselves to the *historical*-grammatical method of exegesis, consideration of the original cultural context is explicitly embedded in the method. But, even though everyone endeavors to read contextually, the results can vary widely due to the manner with which different interpreters draw upon cultural background. This is nowhere more evident than in the interpretation of Old Testament creation texts.[1] By applying to these texts a model of communication called *relevance theory*, I hope to bring a different type of methodological rigor to bear on some long-disputed problems for interpreting these texts.

---

1. E.g., Barton and Wilkinson, *Reading Genesis after Darwin*, esp. chapters 1–4; Charles, *Reading Genesis 1–2*; Halton, *Genesis: History, Fiction, or Neither?*

Reading with Relevance Theory

Relevance theory has been discussed among linguistics and literary critics for decades, but it has received only minor attention in biblical studies. So, for those not familiar with relevance theory, the first part of Chapter 1 provides an introduction. Linguistic discussions are often difficult to follow because of the plethora of technical vocabulary unique to the discipline. I have attempted to reduce technical terms and definitions to a minimum while at the same time remaining true to the theory. Relevance theory's strength is its focus on how discourse relies on contextual assumptions for meaning. This makes it particularly suited to address some of the difficulties at the heart of the disagreement among interpreters of biblical creation texts.

After a linguistic introduction, the bulk of Chapter 1 applies relevance theory directly to specific issues pertinent to this debate, using Genesis 1 as a sample text. The discussion addresses the following questions: What role does literal interpretation play in communication? What can we assume about the accessibility of ancient Near Eastern creation traditions to the Israelite context? How does relevance theory complement already established principles of the comparative method? How does the language of Gen 1 guide contextual inference in Israel's cognitive environment? If discourse is largely dependent on cultural context for meaning, how do we account for Christian interpretation during nearly two thousand years when access to the original cognitive environment of Gen 1 was lost?

Assessing the Ancient Cognitive Environment

One of the difficulties for understanding biblical creation texts is reconstructing the cosmology that is implicit in the background of text. Further complicating this difficulty is the substantial difference between the way modern and prescientific people construct mental models of how the natural world functions. Consequently there is a diversity of opinion among modern interpreters who attempt to reconstruct ancient models of cosmic geography. In past decades modern reconstructions have depicted ancient cosmological models in a rather literal fashion. Recent opinion among specialist is shifting to emphasize a more metaphorical meaning in the way ancient Near Eastern texts and iconography employ cosmology. But in my opinion, this change is often marked by a degree of overcorrection. Chapter 2 revisits the textual and iconographic evidence to discern the basic contours of ancient cosmography, and along with these it examines some Old Testament expressions that might presume similar assumptions about cosmology. This discussion sets the stage for consideration of the doctrine of accommodation, which throughout the history of Christian interpretation has been invoked to account for difficulties between the language of the biblical text and certain real-world perceptions of the physical cosmos.

Divine Accommodation in Historical Perspective

Chapter 3 reviews the doctrine of divine accommodation used by the church throughout its history. In special focus is the church's interpretation of cosmological texts and their relationship to natural science. The history of interpretation is more complex than is usually presumed, and many contemporary discussions regarding the interpretation of Old Testament creation texts offer imbalanced presentations of viewpoints held by church scholars over the centuries. Proper understanding of these complexities is necessary not only for situating modern debate over the interpretation of Gen 1 but also for clarifying the exact nature of divine accommodation. In spite of a long history of use, difficulties remain in debate, such as the supposed distinction between accommodation in *manner* of speech in contrast to *matters* of content. The recently revived distinction between positive and negative accommodation does not offer a satisfying solution either. This chapter-length survey clarifies some problems that remain in discussion.

Accommodation and Relevance

As discussed in Chapter 3, there is a fundamental problem defining exactly what accommodation entails. In addition, when considering matters related to cosmology, most would include the human author with the audience among those for whom the language of Scripture has been adapted by a *divine* author. But since accommodation presupposes the dual authorship of Scripture, how does one maintain the unity in meaning of the text when the divine author and human author have different understandings about the nature of the cosmos to which the biblical text alludes. Relevance theory offers a framework that allows separation between implicit assumptions on the one hand and authorial intent on the other. So chapter 4 introduces some important concepts from relevance theory that were not introduced in chapter 1 and applies them to consider cosmological assumptions that may or may not be implicated by the author's informative intention.

Validation and Theological Implications

Alongside questions about the appropriate reading strategy for creation texts (Chapter 1), reconstructing implicit assumptions about ancient Near Eastern cosmology (Chapter 2), as well as the notion of divine accommodation (Chapters 3 and 4), there are related theological issues for which relevance theory provides guidance. Since judging expectations of relevance for an ancient communication situation is difficult, chapter 5 validates the conclusions of the previous chapters by briefly examining intertextual use of Genesis 1 elsewhere in the Old Testament. Methodologically related to intertextuality *within* the Old Testament, the long-established notion of "polemics" in Old Testament literature extends the consideration of intertextuality *beyond* the Old Testament canon to ancient Near Eastern traditions and literature more generally. Along with the canonical method of reading Genesis 1, this chapter also considers the important doctrine of creation ex nihilo in the light of relevance theory. Finally, relevance theory is germane to the discussion of whether a Trinitarian reading of Genesis 1 is possible. This illustrates the rich potential for incorporating relevance theory in the theological interpretation of Scripture.

Relevance theory is only one hermeneutical tool. It does not replace, contradict, or dismantle other theories, such as speech-act; rather it complements approaches that have already proven useful. However, relevance theory has been under-utilized in biblical studies. Hopefully this application of relevance theory will demonstrate that it offers an important new perspective, not only for advancing the conversation on creation texts, the doctrine of accommodation, and the theological interpretation of Scripture, but also for biblical hermeneutics in general. In relevance theory's own terms, grappling with linguistic theory demands exceptional, mental-processing effort on the part of the reader; however, it rewards such effort with worthwhile cognitive benefits.

1

Reading with Relevance Theory

Communication and Context

Once, on my way out of seminary chapel, I said to a colleague, "I'm going to keep the doctor away." Simultaneously, I held out the apple that was in my hand. My informative intention[1] was reinforced by the fact that chapel lets out just before lunch. My meaning was "I'm going to eat an apple now for lunch." Effective communication depended on three factors in this context: (1) the shared knowledge in our institution that people often eat lunch immediately after chapel, (2) the visual object to which I drew my friend's attention, and (3) the shared knowledge of a commonly known proverb for which he needed to supply the first half.

Now, if the chapel sermon just heard had been about the efficacy of prayer and fasting for healing, my friend might have concluded that

---

1. Throughout this work I use "informative intention" as the *cognitive effect* a speaker/writer hopes to have on an audience. Biblical scholars commonly use the term "communicative intent" to denote the meaning of someone's discourse. But in technical discussion, relevance theorists restrict the term "communicative intention" to the effort of a speaker to make clear to an audience that he or she wishes to communicate something (see Wilson and Sperber, "Relevance Theory," 611; Sperber and Wilson, "Précis of Relevance," 226). In communication, the intention to communicate is mutually manifest between speaker and audience (i.e., the speaker gains the audience's attention). Sperber and Wilson grant this assumption when there is a captive audience, such as in a lecture or for literary texts such as the Bible (Sperber and Wilson, *Relevance* [1986 ed.], 63). The phrase "informative intent" is also used in speech-act theory to denote an illocution involving information transfer. As used in relevance theory, "informative intention" is broader, including any communicative effect, such as emotional impact or declarative performance.

I was going off to pray (to keep the doctor away) instead of eating lunch immediately. Perhaps my lifting the apple was a gesture to offer it to my friend to eat, since I was going to fast (the opposite meaning from the previous paragraph). If my friend had not been familiar with the proverb "An apple a day keeps the doctor away," he would surely have missed the possibility that my words had anything to do with eating an apple. Awareness of context really matters! But in this case, the chapel message was not in any way associated with healing or eating.

More subtle is how my comment related to a discussion in faculty meeting the previous day on the relative importance of backgrounds outside of the biblical text for accurate interpretation. My comment was immediately understood as continuing that discussion, and it left no doubt in my colleague's mind as to where I weighed in on that issue. The communication process he just experienced validated the importance of background assumptions and so conveyed my sentiments. We shall return to this illustration below to consider how listeners overlook trivia in order to maximize the benefit of what they hear.

Communication is a very complex affair, dependent on more than dictionary definitions and matters of grammatical syntax. Understanding a speaker or author necessitates more than linguistic competence; it also requires some knowledge of the cultural and often the situational context that clarifies and enriches the meaning of an utterance. The above example illustrates how assumptions shared between my colleague and me were cultural (a proverb), situational (time of day, a visual object), and dependent on memory (a recent faculty discussion). The fact that this discussion was particularly important to the both of us was also a factor. Furthermore, it required that my colleague make the right connections between all of these elements in order to infer my informative intention. There was nothing in the words of my utterance that conveyed my meaning without the enrichment from cultural and situational context as well as shared interest. All of this demonstrates how effective communication operates through expected inferences from shared context.[2] Many linguists working on the pragmatic[3] side of communication use

---

2. In terms of biblical studies, it involves the "historical" aspect of *historical*-grammatical exegesis as well as the grammatical (i.e., semantic-syntactical) component.

3. The term "pragmatics" refers to how words are being used in real-life discourse, in contrast to the study of the normative grammar of a language in abstraction from everyday use.

what is termed "relevance theory" to explain how this interpretive process operates.

Relevance Theory: An Introduction

Moving beyond the Code

Even though extrabiblical context has always been acknowledged in hermeneutics, the methodological emphasis in the past has focused primarily on semantics and grammar. This is perhaps due to the fact that until the 1950s, communication theory in general worked with a code model that attended to grammatical syntax and to the semantics of words that could be interpreted by dictionary reference. But this did not account well for nonpropositional uses of language (e.g., warnings or questions) or for extratextual effects, such as how the text interacts with material or cultural background.[4]

One successful effort to move beyond the code model is speech-act theory.[5] Theorists noted that the code model alone could not account for a speaker's intention, i.e., the full meaning of the discourse, which includes not just the words uttered (locution) but also the disposition and intention of the speaker (illocution).[6] To illustrate: when someone says, "It's cold outside," does this inform someone about air temperature or does it attempt to direct someone to take action based upon the peril of the cold? Speech-act theory addresses this level of communication. But a limitation of speech-act theory is that it has no mechanism for moving beyond the *general intention* of the speaker (to assert information, direct others, commit to action, make declarations, or express attitudes) to validate the *specific content* of the discourse. Let's assume that the utterance about air temperature is a speech-act of direction. Does it urge someone to put on a jacket before going outdoors or is it a plea to a dog owner to bring the poor dog in from the backyard? If the concern is for the dog, perhaps the remedy is to put a canine blanket on him rather than bring

---

4. For the sketch of history of discussion, see Fantin, *The Greek Imperative Mood*, 42–53; and Cummings, *Pragmatics*, 9–18.

5. Austin, *How to Do Things with Words*; Searle, *Speech Acts*. Austin's work was first published in 1962, and Searle further refined the typology of speech-acts.

6. Speech-act theory also includes a third component, perlocution, to denote the resulting outcome of the communicative act. But perlocution is not pertinent to this discussion.

him inside. Nothing linguistically encoded in the semantics of the utterance suggests any of these interpretations, and speech-act theory cannot help in the choice between giving the dog a coat or bringing him inside. In this example, the specific content of intended meaning depends on a customary action *assumed* between the speaker and hearer for dealing with the dog when inclement weather sets in.[7] Meaning is inferred by the hearer through a link between the semantics of the utterance and their shared context.

The limitation of speech-act theory can be illustrated from discussions about the appropriate reading strategy for interpreting Gen 1. One approach maintains that Gen 1 is historical narrative in which the author intends to inform us about chronologically sequenced actions by God in geological history.[8] In speech-act terms, the illocutionary force of the text is informative. Another approach also argues that Gen 1 is narrative but the meaning of the author is limited to theological history.[9] This also views the illocutionary force of the passage as informative. Both judge the text the same way at the illocutionary level; but they interpret the content of that informative act in radically different ways.[10] So speech-act theory is not an adequate linguistic tool to adjudicate their differences, even though appeal to illocution is often invoked in these discussions.[11]

---

7. This is not simply a matter of "application" (or "significance") of a more general request to protect dogs. The specifics are "built into" the communicative event.

8. Beall, "Reading Genesis 1–2," see esp. 49, 59.

9. Longman, "What Genesis 1–2 Teaches," see esp. 106, 110.

10. The terms "genre" and "figurative" appear regularly in these discussions as well, but they are likewise inadequate categories. Without doubt, genre is an important concept, but it is not precise enough for purposes of determining the referential intention of a text. Narrative and poetry both contain figurative language and have referential intent, pointing to real people, places, and events. For example, Judg 4:16 narrates how all the enemy fell by the "mouth" (*peh*) of the sword. This is both metaphor (because swords do not have mouths) and metonymy (because many enemies also died from spears and clubs). At the same time, the poetic rendition of this battle in Judg 5 reports real events in a sequential fashion. Categories of "genre" and "figurative language" cannot in themselves resolve questions of referential intent, which must be addressed at the level of the interaction between the text and its context. For further discussion on how genre functions in a subordinate manner to contextual expectations of relevance, see Unger, *Genre, Relevance and Global Coherence*, esp. 248–51 for summary.

11. John Walton properly recognizes the difference between illocution (informative) and locution (content) (Walton, "Reading Genesis 1 as Ancient Cosmology," 143–45). He argues that the divine author accommodates at the level of locution but not illocution. All this means in speech-act terms is that the divine

Alongside speech-act theory, there emerged in the 1950s and 1960s the work of Paul Grice. Grice examined how meaning is *inferred* from implicit contextual assumptions (e.g., my illustration opening this chapter).[12] He introduced the notion of inference alongside his "cooperative principles" of communication that guide listeners in their interpretive process. He argued that people naturally expect communication to be economical in the *quantity* of words used, truthful in *quality*, appropriate in *relation* to the need of the listener (i.e., relevant), and clear in *manner* of expression. Assuming these principles, listeners infer implications from a speaker's utterance.

Daniel Sperber and Deirdre Wilson subsequently focused on the inferential element of Grice's model, which they argued is driven by contextual *relevance*.[13] Since illocution (disposition of the speaker) is one component of this, speech-act theory relies on broader consideration of contextual relevance.[14] But in addition to illocution, relevance theory

---

author does not deceive. But this does not address the meaning of the content. Walton later discusses "high context" communication and "low context" communication, invoking language of optimization. At this point, even though he does not use the term "relevance theory," Walton is working with similar categories. Unfortunately, his use of speech-act categories is less clear in another work (Walton and Sandy, *The Lost World of Scripture*, 52).

12. Grice, "Logic and Conversation," 22–40.

13. On the development, see Sperber and Wilson, "Pragmatics," 470–73; Cummings, *Pragmatics*, 114. The classic discussion is Sperber and Wilson, *Relevance* (1986 ed.) with a second edition containing an important postscript (Sperber and Wilson, *Relevance* [1995 ed.]). For biblical studies, concise introductions have been offered by Joe Fantin (*The Greek Imperative Mood*, 43–65), Gene Green ("Relevance Theory and Theological Interpretation," 77–82; see also Green, "Lexical Pragmatics and Biblical Interpretation," 799–812; Green, "Relevance Theory and Biblical Interpretation" [2009], 217–40; Green, "Relevance Theory and Biblical Interpretation" [2013], 266–73), and Stephen Pattemore (*The People of God in the Apocalypse*, 13–22). Brief essays by Sperber and Wilson can be found in Sperber and Wilson, "Précis of Relevance," 220–46 (reprint of a 1987 précis of their 1986 book); Wilson and Sperber, "Inference and Implicature," 377–93; Wilson and Sperber, "Relevance Theory," 607–32; and Sperber and Wilson, "Pragmatics," 468–501. The only general introduction to biblical hermeneutics, of which I am aware, that integrates relevance theory at least to some degree into the hermeneutical task, is that of Jeannine Brown (*Scripture as Communication*, see esp. 35–38, 48). A helpful introduction to relevance theory with application to New Testament exegesis is Sim, *A Relevant Way to Read*.

14. Sperber and Wilson, *Relevance* (1995 ed.), 10–11; Vanhoozer, "From Speech Acts to Scripture Acts," 26. Specifically, a listener or reader adopts "the first assumption that is consistent with the principle of relevance," which includes the illocutionary force of the utterance (Sperber and Wilson, *Relevance* [1995 ed.], 248).

gives more attention to the propositional content of an utterance. If the speech-act asserts something as true, relevance theory attends to the contextual assumptions that inform the propositional content. The link that enables a listener to know which inferences are intended by the speaker is contextual relevance. The terms "context" and "relevance" need further explanation.

Cognitive Environment and Context

It was stated earlier that communication draws not only on dictionary entries but on the "encyclopedic" notions that people hold on a given topic and to varying degrees are shared between the parties in any act of communication—specifically, any information that is available for mental processing. The human brain does not organize definitions in simple entries like a dictionary. Rather, concepts are arranged in schemas that people draw on when stimulated "at a moment's notice" by another person's utterance. Gene Green writes, "No dictionary is capable of embracing all the possible concepts that a lexeme's template may suggest."[15] In terms perhaps more familiar to readers in biblical hermeneutics, Sperber and Wilson use the phrase "cognitive environment."[16] Technically speaking, "cognitive environment" includes anything the audience is *capable* of being aware of, while "context" refers to the subset of the cognitive environment pertinent to a particular communication event. In Sperber and Wilson's words, context is "the set of premises used in interpreting an utterance."[17]

They define context very broadly:

> A context in this sense is not limited to information about the immediate physical environment or the immediately preceding utterances: expectations about the future, scientific hypotheses or religious beliefs, anecdotal memories, general cultural assumptions, beliefs about the mental state of the speaker, may all play a role in interpretation.[18]

---

15. Green, "Lexical Pragmatics and the Lexicon," 323.
16. Sperber and Wilson, *Relevance* (1995 ed.), 38–40.
17. Sperber and Wilson, *Relevance* (1995 ed.), 15.
18. Sperber and Wilson, *Relevance* (1995 ed.), 15–16.

As summarized by Gene Green, context includes "all the assumptions which are accessed in order to interpret an utterance."[19]

This leads to another important consideration of context: the notion of accessibility. Some perceptions or phenomena in an environment may be more manifest than others. Contrast, for example, a conversation in an elevator to the music playing softly from a speaker in the elevator, or the mental accessibility of recent headline news compared to the events of last week. But the attention garnered by each stimulus is relative to each individual. What if the music playing in the elevator is a favorite song, or an event of the previous week was a birth in your family? As Gutt writes, "different degrees of accessibility . . . make themselves felt by the amount of effort their retrieval requires."[20] In the cases just mentioned, the inclination of our thoughts to attend to one stimulus over another is not only a function of audible volume or distance of memory, but is measured by relevance. The greater the relevance, the less effort access requires.

Relevance

How does "relevance" work in communication? Since context has no practical limit, Sperber and Wilson argue that communication must be *optimally* relevant to help the listener navigate effectively through a wide array of possible meanings.[21] First, people expect some cognitive benefit for their attention, whether it be *new information, support for existing*

---

19. Green, "Relevance Theory and Biblical Interpretation" (2009), 235.

20. Gutt, *Translation and Relevance*, 28.

21. Sperber and Wilson are careful to differentiate between two principles. The first is the "Cognitive Principle" whereby "Human cognition tends to be geared to the maximisation of relevance." The second is the "Communicative Principle" whereby "Every act of ostensive communication communicates a presumption of its own optimal relevance" (Sperber and Wilson, "Pragmatics," 260–61). The first principle is an aspect of biological survival and adaptation accompanied by a penchant to optimize use of resources, including cognitive. The second principle is related to the first in that parties of communication generally assume optimization. As Sperber and Wilson describe it, "the First Principle does indeed make the cognitive behaviour of another human predictable enough to guide communication" (Sperber and Wilson, "Pragmatics," 263). They write, "interlocutors always share at least one common goal, that of understanding and being understood" (Sperber and Wilson, "Pragmatics," 268). What constitutes "optimal" will vary from culture to culture. For example, communicators are ordinarily expected to follow rules of etiquette (Wilson and Sperber, "Truthfulness and Relevance," 65), but these are culturally relative.

beliefs, or *correction of mistaken ideas*.[22] Their attention is attuned to look for some benefit in the discourse, not just trivia; in this sense it is "relevant." Second, people naturally begin a conversation with contextual awareness organized in the order of mental accessibility (whether immediate environment or memory as illustrated above).[23] What an utterance does is draw an audience's attention to certain elements in the cognitive environment to make them mutually manifest to all parties.[24] The utterance creates a subset from the cognitive environment to be used in mental processing, that is, it creates a more specific context.[25] This guides the audience to link those contextual elements necessary to infer meaning. When successful, this results in the cognitive effects that the speaker wishes to bring about in the minds of audience members (e.g., information transfer, emotional impact, persuasive force). Along with this, a speaker is also expected to use words judiciously and not to place an unnecessary burden on hearers to process the information.[26] So a speaker chooses an utterance that is adequate to guide the hearers in their choice of contextual elements but requires a minimal effort from the hearers to process.[27] In this sense, communication is "optimal." In Sperber and Wilson's words, an audience "will follow a path of least effort in computing cognitive effects: Test interpretive hypotheses (disambiguations, reference resolutions, implications, etc.) in the order of accessibility" [i.e., what first comes to mind], and processing will "stop when [their] expectations of relevance are satisfied (or abandoned)."[28]

22. Gutt, *Translation and Relevance*, 29; Sperber and Wilson, "Pragmatics," 473.

23. Gutt, *Translation and Relevance*, 28. Gutt writes, "The crucial point is that all this information is *ordered* in terms of degrees of *accessibility*: the initial context is the most accessible information, followed by encyclopaedic information directly associated with the concepts in the stimulus; any further extensions of the context, e.g., via concepts in those encyclopedic entries are less accessible, and incur extra processing cost and so forth" (Gutt, "Aspects of 'Cultural Literacy'," 5).

24. Sperber and Wilson, *Relevance* (1995 ed.), 61–63.

25. Green, "Relevance Theory and Biblical Interpretation" (2009), 229.

26. As noted above regarding optimal relevance, what constitutes an "unnecessary burden" is culturally relative. This becomes important in later discussion regarding why modern audiences might fail to understand what was obvious to an ancient audience. The ancient author is at liberty to take shortcuts, so to speak, in communicating with the ancient audience; but we moderns experience the brevity as a burden. Conversely, moderns impose assumptions on ancient texts that are foreign to their context. It is simply the reality of secondary-communication situations discussed below.

27. Gutt, *Translation and Relevance*, 31–32.

28. Wilson and Sperber, "Relevance Theory," 613; Sperber and Wilson,

They add, "when a hearer following the path of least effort arrives at an interpretation that satisfies his expectations of relevance, in the absence of contrary evidence, this is the most plausible hypothesis about the speaker's meaning."[29] Experimental testing has confirmed the outcomes predicted by relevance theory.[30] One might use the analogy of an internet-capable device searching for an accessible Wi-Fi network in the order of network names prioritized by the device's network settings. The device connects to the first available network in the order listed.

Returning to our opening illustration, my utterance about "keeping the doctor away" was initiated independently of what my colleague and I were just chatting about. However, my friend immediately inferred from contextual factors, including the apple, the proverb, and the time of day, that I was stating my intention to eat an apple for lunch. However, this in itself might be a rather trivial proposition. So my colleague did not stop processing my comment. He was looking beyond the trivial for more cognitive benefit. Given our shared interest in the current faculty discussion about the role of context, my friend understood my utterance as a reassertion by example of the importance of context in exegesis. That constituted a more significant cognitive effect, and he replied with a smile and a friendly chuckle because we happened to disagree to some extent on this issue. As Robyn Carston notes, speakers provide adequate, quality stimulus to guide the listener, and listeners are "entitled to expect . . . a worthwhile range of cognitive effects."[31] Sperber and Wilson conclude, "Our central claim has been that in normal circumstances the deductive processing of an assumption involves computation of its non-trivial implications, never of its trivial ones."[32]

From Conversation to Literature

Most linguistic discussions on relevance theory involve communication in an oral, conversational setting. Communication in these situations tends to be much more dependent on nonverbal context, including objects in the vicinity, gestures, voice intonation, and the interests of those

---

"Pragmatics," 474–75.
29. Wilson and Sperber, "Relevance Theory," 614.
30. Henst and Sperber, "Testing the Cognitive," 279–306.
31. Carston, *Thoughts and Utterances*, 2–3.
32. Sperber and Wilson, "Pragmatics," 103.

involved in the specific situation. Written communication has fewer of these sorts of contextual factors upon which to draw. Nevertheless, the same principles of relevance are in play. Sperber and Wilson write, "lengthy and highly self-conscious processes of textual interpretation that religious or literary scholars engage in are governed just as much by the principle of relevance as is spontaneous utterance comprehension."[33] In other words, literature creates the same expectation of relevance as normal, oral utterances.[34]

Linguists often understand "texts" as either oral or written, the latter being simply a material trace of a person's utterance.[35] A written text allows spacial distance between speaker and audience, but it nevertheless preserves the discourse of a communicative act.[36] That this distance does not in principle change the communication process, consider that the gap disappears when an author performs his or her manuscript in front of a live audience (e.g., preaching from a manuscript, which is a communicative act comparable to biblical literature). Sophisticated literature often challenges readers with a style that necessitates greater processing effort. However, rather than serving as an example against relevance theory's axiom regarding maximum cognitive effect for minimum processing effort, sophisticated literature actually reinforces the axiom. Even the most underdetermined literature, such as James Joyce's *Ulysses*, utilizes inferential processes based on context; as David Trotter notes, "Writers frequently raise the costs of processing their 'utterances', and promise in exchange a yet richer contextual effect. They do not so much abandon as complicate the principle of relevance."[37] Poetry works in this manner;

---

33. Sperber and Wilson, *Relevance* (1995 ed.), 75.

34. Wilson, "Relevance Theory and Literary Interpretation," 185–204 (cf. Wilson and Sperber, "Relevance and the Interpretation of Literary Works," 76), and Pattemore, *The People of God in the Apocalypse*, 22–23.

35. Unger, *Genre, Relevance and Global Coherence*, 5–6.

36. Understanding text as *discourse* by a *communicative agent* is important for avoiding intentionality fallacies (Vanhoozer, "From Speech Acts to Scripture Acts," 32; Vanhoozer, *Is There a Meaning in This Text?*, 214–18). Furlong notes that texts differ from mere objects subject to the whim of the reader in that they are also communicative acts performed by another agent (Furlong, "A Modest Proposal," 336–37). Cf. Pattemore, *The People of God in the Apocalypse*, 47.

37. Trotter, "Analysing Literary Prose," 11. It is more common now to see use of the term "cognitive effect" than "contextual effect." The older term, contextual effect, stresses the role of inference from contextual assumptions on the act of communication. The newer term, cognitive effect, stresses the benefit derived by the audience.

and similarly, elevated literary prose intentionally invites a reader to explore the context more intensely in order to achieve the cognitive reward offered by the author. Processing might take greater effort, but the cognitive effects are achieved in the same way as in conversational communication.

Paul's Corinthian correspondence illustrates how written communication can be highly dependent on a contextual situation. Most illustrative is Paul's clarification in 1 Cor 5:9–11 of the meaning expressed in an earlier letter. In this case, an implicit link to people in the social context was missed by the Corinthians. They failed to properly disambiguate Paul's reference to those from whom he wanted them to disassociate.[38] Epistles, by their very nature, are situational, as are prophetic oracles (or psalms) delivered in their original setting. These are more situational than legal discourse, which has a broader audience in mind from the outset. Prophetic oracles, in turn, can be resignified when edited for final canonical presentation to a secondary audience; and so the implied audience is now broader than the original. Meaning often becomes more underdetermined in extended communication situations than it would have been in the original setting. So, it is not a question of whether pragmatics are important in understanding written texts; inference from context is at work. It is worth recalling at this juncture that relevance theory does not deny the importance of the verbal utterance; rather it views the wording as a guide that triggers cognitive effects from context in the encyclopedic entries of the reader's mind. So relevance theory does not discount the primacy of the words in an act of communication; it only highlights the interaction between the utterance of words and their broader context.

Relevance Theory and Genesis 1

The importance of historical context for biblical interpretation generally, and for our understanding of creation texts in particular, is not a new topic. What relevance theory does is reapproach the discussion in the light of contemporary understanding of how communication actually works in practice. There are at least three important applications to the question of biblical cosmology: (1) Relevance theory contributes to the discussion about "literal interpretation"; (2) Relevance theory helps us think about what elements of the cognitive environment contribute to

38. We will return to this example later for further discussion.

correct interpretation; (3) Relevance theory assists in unpacking the nature of divine accommodation. The first two applications are considered in this chapter; the third application will be the subject of chapter 4. For illustrative purposes, and for the sake of brevity, application of relevance theory in this chapter will be restricted to Gen 1 (a shorthand designation for Gen 1:1—2:3).

Literal Interpretation

Relevance theory shifts the emphasis away from *decoding* dictionary meanings of words toward *inferring* from statements in broader contexts. Regarding this process Sperber and Wilson write, "there is no reason to think that the optimally relevant interpretive expression of a thought is always the most literal one. The speaker is presumed to aim at optimal relevance, not literal truth."[39] What Sperber and Wilson mean by "literal" here is the ordinary use of a word found at the initial entry of a dictionary—its most basic sense. They are not embroiled in battles over biblical hermeneutics; rather, they are merely using linguistic theory to address how human communication actually works, whether conversations or literary texts. "Literal," in its narrow sense, is not the "normal" way of understanding speech or texts, nor is it the default assumption in communication.[40] This recognition is not unique to relevance theory, but is demonstrated by linguists working from other theoretical angles as well.[41] Because relevance theory accounts for how readers comprehend

---

39. Sperber and Wilson, *Relevance* (1995 ed.), 233. Cf. Wilson and Sperber, "Truthfulness and Relevance," 50, 79–80.

40. In biblical hermeneutics, "literal" is sometimes used in contrast to "figurative," as in the quotation of Sperber and Wilson above (e.g., Mickelsen, *Interpreting the Bible*, 179). But it is also common in literature on hermeneutics to see "literal" interpretation as taking language in its normal sense—grammatically, historically, *and* including figurative meanings or other uses that are socially constructed by culture (Mickelsen, *Interpreting the Bible*, 33; Kaiser and Silva, *An Introduction to Biblical Hermeneutics*, 33, 141–42; Bartholomew, *Introducing Biblical Hermeneutics*, 127). Some shift the emphasis to "literary" in order to capture this broader sense of "literal" (Johnson, *Expository Hermeneutics*, 31 with 42, 209; Klein, et al., *Introduction to Biblical Interpretation*, 8–10). Vanhoozer uses the term "literalistic" interpretation to denote being overly fixated on the literal meaning of individual words rather than the "whole meaning of the writer, including his metaphors and figures." In his definition, the "literary sense is the sense of a literary act" (Vanhoozer, *Is There a Meaning in This Text?*, 117, 312).

41. E.g., Glucksberg, *Understanding Figurative Language*, 10–12. He specifically rejects the claim that literal meaning is basic and has unconditional priority (3).

texts, it is useful for understanding how readers might intuitively adopt interpretations that are "literal" or "nonliteral."

Laboratory testing by cognitive linguists has demonstrated that people process literal and figurative possibilities of interpretation in parallel, *not* in series.[42] In other words, in normal human communication, we do not assume a literal interpretation and then switch to an alternate possibility only after perceiving that the literal makes no sense in context. In fact, some experiments have shown that people default to metaphorical interpretations whenever such are available. So the burden is actually on the interpreter to demonstrate literality. As Sperber and Wilson maintain, "the hearer should take an utterance as fully literal only when nothing less than full literality will confirm the presumption of relevance."[43] This is a different approach from what is commonly assumed—that literal interpretation is default unless it makes no sense. Whether a person interprets a word literally or figuratively depends on which assumptions they select in the process, assumptions driven by their individual contextual relevance.[44] Relevance theory, then, merely places inference in a cognitive environment at the center of its interpretive model.[45] Literal interpretation, in the sense of initial dictionary meanings of words, has no privileged place in communication, including that of the Bible.

---

42. Glucksberg, *Understanding Figurative Language*, 16–28. For parallel processing in human cognition generally, see Sternberg and Sternberg, *Cognitive Psychology*, 319–22. Stemmer summarizes the neuroimaging research that "information about phonology, syntax, and semantics of single words and sentences as well as discourse information, world knowledge, and non-linguistic context information immediately converge to support interpretation" (Stemmer, "Neuropragmatics," 9). She continues, "The evidence thus speaks against a literal-figurative dichotomy... and is also difficult to reconcile with the classical right-hemisphere hypothesis which was based on such a dichotomy" (Stemmer, "Neuropragmatics," 12). In conclusion, she writes, "From a chronological point of view, metaphoric meanings are activated very early in processing, suggesting that metaphor comprehension and literal language share qualitatively similar processing mechanisms, thus speaking against a literal–figurative dichotomy" (Stemmer, "Neuropragmatics," 18). See also Carston's discussion of processing of polysemous words (Carston, "Word Meaning," 190–91). There are even earlier studies (Rumelhart, "Some Problems," 75–76).

43. Sperber and Wilson, *Relevance* (1986 ed.), 234. Cf. Lowery, *Toward a Poetics of Genesis 1–11*, 63–64.

44. Wilson and Sperber, "Relevance Theory," 619–20. Wilson and Sperber argue that *all* inferential processes, not just literal versus some other, run concurrently (Wilson and Sperber, "Relevance Theory," 615–17).

45. Similarly, Rumelhart argues for the centrality of context from the standpoint of schema theory (Rumelhart, "Some Problems," 71–82).

Guiding Contextual Inference

Most of the time, we process communication in our primary cultural context with intuitive ease. A communicator is aware of what is accessible knowledge to his or her audience and makes appropriate word choices based on assumptions about degrees of cognitive access.[46] The language of an utterance serves to guide the audience, leading them to contextual inferences and resulting in the cognitive effects intended by the speaker.[47] In such "primary communication situations," people experience most utterances as adequate to trigger those dictionary and encyclopedic entries of the mind that are necessary to infer meaning. But, because communication is so dependent on assumptions within a shared context, "secondary communication situations" (such as modern Western versus ancient Near Eastern) are inherently problematic because of the different, instinctual, contextual, or cognitive effects.[48] There is a degree of mismatch in assumptions from two different cognitive environments. When listeners or readers fail to recognize the contextual assumptions intended by the communicator, misunderstanding often results. In Gutt's words, "ambiguities can be resolved the wrong way, metaphorical expressions can be taken literally, implicatures can be missed."[49] Therefore, competent listening and reading necessitates familiarity not only with the *language* of original communication but also its *historical, geographical, and cultural setting*.

A quick read of Luther's commentary on the first chapter of Genesis nicely illustrates this problem. Luther, working with an Aristotelian natural philosophy, interpreted the "waters above the firmament" as a layer of ice that cooled the spheres that were rotating around the earth.[50] He notes that this was the opinion of the "majority of the theologians" in his day. Luther responded to the utterances of Gen 1 based upon the cognitive effects of the text on *his* assumptions about cosmic geography.[51]

46. Gutt, "Aspects of 'Cultural Literacy,'" 6.

47. Sperber and Wilson, "Pragmatics," 470, 488; Fantin, *The Greek Imperative Mood*, 59.

48. Gutt, *Relevance Theory*, 27; Gutt, *Translation and Relevance*, 76–77; Pattemore, *The People of God in the Apocalypse*, 29; Green, "Relevance Theory and Theological Interpretation," 84 n. 27; Lowery, *Toward a Poetics of Genesis 1–11*, 29.

49. Gutt, *Translation and Relevance*, 77.

50. Luther, *Lectures on Genesis Chapters 1–5*, 26, 31.

51. Luther chose to reject the possibility that the waters above the firmament are clouds: "But Moses says in plain words that the waters were above and below the

In contrast, the proper focus of interpretation must be on the cognitive environment of the *original* audience. Relevance theory is not a method of interpretation; rather it is a model of communication that accounts for how different interpretations arise in various contexts. This will be revisited at the end of this chapter in consideration of the church's lost access to the ancient Near Eastern culture.

According to relevance theory, how might the language of Gen 1 access encyclopedic knowledge in the primary communication context? Recall that the mind draws inferences derived from contextual assumptions *in the order of accessibility*. An initial range of interpretive possibilities is immediately present to the audience's mind based upon a heuristic expectation. The mind chooses from among heuristic possibilities based upon relevance, as guided by the utterances of the speaker (i.e., a "best fit"). One might say that the speaker or author pulls the background into the foreground. How does this work for Gen 1 in its original context? First, one must establish that Israel had shared access to ancient Near Eastern traditions about creation.

Israel's Access to the Ancient Cognitive Environment

There is evidence for direct scribal knowledge of Mesopotamian cuneiform *texts* with cosmological importance in the Levant and Egypt. Fragments of the Gilgamesh Epic and Atrahasis were found at Ugarit (northern Levant).[52] Discoveries at Megiddo (southern Levant and eventual Israelite territory) revealed a fragment of Gilgamesh,[53] as well as a fourteenth-to-twelfth-century ivory that depicts a Hittite cosmological

---

firmament. Here I, therefore, take my reason captive and subscribe to the Word even though I do not understand it" (Luther, *Lectures on Genesis Chapters 1-5*, 26).

52. One Gilgamesh fragment with additional paraphrases from the Epic in other texts at Ugarit (George, *The Babylonian Gilgamesh Epic*, 24, 26-27). Originally classified as a fragment of Gilgamesh, RS 22.421 is now shown to be from Atrahasis (Kämmerer, "Das Sintflutfragment aus Ugarit," 189-200).

53. George, *The Babylonian Gilgamesh Epic*, 339-47; Horowitz et al., *Cuneiform in Canaan*, 102-5. Although discovered in the vicinity of Megiddo, based on petrographic analysis of the clay in the tablet it is not likely that the text was written at Megiddo. Rather it probably originated at a coastal town such as Gezer (George, *The Babylonian Gilgamesh Epic*, 1:340; Goren et al., "A Provenance Study of the Gilgamesh Fragment," 763-73). From there the tablet was brought to Megiddo. This highlights the exchange of these texts and traditions.

tradition.⁵⁴ Textual remains of Adapa and the South Wind, which describes a flight from earth to heaven, as well Nergal and Ereshkigal, a primary source for beliefs about the underworld, were found in Egypt (Amarna), even more distant from Mesopotamia than the Levant.⁵⁵ These artifacts probably underrepresent the full range of texts, and those relevant to cosmology, that were known by an internationally competent scribal class.⁵⁶

Including these cosmologically significant texts, from the southern Levant alone (Israel's homeland) the extant cuneiform texts number over ninety and include literary texts, letters, administrative documents, royal inscriptions, magical incantations, among other writings. These were written on a variety of media, including tablets, cylinder seals, votive objects, and ceramic vessels. The finds are well distributed over the entire southern Levant. Most of the material stems from the Late Bronze Age (1550–1200 BCE) and the period of Assyrian occupation (745 BCE to c. 640 BCE).⁵⁷ Cuneiform texts are, so far, missing from the period after the collapse of Bronze Age civilization until the Assyrian conquest. During this gap alphabetic scripts dominated (e.g., Hebrew and Aramaic).⁵⁸ For this reason, Byrne cautions, "We do not know how much of this Late Bronze literary culture survived in public memory as the city-states of Canaan gave way to the successor petty states of Judah and Israel."⁵⁹ However, a trained scribal class was active in the southern Levant from the eleventh century onward, as attested by extra-biblical Semitic inscriptions from this period.⁶⁰ Rollston expects that knowledge of the lore in foreign languages would have been part of scribal training.⁶¹ These traditions would have been handed down from the internationally

---

54. Loud, *The Megiddo Ivories*, 10, no. 44a–h, pl. 11; Alexander, "Šaušga," esp. 179; B. J. Collins, *The Hittites*, 138 (fig. 3.10), 192.

55. EA 356 and 357 respectively (Izre'el, *The Amarna Scholarly Tablets*, 43–61; Horowitz et al., *Cuneiform in Canaan*, 17).

56. Scribal culture was both international and collegial. Scribes at times appended personal greetings to one another in international correspondence (Cohen, *Wisdom*, 24).

57. Horowitz et al., *Cuneiform in Canaan*, 4–7.

58. Horowitz et al., *Cuneiform in Canaan*, 19.

59. Byrne, "Self, Substance, and Social Metaphysics," 109.

60. Rollston, "Scribal Curriculum," 71–101; Rollston, "Inscriptional Evidence for the Writing," 17, 27, 37, 45.

61. Rollston, "Scribal Curriculum," 92.

knowledgeable scribes of the immediately preceding period, a survival of the Late Bronze Age collapse in the region. So Mesopotamian *traditions* at least were probably known among educated people throughout the Levant, including the regions and periods of Israel's emergence and flourishing as a nation.

Egyptian traditions were familiar to Israelites from both their historical roots in Egypt[62] and ongoing cultural exchange.[63] Israelite tradition itself places the formal education of Moses in the Egyptian royal house (Exod 2:10), which would have entailed direct exposure to Egyptian texts and religious traditions. Court exchanges between Egypt and the Solomonic administration point to continued cultural interaction (1 Kgs 3:1; 9:16; 10:28-29).[64] This is best illustrated for wisdom traditions.[65] Most notable is the textual dependence of Proverbs 22-24 on the Egyptian Proverbs of Amenemope, which has been conclusively demonstrated, in my view, by Paul Overland based on arguments usually overlooked in discussion.[66] Therefore, literary intertextuality was not inherently problematic. Cultural influence is evident from the many motifs used in Israelite iconography that adapted Egyptian art.[67] This is not surprising

---

62. See, for example, Hoffmeier, "Egyptian Religious Influences," 3-35. For a minimal historical core for the exodus tradition, see Davies ("Was There an Exodus?," 23-40).

63. International trade flourished in Solomon's reign, both northward, where Mesopotamian traditions were more closely shared, and southwestward, to Egypt (Lemaire, "The United Monarchy," 108-12). For interconnections, see Kitchen, "Egypt and East Africa," 116-23; and Currid, *Ancient Egypt*, 162-68.

64. Currid, *Ancient Egypt*, 167-68.

65. See Shupak for comparisons (Shupak, "The Contribution of Egyptian Wisdom," 284-97); although Shupak sees more direct influence in the late eighth century than at Solomon's time.

66. Overland, "Structure in the Wisdom," 275-91. There are more than just thematic and verbal parallels. For example, in many instances, the verse sets in Proverbs were compiled by combining carefully selected cola from Amenemope that correspond to the opening (and sometimes closing) line of chapters in the Egyptian text (i.e., "telescoping"). Thus, Proverbs shows awareness even of the *structure* of Amenemope. Overland's recent paleographic study of a Cairo Museum ostracon (EM 1840-44) of Amenemope demonstrates a date centuries *before* the Solomonic era. Neither the intertextuality nor direction of dependence is in doubt (Overland, "Paleographic Dating"). For other supportive discussion, see Shupak, "The Instruction of Amenemope," 203-20.

67. Beck, "The Art of Palestine," 203-22. Examples of Egyptian motifs on Israelite art are illustrated throughout the work of Keel and Uehlinger (*Gods, Goddesses, and Images of God*). Influence on pottery style is also significant.

in view of Egypt's Late Bronze Age colonialism that lasted well into the Iron I Period and left an indelible mark on the culture of Canaan within which Israel was immersed.

Alongside Egyptian influence, there are examples of iconographic style from Phoenicia, inland Syria, and Mesopotamia. These also have continuity with Late Bronze Age art.[68] Israel's exposure to foreign culture is revealed by Solomon's acquisition of Phoenician artisans for the temple (1 Kgs 5). Whether one evaluates such openness positively or negatively (e.g., 2 Kgs 16:10–11), the point is that Israel had access to international culture throughout its history.[69]

This evidence suggests the likelihood that specific texts were known by scribes in Israel. But when considering a possible relationship between foreign traditions and biblical literature, it is not necessary that specific, foreign *texts* be in view. *Traditions* represented by these texts were part of common knowledge across the ancient Near East and likely known by the educated class. But cognitive environment is more subtle than just intellectual tradition, as John Walton stresses, since *many ideas about the world are simply assumptions shared popularly across cultures, often without people even considering any question of source.*[70] He correctly notes, "Israelite literature reflects the broad ancient stream of culture from which it was watered in the course of centuries or even millennia."[71] This applies to anthropological constructs such as honor and shame, and to cognitive frameworks like cosmology. Recalling the definition of cognitive environment used in relevance theory, assumptions about the natural world ("science") and religious beliefs play an important part. Israelites, especially those responsible for composing biblical literature and educating social leadership, had knowledge about cosmology, religion, and probably specific textual traditions that were part of a common ancient

---

68. Beck, "The Art of Palestine," 205, 212, 215–17.

69. This is illustrated by Keel's correlation between the imagery in biblical texts and ancient Near Eastern iconography in general (Keel, *The Symbolism of the Biblical World*). A more current and comprehensive presentation is currently appearing, three volumes of which were available at the time of this writing. See Schroer and Keel, *Die Ikonographie Palästinas/Israels*, vol. 1; Schroer, *Die Ikonographie Palästinas/Israels*, vol. 2; Schroer, *Die Ikonographie Palästinas/Israels*, vol. 3.

70. Walton, *Genesis 1 as Ancient Cosmology*, 2–5.

71. Walton, *Genesis 1 as Ancient Cosmology*, 13. Along the same lines as Walton's point, Pattemore notes that some assumptions are "contextually evoked" but often they are only "used conventionally" (Pattemore, *The People of God in the Apocalypse*, 41–42).

Near Eastern cognitive environment. Knowledge of this sort invariably permeates the broader culture, extending to average people to varying degrees.

Relevance Theory, Comparative Method, and "Echo"

Relevance theory reinforces from linguistic theory the guidelines for discerning intertextuality, or "echoes," that have been set forth by Richard Hays.[72] The methodological overlap is brought even closer to our interest in a helpful essay by Christopher Hays, who applied Richard Hays's notion of echoes to the comparative method in biblical and ancient Near Eastern studies.[73] In answer to the question "When, and on what grounds, is comparison valid?" Christopher Hays restates the criteria for judging echoes, to which I will add comment from relevance theory:

(1) *"Availability: Was the proposed source of the echo available to the author and/or his original readers?"*[74] This consideration is related to relevance theory's notion of accessibility discussed above.

(2) *"Volume: How 'loud' is the echo; that is, how explicit and overt is it?"*[75] In relevance theory terms, this corresponds to the actual wording of an utterance that a speaker chooses in order to draw elements from the cognitive environment to the attention of the audience. By making *more* manifest certain background assumptions, a speaker increases the volume (to use Hays's term). This category is related to the explicit/implicit distinction in relevance theory, which is a topic taken up in chapter 4. The more explicit the language, the more salient the echo.

(3) *"Recurrence or Clustering: How often does the author cite or allude to the same text?"*[76] This actually explicates *one* way an author can "adjust the volume" (i.e., increase cognitive accessibility) of the echo. In other words, by repeating a word or by incorporating schemas of words and motifs, specific components are made more manifest.

---

72. R. B. Hays, *Echoes of Scripture*, 29–32. I thank C. John Collins for drawing my attention to the connection between relevance theory and Hays's work. Pattemore summarizes Richard Hays's criteria in two categories of relevance theory: processing effort (1–3) and contextual effects (4–5) (Pattemore, *The People of God in the Apocalypse*, 38).

73. C. B. Hays, "Echoes of the Ancient Near East?," 20–43.

74. C. B. Hays, "Echoes of the Ancient Near East?," 36.

75. C. B. Hays, "Echoes of the Ancient Near East?," 36–37.

76. C. B. Hays, "Echoes of the Ancient Near East?," 37–38.

(4) *"Thematic Coherence: How well does the alleged echo fit into the line of argument of the passage in question? Does the proposed precursor text fit together with the point the author is making?"*[77] Relevance theory emphasizes a listener's effort to make sense of the *whole* of the discourse. Interpretive processing continues until all the parts of the whole make sense in a relevant way, including not only context (immediate textual context) but also elements of the cognitive environment that are inferentially related.

(5) *"Historical Plausibility: Could an author in fact have intended the alleged meaning effect of any proposed allusion, and could contemporaneous readers have understood it?"*[78] Also related to accessibility, this is a central concern of relevance theory for *optimal relevance*. Speakers who succeed in producing a cognitive effect on their audience cooperate with the audience's expectations of relevance as well as their capacity to draw inferences between the utterance and their encyclopedic entries. *Optimal* communication means that if information is not part of the shared encyclopedic entries, the speakers must supply the missing pieces. But *optimal* communication is also *efficient*, that is, it supplies only the words and pieces that are necessary. Hays's use of the word "effect" at this point conforms well with relevance theory's definition of communication as involving cognitive effects.

(6) *"History of Interpretation: Have other readers in the tradition heard the same echoes that we now think we hear?"*[79] Validation for modern interpretation, which is a distant, *secondary* communication situation relative to the ancient Near East, is strengthened when one finds matching interpretations in the *primary* communication situation of ancient Israel. Even by late Second Temple times, the communication situation was already *secondary*. In chapter 5, I will briefly examine the use of creation texts from Genesis within the Old Testament itself. This consideration relates as well to the reception history of Genesis in the church, which I address at the end of this chapter and in more length in chapter 3.

(7) *"Satisfaction: Does the proposed intertextual reading illuminate the surrounding discourse and make some larger sense of the author's argument as a whole? Do we find ourselves saying, 'Oh, so that's what the author*

---

77. C. B. Hays, "Echoes of the Ancient Near East?," 38-39.
78. C. B. Hays, "Echoes of the Ancient Near East?," 39-40.
79. C. B. Hays, "Echoes of the Ancient Near East?," 40-41.

meant'"?⁸⁰ As Hays admits, this is an especially subjective test. However, it does reflect the concern of relevance theory, already mentioned for number 4 above, that processing stops only when the audience's expectation of relevance is satisfied (an aha moment). To the extent that we endeavor to become competent readers of ancient literature, we should stop processing at the moment all the pieces of the text, cotext, and context fall into place as a sensible whole, *given the expectation of ancient readers*. Such moments in the realization of modern interpreters match the point when ancient readers would stop processing.

These tests for echo are written primarily with respect to formal intertextuality where there is interplay between two specific texts. However, like Walton, Christopher Hays stresses that an "echo" need not be sourced in a *text* at all; rather, it may be an utterance that attaches an idea from the broader cultural context. As noted above, relevance theorists consider the "cognitive environment," which includes anything mentally accessible to an audience.

Echoes of Ancient Near Eastern Traditions in Genesis 1

Ancient Israelites had access to ancient Near Eastern traditions about creation. This probably included texts, but for the question of echoes in the biblical text, it is only necessary that Israelites were aware of how other cultures expressed their beliefs, even if transmitted orally. Is there specific language in the text of Gen 1 that encouraged ancient Israelites to draw consciously on these traditions for interpretation and cognitive effect? As noted above, one need not propose any direct intertextual links between Genesis and specific ancient Near Eastern texts in order for these cosmological traditions to be echoed in the looser sense just discussed. Indeed, much of the cosmological language in the Old Testament probably had no conscious association for Israelites with foreign traditions; rather, it simply reflects the assumptions of the broader culture with regard to their cognitions about the world of nature. The way the language of the Old Testament reflects only incidentally this "world picture" of cosmic geography will be addressed at length in the next chapter. Here, the following examples highlight a sufficient number of motifs, even if not exhaustive, to show that echoes of specific foreign traditions about creation are likely in Gen 1.

80. C. B. Hays, "Echoes of the Ancient Near East?," 41–42.

In the beginning . . . heavens and earth[81]

One of the ways a speaker will guide an audience with minimal processing effort is by use of a topic sentence.[82] This gives the audience immediate access to the encyclopedic information that will be crucial for understanding the discourse. The opening verse of Gen 1 functions in this way. It would immediately draw the audience's attention to a range of thoughts from their cognitive environment about this topic. Two Mesopotamian texts relating to creation open with a similar expression: "in the beginning" (*ina reš* [cognate to *re'šit* in Gen 1:1]; *ina šurri*).[83] However, a more common opening reference is to "heaven and earth," in particular their separation, a notion found also in the Hittite Song of Illikummi, an Old Hattian ritual, as well as in Egyptian tradition.[84] In each case, the word pair, "heaven" and "earth" denote the totality of the universe as a structured whole. For example:

> When the heavens above did not exist,
> And earth beneath had not come into being–
> (Enuma Elish)[85]

> In former days, in distant former days,
> In former nights, in distant former nights,
> In former years, in distant former years, . . .
> After heaven had been separated from earth,
> After earth had been separated from heaven . . .
> (Gilgamesh, Enkidu, and the Nether World)[86]

---

81. Unless otherwise indicated, all Bible translations are my own. The syntactical issues involved in translating Gen 1:1–3 are discussed in chapter 5. The translation adopted here assumes that Gen 1:1 is an absolute clause and functions as a summary statement for the creation account that follows. Although less likely in my opinion, if the translation as a relative clause is correct ("When God began to create"), then Genesis still parallels other Mesopotamian creation traditions rather closely, e.g., *Enūma eliš*, "When on high." The point of my discussion that follows remains valid.

82. Sperber and Wilson, *Relevance* (1995 ed.), 216.

83. Lambert, *Babylonian Creation Myths*, 393, 399. The first reference, from the Theogony of Dunnu is partially but plausibly reconstructed.

84. Lambert, *Babylonian Creation Myths*, 169–71. For Egypt, see below. More will be said of this Hittite tradition in the next chapter.

85. Lambert, *Babylonian Creation Myths*, 51.

86. Lambert, *Babylonian Creation Myths*, 170.

[On that day], the day when heaven was [separated] from earth,
[On that night], the night when heaven and earth were established...
(Enki and Ninmah)[87]

When heaven was separated from earth, its faithful companion,...
When heaven was set up and earth was made...
(A Unilingual/Bilingual Account of Creation)[88]

When Anu, Enlil, and Ea,
The great gods, in their sure counsel
Had fixed the designs of heaven and earth...
(*Enuma Anu Enlil*)[89]

This last example is one of several versions of *Enuma Anu Enlil*, all of which incorporate the word pair, "heaven and earth," as an idiom for the ordered universe, complete with fixed appointment of all astral objects.[90]

A conceptually parallel phrase, "first occasion" (*sp tpy* [*tp* = "head," analogous to *roʾš* in biblical Hebrew *reʾšit*, Gen 1:1]), is used in Egyptian texts for the beginning of creation.[91] Common in Egyptian tradition is also the idea of the god Geb (earth) being separated from the goddess Nut (sky):

I have lifted my daughter Nut top me...
I have put Geb under my feet
(Coffin Text Spell 76, II.2c, e)[92]

It is of interest that creation according to Egyptian tradition was framed in terms of solar revolution, similar in this respect to Gen 1; but in the case of Egypt it was only a *one-day* process.[93]

An Egyptian account of the creation of the gods (the Ptah section of the Memphite Theology) employs a topic-sentence opening as well as

87. Lambert, *Babylonian Creation Myths*, 335, 498–99.
88. Lambert, *Babylonian Creation Myths*, 353.
89. Lambert, *Babylonian Creation Myths*, 176.
90. See variations in Lambert, *Babylonian Creation Myths*, 176–77.
91. Hoffmeier, "Some Thoughts on Genesis 1 & 2," 42; Faulkner, *A Concise Dictionary of Middle Egyptian*, 222, Book of the Dead 9.1.
92. E.g., Allen, *Genesis in Egypt*, 18 (Buck, *The Egyptian Coffin Texts*, II.2c, e; cf. CT 78, II.19).
93. G. H. Johnston, "Genesis 1 and Ancient Egyptian Creation Myths," 192.

a summary conclusion, forming an *inclusio* similar to the stylistic device in Gen 1:1 and 2:1:

> The gods have come into existence from Ptah (line 48) . . .
> They came into existence there (line 61)[94]

The column layout of the Ptah section is vertical throughout, except line 48, which stands conspicuously across the opening of the account in horizontal fashion, making the topic-sentence function of line 48 especially manifest.[95]

formless and void . . . darkness . . . the deep

Although the underworld waters is a standard feature of cosmic geography,[96] preexisting waters were not as common an element in Mesopotamian creation texts (the only exceptions being Enuma Elish and the Eridu Genesis, lines 10, 17). For Egyptian cosmogony, however, this is the standard state of affairs at the beginning of creation, which also names other primordial conditions:

> on the day that Atum evolved,
> out of the Flood, out of the Waters,
> out of darkness, out of lostness . . .
> (Coffin Text Spell 76, II.4d)[97]

> "Flood" (*ḥḥw*, "millions," hence, boundless expanse;
>   or [primeval] Flood waters of Nile)[98]
> "Waters" (*nw*; "cosmic waters")[99]

---

94. See the observations of Finnestad, "Ptah, Creator of the Gods," 87, 94, 97.

95. For visual layout of the text, see Breasted, "The Philosophy of a Memphite Priest," pl. I & II, col. 48.

96. Horowitz, *Mesopotamian Cosmic Geography*, 334–47. See discussion in chapter 2.

97. Allen, *Genesis in Egypt*, 18 (Buck, *The Egyptian Coffin Texts*, II.4d).

98. "infinity," "endless space" (Molen, *A Hieroglyphic Dictionary*, 353). For Allen's commentary on these terms, see Allen, *Genesis in Egypt*, 14, 20 and 68 n. 80 or *COS* 1.6: 10. Rather than related to *ḥḥ* ("millions"), Allen relates the term *ḥḥw* to the word *ḥḥ(j)*, which denotes the flood waters of the Nile (cf. Molen, *A Hieroglyphic Dictionary*, 354). He notes that in the Book of the Dead 175, all creation returns to the primeval waters (*nw*) and the "Flood" (*ḥḥ(j)*), which offers an appropriate association with the original emergence of land from the cosmic waters (for the beginning out of waters, see also Buck, Coffin Text 714; Allen, *Genesis in Egypt*, 13).

99. "primeval waters," "Abyss" (Molen, *A Hieroglyphic Dictionary*, 203).

"darkness" (*kkw*; "darkness")[100]

"lostness" (*tnmw*, "confusion" or "chaos" [related to the verb "to become lost, confused"])[101]

Many have observed a similarity to Gen 1:2.[102] The parallels, darkness and the boundless waters, are clearest. Whether "formless and void" (*tohu wabohu*) is parallel is more difficult. Some interpreters avoid associating this Hebrew word pair with "chaos" altogether; rather, something more neutral, i.e., "unproductiveness and emptiness"[103] or "nonexistent (nonfunctional) cosmos."[104] If this line of interpretation is accepted, there is no good parallel between the Egyptian description and *tohu wabohu*, unless one follows Walton's suggestion that both the Egyptian text and *tohu wabohu* in Gen 1:2 denote that which is "nonfunctional" and therefore "nonexistent."[105]

However, in spite of careful arguments against the notion "chaos," there are reasons to retain this English gloss. Detailed argument will be taken up in chapter 5 in connection with echoes of Gen 1 in Jer 4:23. Briefly here, the ancients regarded anything at the periphery of inhabitable land, whether boundless ocean or desert expanse, to be hostile to life—not a neutral association. Such an empty and disordered state is "chaos" in the *connotations* of ancient cosmology. The use of the word "chaos" does not necessitate a cosmic battle between God and personified forces in Gen 1:2, only that the conditions described were discombobulated and inimicable to life, yet transcended and superintended by the Spirit of God.[106] If this is the case, then *tohu wabohu* contributes to the cluster of motifs that echo the primordial conditions in Egyptian thought.

100. "darkness" (Molen, *A Hieroglyphic Dictionary*, 677).

101. "darkness," "gloom" (Molen, *A Hieroglyphic Dictionary*, 738). Allen also glosses this "chaos" (Allen, *Genesis in Egypt*, 20).

102. E.g., Hoffmeier, "Some Thoughts on Genesis 1 & 2," 43; G. H. Johnston, "Genesis 1 and Ancient Egyptian Creation Myths," 185–86; Walton, *Genesis 1 as Ancient Cosmology*, 151–52; Miller and Soden, *In the Beginning*, 83–87. Cf. James Allen's cross-references in *COS* 1.6: 10; 1.8: 11.

103. Tsumura, *The Earth and the Waters*, 41 (with some updating in Tsumura, *Creation and Destruction*, 35; cf. R. S. Watson, *Chaos Uncreated*, 16, 269–70).

104. Walton, *Genesis 1 as Ancient Cosmology*, 144.

105. Walton, *Genesis 1 as Ancient Cosmology*, 141, 143–44.

106. Rebecca Watson, who advocates *avoiding* the term "chaos" altogether in discussion of any biblical texts, draws a helpful distinction between "battle," "creation," and "chaos," which the literature has tended to blur (R. S. Watson, *Chaos Uncreated*, 16, 367–99). Not only can creative acts be separated from cosmic battle, but there

Another possible parallel has been suggested for the Egyptian primordial state and Gen 1:2. A later Egyptian tradition substitutes the name of the god Amun for "lostness." Since Amun is associated with the wind, some have suggested a closer parallel to "wind/Spirit of God."[107] Whether a valid comparison or not, it seems unnecessary that all four Egyptian terms have exact semantic glosses in the Hebrew text for a comparable state of affairs to be shared between them.

... separated ...

The use of the word-pair "heaven and earth" as a topical introduction, along with mention of their separation, was discussed above. But the organization of the universe, expressed by the motif of separation, also extends to other aspects of creation. This is comparable to the first three days of Gen 1 that describe the separation of light and darkness, the waters above and below, and the land and sea respectively.

Distinction between day and night is illustrated in two texts already cited above, Gilgamesh, Enkidu and the Netherworld, and Enki and Ninmah. A similar distinction, as well as separation, are described in several other texts:

> "The reliable god, who interchanges day and night, who establishes the month, and keeps the year intact" (actions of Nanna in a dedication inscription).[108]

---

needs to be a distinction between cosmic origins and God's ongoing role in cosmic stability (377). However, I would argue that the latter is nonetheless an exercise of divine power to prevent what I think we can properly call "chaos" from reemerging. Methodologically, Watson eschews the comparative method, which in my view is essential for reconstructing the cognitive environment necessary for enriching the biblical text. She asserts that the result of her analysis, "without recourse to extrabiblical parallels, confirms that the traditional interpretation has grossly overplayed any indications which could be compatible with the presence of the *Chaoskampf* theme" (R. S. Watson, *Chaos Uncreated*, 259; cf. 261–62). (*Chaoskampf* means "God's battle against chaos.") So while she is correct that the application of this theme has been simplistically overused, in my view she has overstated her own case to deny the propriety of the term "chaos." For a well-reasoned challenge to Watson on numerous biblical texts where she denies the motif of divine battle with chaos, see Batto, "The Combat Myth," 217–36. However, Batto's attempt to reassert this for Genesis 1 (pp. 233–36) does not produce any evidence that the battle motif is implicated in that context.

107. Hoffmeier, "Some Thoughts on Genesis 1 & 2," 43–44.
108. Lambert, *Babylonian Creation Myths*, 172.

"... the great gods ... divided night from daylight ..." (*Enuma Anu Enlil*)[109]

"unchanging stars (shine) by day and night" (A Unilingual/Bilingual Account of Creation)[110]

Along with separation of day and night, there is also the separation of waters. This is found in Mesopotamian tradition only in Enuma Elish, where it is explicit:

> Bēl rested, surveying the corpse [of Tiamat the cosmic ocean]
> In order to divide the lump by a clever scheme.
> He split her into two like a dried fish:
> One half of her he set up and stretched out as the heavens.
> He stretched the skin and appointed a watch
> With the instruction not to let her waters escape.[111]

In Egyptian cosmology, which invariably opens with preexisting waters, the motif of separation is only implicit in the enigmatic language describing the god Shu (atmosphere) emerging between the waters.[112] But separation is also implicit in the *result* of creation, described as waters above and below in Egyptian tradition.[113]

While not explicitly described with the word "to separate" in Gen 1:9–10,[114] the emergence of land with respect to the seas has counterparts in Mesopotamian and Egyptian text traditions. Mesopotamian tradition is not expressed in terms of gathered waters. Rather, Enuma Elish has Marduk creating earth from half of the carcass of Tiamat, which he places over what would become the subterranean waters; and another Marduk tradition describes him building earth like a raft on the cosmic waters.[115]

---

109. Lambert, *Babylonian Creation Myths*, 177, cf. variant on p. 179.

110. Lambert, *Babylonian Creation Myths*, 359.

111. Enuma Elish iv 135–140 (in Lambert, *Babylonian Creation Myths*, 95). Cf. Horowitz, *Mesopotamian Cosmic Geography*, 114–15.

112. Allen, *Genesis in Egypt*, 16–17. Allen compares this to Gen 1:6–8 (Allen, *Genesis in Egypt*, 4–5).

113. Allen, *Genesis in Egypt*, 4–5, 9, pls. 1–3. The position of cosmic waters is discussed in the next chapter.

114. The verb *bdl* is not used as it was for light/darkness and the waters (Gen 1:4, 7).

115. Horowitz, *Mesopotamian Cosmic Geography*, 118–19, 130–32. Treated in more detail in the next chapter.

But close to the biblical description is Egyptian belief that a primeval hill emerged out of the cosmic waters, like the first appearance of dry ground when the flood waters of the Nile recede annually. This motif is common in Egyptian tradition, e.g.:

> Atum Scarab!
> When you became high, as the high ground—
> when you rose, as the benben [primeval hill][116]

These three domains—light, water, and arable land—were of prime relevance to agrarian societies and for this reason are important in their accounts of creation. The same concern expressed in Mesopotamian and Egyptian creation accounts corresponds as well to the Ugaritic myths about Baal, which are not about the *process* of creation; nevertheless, they attend to the same concerns in the ongoing *maintenance* of creation.[117]

... lights ...

Astral objects (i.e., sun, moon, stars) are of great importance in ancient creation accounts, not surprisingly, since they are fundamental to human orientation to time and the cycles of life—not to mention the divine status of these objects in religious context. Enuma Elish describes Marduk's organization of the heavenly bodies (stars ["great gods"], moon ["Nannar"], sun ["Shamash"]) as orientation points for the calendar.[118] His own star is the center of this regulatory control.[119] In *Enuma Anu Enlil*, the creator gods establish the "stellar-positions/locations," which are equated with the "gods of the night."[120] Egyptian creation accounts are less descript about the *process* of astral organization, but its organization is very important and inherent in the final structure in which the movement of sun and stars are fixed relative to the goddess of the sky, Nut.[121]

---

116. From PT 600 (Allen, *Genesis in Egypt*, 13–14). See also Allen's commentary in COS 1.4: 7 n. 2 and Hoffmeier, "Some Thoughts on Genesis 1 & 2," 46.

117. Averbeck, "The Three 'Daughters' of Baʿal," 237–56. This topic will be taken up again in the next chapter.

118. Enuma Elish v 1–26 (in Lambert, *Babylonian Creation Myths*, 99).

119. Enuma Elish v 6–7; vii 126–31 (in Horowitz, *Mesopotamian Cosmic Geography*, 116).

120. Horowitz, *Mesopotamian Cosmic Geography*, 147.

121. Allen, *Genesis in Egypt*, 3, 5; Hornung, *The Ancient Egyptian Books of the Afterlife*, 114–16.

... humanity/image of God ...

Mesopotamian tradition presents the creation of humans as chattel-labor for benefit of the gods, but the concept of humans as the "image" of the gods does not appear in Mesopotamian creation contexts.[122] This dignity is reserved for special representatives of the god (almost exclusively the king) as the "image of god."[123] Egyptian royal texts likewise assign to the king the status of god's "image." But Egyptian belief extended this title in some degree to all humans. Wisdom tradition associates it with the god's creative acts:

> Well tended is mankind—god's cattle,
> He made the sky and earth for their sake,
> He subdued the water monster,
> He made breath for their noses to live.
> They are his images,[124] who came from his body,
> He shines in the sky for their sake;
> He made for them plants and cattle,
> Fowl and fish to feed them . . .[125]

This text alludes to another Egyptian tradition related to the creation of humanity, giving breath to human nostrils, but this pertains to Gen 2:7, not the imagery in Genesis 1.[126]

... rested ...

This motif has counterparts in Mesopotamian and possibly Egyptian creation tradition as well. Walton has summarized well the temple theology associated with creation and divine rest for both the Mesopotamian tradition as well as the Old Testament.[127] Upon taking up residence

---

122. Atrahasis i 1–4, 195–197 (in Foster, *Before the Muses*, 229, 235); Enuma Elish v 7–8 (in Lambert, *Babylonian Creation Myths*, 111).

123. Clines, "The Image of God," 83; Garr, *In His Own Image*, 144–49. These texts use the Akkadian, ṣalmu, which is cognate to the Hebrew word for image (ṣelem).

124. The Egyptian *snn* denotes among other things, divine images in statues (Faulkner, *A Concise Dictionary of Middle Egyptian*, 232; cf. Hoffmeier, "Some Thoughts on Genesis 1 & 2," 47); hence, conceptually parallel to the Akkadian ṣalmu and Hebrew ṣelem.

125. Instruction of Merikare (in *COS* 1.35:65).

126. The derivation of humans from the god's body also finds no parallel in Gen 1. It alludes to the creation of humans from the tears of the god (*COS* 1.9: 15).

127. Walton, *Genesis 1 as Ancient Cosmology*, esp. 110–16.

in the completed temple (for Genesis, it is the cosmic temple), the deity has ceased building activity but commences administrative oversight of creation. In Mesopotamian religion, the final purpose of creation is to provide temples for the gods to rest:

> [Marduk] created dirt and heaped it on the raft.
> In order to settle the gods in a comfortable dwelling,
> He created humankind.[128]

According to Enuma Elish, Marduk's finished temple would provide an evening rest stop for the gods on their travels:

> Let us make a shrine of great renown:
> Your chamber will be our resting place wherein we may repose
> Let us erect a shrine to house a pedestal
> Wherein we may repose when we finish (the work).[129]

The Akkadian word translated "repose" (*pašahu*) can mean to rest after exerting oneself, which fits the context in Enuma Elish where the gods find refreshment at the house of Marduk after a day of travel.[130] This corresponds to the sense of Gen 2:3, amplified in Exod 31:17, in which God's rest is restorative.[131]

A parallel exists between Gen 2:2–3 and the Memphite theology:

> So has Ptah come to rest after his making everything . . .[132]

It is possible that the word translated "rested" (*ḥtp*) could be rendered "was satisfied."[133] But even if it denotes the satisfaction taken by

---

128. Marduk, Creator of the World, lines 17–20 (in Foster, *Before the Muses*, 488).

129. Enuma Elish vi 51–54 (in Lambert, *Babylonian Creation Myths*, 113).

130. *CAD* 12:232–33 (5.a.1—the god Ea restoring himself after battle; 5.c—rest for feet of weary traveler; 6—used in our passage intransitively in the sense of relaxation after travel).

131. Niphal of *npš* denotes restorative refreshment (Exod 23:12; 2 Sam 16:14).

132. Allen, *Genesis in Egypt*, 44 (*COS* 1.15:23). See also Finnestad, "Ptah, Creator of the Gods," 97–98. I thank James K. Hoffmeier for directing my attention to Finnestad's work.

133. The Egyptian word *ḥtp* can mean "to be pleased," "to become calm," or "to rest" (Faulkner, *A Concise Dictionary of Middle Egyptian*, 179–80). Lichthiem translates the phrase, "Ptah was satisfied" (Lichthiem, *Ancient Egyptian Literature*, 1:55). John A. Wilson's translation in *ANET*, 5, offers both possibilities—"was satisfied" or "rested," n. 19). James K. Hoffmeier (private communication) notes that the notion "satisfied" is common in personal names employing a divine name with *ḥtp*. On the

Ptah in his creative activity ("he was satisfied after his making everything"), it would then be conceptually comparable to God's assessment that his work was "very good" (Gen 1:31). Ptah's "rest" occurs at the end of six creative movements, on the seventh of which the gods take up their temple abodes.[134]

... xth day ...

One of the crux issues in the interpretation of Gen 1 is understanding the sense of "day." The question is more difficult than discerning whether twenty-four-hour days are meant. Those who purport to read Gen 1 "literally" and those who read it "literarily" both recognize that six twenty-four-hour periods are presented in the text. The phrase "and there was evening and morning" strongly supports this understanding of the sense of "day." The question is whether or not we should infer chronological implications beyond literary structure. In view of the cognitive environment of the original audience, what would they have inferred? Three considerations from relevance suggest that chronological concord with earth history was not in view.

First, it is important to keep in mind that there is no ancient Near Eastern creation account per se, whether one considers Mesopotamia, Egypt, Anatolia, or the Levant. Various traditions that are *related* to creation were put into the service of texts with other interests. This in itself is instructive, since it shows that the interests of the ancients revolved around questions such as theogony, cultic order, the relationship between gods and humans, magic, participating in creation cycles to overcome death, or the concerns of agriculture—not the age of the earth or how earth's natural history unfolded. What was important to the ancients was the final order of the universe as it pertains to time, weather, and food production as well as implications for temple service.[135] In terms of relevance theory, it is inherently improbable that Gen 1 addresses chronology of *natural* history or any question of interest to modern science. The parallels just discussed suggest that Gen 1 guided the attention of the original audience to those concepts of creation that were pertinent

---

other hand, gods "rest" (*ḥtp*) in their temples (Görg, *Gott-König-reden*, 158). See Breasted (*Ancient Records of Egypt*, vol. 4 §§9, 250, 252, 311, 312) where he translates *ḥtp* as "rest" (for the Egyptian text, see Erichsen, *Papyrus Harris I*, p. 29, line 16; p. 30, line 9; p. 50, lines 9, 17).

134. Finnestad, "Ptah, Creator of the Gods," 97.

135. Walton, *Genesis 1 as Ancient Cosmology*, 119–21, 161–62, 170; Averbeck, "The Three 'Daughters' of Ba'al," 237–56.

in their day. It is not that the ancients were *incapable* as human beings of grasping rudimentary, modern scientific notions, if sufficient effort were spent to explain things to them.[136] Nor is it that God could not have revealed a concordant version of earth history in terms understandable to the ancients. But, as Daniel Lowery notes, *the language of Gen 1 was optimized for other cognitive effects.*[137] The authors of Genesis chose language that activated comparative-religious cognitive effects. One should not expect a chronology of natural history.

Second, contextual clues within Gen 1 and 2 lead away from reading the six days of creation in a historically referential manner. In the words of Sperber and Wilson, "When a hearer following the path of least effort arrives at an interpretation that satisfies his expectations of relevance, in the absence of contrary evidence, this is the most plausible hypothesis about the speaker's meaning."[138] The qualifying phrase, "in the absence of contrary evidence," is important. There are problems, long-recognized across the entire history of interpretation, in reconciling days 1 and 4 (light/sun) and in reconciling days 3 and 4 (plants/sun), as well as inconsistencies between Gen 1 and 2.[139] These inconsistencies create excessive processing effort for interpreting the days historically, and it likely would have done the same for ancient Israelites. As Sperber and Wilson note, consistency of assumptions is a key to the loose logic used in inferential processing.[140] Even *if initially* assuming historical creation days, an ancient reader would quickly abandon such an inference, particularly in view of the elegant paneling of days 1–3 with 4–6 that resolves the tension by literary style.[141] However, natural history is unlikely to be an

---

136. The nature of ancient science is discussed at length in the next chapter.

137. Cf. Lowery, *Toward a Poetics of Genesis 1–11*, 70.

138. Wilson and Sperber, "Relevance Theory," 614.

139. Interpretation of Gen 1 throughout church history is discussed in more detail in chapter 3.

140. Sperber and Wilson, "Précis of Relevance," 228–29.

141. In the history of interpretation, this appears as early as Peter Lombard (c. 1100) (A. J. Brown, *The Days of Creation*, 69–70) but with more ancient antecedents. Its re-emergence to popularity in contemporary discussions is due to the compelling nature of its elegance. The framework model has received criticism (McCabe, "A Critique of the Framework Interpretation," 211–49). But the model appeals to literary artistry, which functions at a control level in interpretation above the mere observation of "narrative" style. In brief, one can grant that *narrative* sequence is *presented* in Gen 1, based on both the *waw*-consecutive verb sequence as well as the use of ordinal numbers for the days; but that these observations indicate only that Gen 1 *presents*

initial assumption in any event, since an ancient audience would be in search for (to them) less trivial matters found in comparative theological interpretation.¹⁴²

Third, many have pointed to the frequent use of a sevenfold pattern in ancient Near Eastern and Old Testament literature. Seven of any object or activity, in literature or in practice, guided an audience to infer effective completeness. It was a schema by which one organized a narrative, poetry, or planned ritual. As a literary schema, it did not necessarily correspond to real passage of days; rather, it was simply the way one structured thought.¹⁴³ This schema was common and it likely held a very

---

creation in narrative sequence, not that this necessarily coheres with chronological sequence in actual earth history. In other words, narrative presentation cannot be confused with historical sequence. The former pertains to literary style and the latter to historical referentiality. The Synoptic Gospels, for example, *present* the life of Jesus in narrative fashion, but none teaches the actual, chronological sequence of historical events, apart from the very general course of Jesus' life. The question for Gen 1 must be resolved at the level of contextual relevance, not at the level of linguistic register (i.e., narrative versus poetry). Therefore, arguments by McCabe and others for historical referentiality based on narrative sequencing beg the question of stylistic intent.

142. Cummings discusses how people will suspend certainty about an assumption until contextual evidence disambiguates the intended meaning ("backward inference"), or in some cases, they entertain an inference "subject conditionally to future evidence" (Cummings, *Pragmatics*, 95–96, 109–10).

143. Sometimes an actual sequence of days might be in view, but even these examples help demonstrate the symbolic significance of the schema, whether used in real time or as a literary device. The Memphite Theology summarizes Ptah's creative work in seven movements by which "Ptah organizes and equips the Egyptian cultus in its totality" (Finnestad, "Ptah, Creator of the Gods," 97). Richard Averbeck (unpublished paper) lists the following examples: (1) a six-plus-one pattern is utilized in Exod 24:16 and Job 5:19; Prov 6:16–19 (cf. three-to-four pattern in Prov 30:15, 18, 21, 29); (2) seven-day periods surround temple construction and dedication (1 Kgs 8:2, 65 [seven days in seventh month]; 2 Chr 7:8–10); it took seven years to build the temple (1 Kgs 6:38); seven petitions dedicate the temple during this time (1 Kgs 8:31–53); (3) the tabernacle instructions are given in groups of seven: each set of seven instructions begins with the formula "the Lord said to Moses" (Exod 25:1; 30:11, 17, 22, 34; 31:1, 12), and the last deals with the Sabbath (Exod 31:12–17); (4) a seven-day ritual occurs for Israelite priestly ordination (Lev 8:33–35); (5) seven-day rituals dedicate the temple in Ezekiel's vision (Ezek 45:21–25); (6) a seven-day temple dedication sets apart Gudea's temple in Mesopotamia (Gudea Cylinder B xvii 12—xxiv 8; *COS* 2.155:432 n. 74); (7) a six-then-seven-day pattern appears around the flood in Gilgamesh (*COS* 1.132:459–60); (8) Baal takes seven days to build his palace (*COS* 1.86:261 n. 175); (9) the Ugartic Kirta epic features a six-then-seven motif in the hunt for the king's wife-to-be (*COS* 1.102: 333–36). From the list offered by Mark Smith, one can add the following: (10) Samson's wedding feast (Judg 14:12); (11) the duration of Job's friends' lamentation with Job (Job 2:13); (12) the distribution of a donation or venture (Eccl 11:2); (13)

accessible position on the list of cognitive assumptions shared between writer and audience of Gen 1. Therefore, the use of a sevenfold pattern in Gen 1 would lead to inferring effective completeness for creation, not necessarily a creation sequence in real world terms.[144]

Summary

It is not the purpose of this section to expand upon the theological implications of these comparisons. Rather, in examining how Gen 1 guided contextual inference, two points are outstanding. First, Israel had *access* to ancient Near Eastern creation traditions. Second, the examples cited above illustrate how the language of Genesis offered stimulus for the audience to access those elements in their knowledge of creation traditions that they shared with the broader cognitive environment, from Mesopotamian to Egyptian. The author guided Israel's contextual inferences toward relevance in an agrarian society but also in a competitive, pluralistic religious milieu. Similarities might be expected, for in an agrarian society there are common elements of fundamental importance. However, it is not just the topics of creation, but also the nature of the descriptions—the wording of Genesis incorporates quite manifestly a cluster of motifs used also by Israel's neighbors. In relevance theory terms, the language of Genesis was *optimized* to encourage comparison between Gen 1 and the foreign traditions. Gen 1 offers a similar but alternate narrative of

---

the lamentation right of Ugaritic hero Danil (*KTU* 1.17 i 15–16); (14) Jericho's fall after seven days in which seven priests with seven trumpets march around the city seven times (Josh 6:15–16); (15) the number of times for perfect refinement of gold (Ps 12:6; Heb. 7); (16) the complete number of abominations (Prov 26:25); (17) the work-regimen on the priestly calendar (Lev 23:3, 7, 36; Num 29:17–32) (Smith, *The Priestly Vision of Genesis 1*, 87–88). In Ezekiel's oracles against the nations (Ezek 25:1–32:32), Block notes seven oracles against Egypt, which itself is the seventh and final nation addressed (Block, *Ezekiel 25–48*, 128). It takes six days and seven nights for the woman in the Gilgamesh story to tame Enkidu (Epic of Gilgamesh, i 191–94; George, trans., *The Epic of Gilgamesh*, 8). These examples are far from a complete listing, but they span a considerable breadth of literature, by geography as well as genre. Just as important, within Gen 1 itself, the sevenfold schema extends far beyond the seven days into an elaborate web of word-count patterns. The following list is also not exhaustive: seven words in v. 1; fourteen words in v. 2; "God" appears thirty-five times; "heaven" and "earth" appear twenty-one times each; the declaration "it was good" appears seven times. For concise summary, see Levenson, *Creation and the Persistence of Evil*, 67.

144. For consideration of Exod 20:11, see the discussion of reception history in chapter 5 (below).

creation to that of Israel's neighbors, and recognizing these similarities and differences would satisfy Israel's expectations for relevance. Processing would likely stop there, since it was *optimized* for these cognitive effects, not for questions about the natural history of the earth, for which there is no trace of interest in ancient Near Eastern traditions.[145]

Lost Accessibility for the Church

Relevance theory accounts for how the church understood the essential theology of Gen 1 while misreading the text in a concordant fashion.[146] As mentioned earlier, relevance theory explains how audiences process input based on their expectations of relevance. As Sperber and Wilson note, an audience will "follow a path of least effort in constructing an interpretation of an utterance," and they will "stop when [their] expectations of relevance are satisfied."[147] As just discussed, an ancient Near Eastern audience would recognize the motifs (topically and stylistically) commonly used to express origins in their culture, draw significant theological inferences that satisfy their expectation of relevance, and stop processing—especially in the light of the excessive processing effort needed to harmonize the account internally when read in literalistic fashion. But an audience not acquainted with ancient Near Eastern creation traditions would *not* stop processing at the level of comparative religions, because they would have missed the cues to consider these comparisons and their implications. To put this in common terms, questions related to what we moderns would call science were not even on the radar screen, so to speak, until the emergence of Greek science and the interaction of Jewish and Christian interpreters with Greek philosophy in late antiquity (see below).

A New Testament example is illustrative. Regarding ancient traditions relevant to the interpretation of the book of Revelation, Pattemore

---

145. There was some interest in the origins and history of kingship. Of note here is the Sumerian King List (Glassner, *Mesopotamian Chronicles*, 117–26), which offers long reigns for the antediluvian kings. But these numbers are themselves highly symbolic, featuring years calculated in multiples of a base-six numeric system. There is no relevance of this royal chronology to questions of natural history.

146. By "concordant" I mean specifically in reference to natural history, not "concord" in the looser sense used by Alvin Plantinga in his helpful work on the relationship between theology and science (Plantinga, *Where the Conflict Really Lies*).

147. Sperber and Wilson, "Pragmatics," 474.

ponders, "How many more examples of metalepsis [indirect intertextuality] are we missing simply because we do not know the texts they link to?"[148] In similar manner, Pattemore writes, "The difference between [an uninformed reader and a competent one] is that while spontaneous interpretation (such as a casual reader or inexperienced reader might make) may reach optimal relevance for that reader, insufficient effort has been expended to achieve an optimally relevant interpretation of the text."[149] It is not that the wording was not optimal for the original audience; rather, for a secondary audience, the wording does not satisfy the relevance expectations that the author intended to raise. The problem of uninformed readers describes the situation prior to the rediscovered understanding of the ancient sources beginning in the late nineteenth century for reading Genesis.

A very limited and vague knowledge of Mesopotamian traditions was accessible to the early Jewish community and the church through Berossus, but even his interpretative presentation of Mesopotamian tradition also infused Greek rationalism.[150] This conflation misled readers, such as Greek natural philosophers and the church fathers, about the nature of ancient Near Eastern cosmology.[151] New categories of thought about the nature of the physical universe were emerging in Greek natural philosophy.[152] So, for example, the theological emphasis on creation ex nihilo in rabbinic and Christian discussions resulted from their anxiety over Aristotle's eternality of matter.[153] But natural philosophy as such was not a category of ancient Near Eastern thought.[154] In addition, the church fathers operated under the assumption that the canon was self-contained

---

148. Pattemore, *The People of God in the Apocalypse*, 43.

149. Pattemore, *The People of God in the Apocalypse*, 27.

150. Breucker, "Berossos," 648–49.

151. Berossus's narration of creation, based on Enuma Elish, diverges from the cuneiform account in important ways (Dillery, *Clio's Other Sons*, 227–40). Furthermore, it is difficult to be certain in some cases what Berossus actually transmitted, since Christian and Jewish authors, to whom we are indebted for our knowledge of him, adapted and often corrupted Berossus for apologetic and chronological purposes (Breucker, "Berossos," 642–44). The flood narrative offers more detail for consideration than the creation accounts (see Day, "The Flood," 211–23; C. J. Collins, "Noah," 403–26), and the intertextual issues are even more complex; but these considerations are outside the scope of this discussion.

152. Lindberg, *The Beginnings of Western Science*, 25–27.

153. Bauks, *Die Welt am Anfang*, 63. This question of creation ex nihilo will be revisited in chapter 5.

154. For further discussion, see the next chapter.

interpretively, that is, they did not need external data.[155] Even if they had known of the ancient Near Eastern worldview, it is unclear if it would have mattered in their interpretation. In other words, without recognizing alternative ancient Near Eastern traditions against which Genesis is a competing account, one would continue to process for relevance. In the absence of more accessible contextual associations, a concordant reading is understandable, particularly in view of emerging Aristotelian natural philosophy ("science") among early church scholars.

In the history of interpretation, church scholars recognized the clues in Gen 1 that led away from a literalistic reading as they wrestled to account for the internal inconsistencies within the text. But not until the rediscovery of ancient Near Eastern backgrounds did assumptions emerge for a reading strategy that offered an alternate, more manifest path involving less processing effort. In the aftermath of nineteenth- and twentieth-century discoveries, concordance with natural history is no longer the most accessible strategy for reading Genesis; rather, the associations are of a comparative religious nature, as in the original communication setting. This does not mean that the basic message cannot be understood apart from ancient Near Eastern background. It is still clear that a transcendent and sovereign God created the universe as a place conducive to human life that is fundamentally "good." There is adequate wording ("code") in the utterances of Gen 1 to convey this message. However, the literary clothing in which this message is couched was crafted for the cognitions of an ancient Near Eastern audience who would enrich the text with associations missed by an audience not familiar with the ancient Near Eastern cognitive environment. It is often asked, How then could God have allowed his church to miss the interpretation of Gen 1 for two thousand years? The answer is that he didn't; the central meaning has been clear. But layers of richness in the text were indeed lost. This is true not just for Gen 1 but for very many texts in both Testaments of the Bible that have been enriched by modern background studies.

Conclusions

An Inferential-Contextual Model of Communication

Relevance theory provides a model of communication that integrates linguistic code with the cognitive environment of the primary

155. Norris, "Augustine," 390.

communication situation. Within a shared cognitive environment, a writer's discourse guides an audience to those elements that are contextually relevant to infer meaning. Faithful readers attend to those elements of the cognitive environment that a writer's discourse makes manifest to constitute the proper context for interpretation. In attending to context, readers (1) assign references to objects, events, or ideas, (2) disambiguate polyvalence of words, and (3) enrich meaning. Both parties in the communication situation are guided by *optimal relevance*—that is, writers *adequately* guide readers to contextual assumptions necessary to infer meaning yet *efficiently* require minimal processing effort from readers, since readers expect cognitive benefits commensurate with the amount of processing effort they expend. In this sense, good communication is optimally relevant.

No Privileged Role for Literal Interpretation

Normative reading does not default to literal meaning; rather, it processes simultaneously all possible options by narrowing the interpretation to the "best fit" within the context made manifest by the author. Literal interpretation, in the sense of initial dictionary meanings of words, has no privileged place in communication, including that of the Bible.

Israel's Accessible Cognitive Environment

For ancient Israel, Gen 1 echoed the stream of ancient Near Eastern creation traditions; and its language was optimized for theological comparison with these traditions, none of which exhibited interest about natural causes or the chronology of earth history. In other words, it was optimized for cognitive effects other than natural history. The author guided Israel's contextual inferences toward relevance in an agrarian society but also in a competitive, pluralistic religious milieu. Yet, embedded in these traditions is language that reveals implicit assumptions about cosmic geography of the natural world. How we should assess mental constructs about the natural world within this ancient cognitive environment is the subject of the next chapter.

2

Assessing the Ancient Cognitive Environment

Encyclopedic Entries and Cognitive Assumptions

The previous chapter introduced the idea that words and phrases have the potential to activate a wide array of ideas in the mind of a reader or listener. This includes the basic uses of a word (what is typically defined by a dictionary); but when consideration is given to the connotations of words and all the associations of those words in the experience of an individual or in the broader culture, the "dictionary entry" expands to "encyclopedic" proportions. This encyclopedic entry constitutes the cognitive environment for any communication event. But the range of possible assumptions for communication is narrowed by a speaker or author, who chooses words that guide an audience to what is contextually relevant.

Evidence indicates that ancient Near Eastern creation traditions were both accessible in Israel's cognitive environment and at play in the composition of Old Testament texts. But echoes need not be sourced in a specific text or tradition, rather they may only incidentally reveal assumptions from the broader cognitive environment that are not part of the informative intention of a text. This chapter examines more broadly the ancient Near Eastern cognitive environment regarding cosmology and considers some Old Testament expressions that presume similar assumptions.

Ancient Near Eastern Cosmology

One of the challenges of studying ancient cosmology is the difficulty validating cognitive assumptions for such a distant culture. How might an ancient Mesopotamian or Egyptian have conceived of the physical structure of the universe? One cannot read the minds of ancient people to know what mental picture they might have entertained regarding cosmic geography. However, this problem does not differ in principle from the problem of knowing the mind of any other person today.[1] We depend on language as an adequate means for sharing thoughts. For the ancient context, what makes the problem more difficult, but only in degree, is the absence of linguistically and culturally competent native speakers from whom we can seek clarification. But ever since the late nineteenth century, when ancient Near Eastern texts began to be deciphered, ancient concepts regarding cosmology have become more accessible. These texts, coupled with iconographic material, provide the data to attempt reconstructions of the world picture, or mental map of cosmic geography, that might have been entertained.[2]

General Considerations

Physical Depictions of Cosmic Geography

It is common to see visual representations of ancient cosmography constructed by modern, literalistic readings of ancient texts. Figure 1 is typical.[3]

---

1. Lloyd observes the same difficulties with respect to ancient Greek and Chinese "science," but he also notes that understanding ancient societies is not much different than understanding our own, except in the degree of cultural fluency (Lloyd, *Ancient Worlds*, 9–11).

2. Janowski defines "mental map" as "a type of 'inner model' that serves the individual and the community to perceive, interpret, and evaluate their environment" (Janowski, "Das Biblische Weltbild," 20). "Mental map" is Janowski's phrase; the rest of the quotation here is my translation.

3. See also examples reproduced in Cornelius, "The Visual Representation," 211, fig. 1; and Wright, *The Early History of Heaven*, 90–92, figs. 3.20–22—albeit with helpful criticism and discussion. Cf. Lamoureux, *Evolutionary Creation*, 108 (with pillars); Miller and Soden, *In the Beginning*, 44, 79, 118 (with windows and pillars); Enns, *Inspiration and Incarnation* (2005 ed.), 54; Enns, *Inspiration and Incarnation* (2015 ed.), 43 (with windows and pillars); Greenwood, *Scripture and Cosmology*, 26, fig. 1.1 (with windows).

FIGURE 1: COSMIC GEOGRAPHY

Artwork by Michael Paukner, after George L. Robinson, *Leaders of Israel* (1913), 2.
Used with permission.

Decades ago Othmar Keel correctly stressed that for the ancients there was no clear separation between the physical cosmos and the divine beings manifested in it; and consequently, visual illustrations often fail to portray the divine realities that animated the physical features which the ancients described.[4] Keel endeavored to correct this oversight

---

4. Keel, *The Symbolism of the Biblical World*, 56–57. The numinous aspect of creation is the controlling theme of Keel and of Schroer, *Creation*, xi (originally published 2002). Keel maintains that if our modern portraits were accurate in detail, one would find closer correspondence in ancient art itself. Instead, in ancient art one finds a greater mixture of physical reference with religious symbolism (Keel, "Das Sogenannte

by introducing more overt divine symbolism into such diagrams.[5] Such visualizations are also more vague in the details of presentation, leaving out features such as "windows" in heaven, separate "storehouses" for various meteorological phenomena, or overliteralized "pillars." Nevertheless, intended or not, these diagrams still leave a visual impression of photographic-like detail. Although not offering visual diagrams—perhaps wisely—others have maintained a similar "world picture" for the ancient Near East and the Old Testament in their verbal descriptions.[6]

Many scholars have noted that the ancients themselves did not offer *one* consistent description of the physical (divinely manifest) universe. Bernd Janowski observes that this inconsistency creates difficulty for anyone attempting to pull together disparate elements into *one* image.[7] Along with Keel and others, he stresses that the ancient world employed rich symbolism that pointed beyond the superficial impression of physicality left upon us moderns by their language and art. Religious ideas were inseparably bound with empirical observation of the natural world.[8] With even more hesitance, Cornelius Houtman voiced doubts that *any* "world picture" can be ascribed to the Israelites but only a "worldview" in which Israel's God takes center stage for the origin, existence, and maintenance of the cosmos.[9]

Altorientalische Weltbild," 157). Cf. Cornelius, "The Visual Representation," 203; and Wright, *The Early History of Heaven*, 89.

5. Keel's 1985 illustration is reproduced in Keel and Schroer, *Creation*, 83, fig. 85; followed and modified in Cornelius, "The Visual Representation," 217–18, figs. 9 and 10; and in Wright, *The Early History of Heaven*, 93, fig. 3.23.

6. E.g., Stadelmann, *The Hebrew Conception of the World*; Seely, "The Firmament-1," 227–40; Seely, "The Firmament and the Water Above-2," 31–46; Seely, "The Geographical Meaning of 'Earth,'" 231–55; Walton, *Genesis 1 as Ancient Cosmology*, 86–100.

7. Janowski, "Das Biblische Weltbild," 13. He adds that the potential for chronological change in ancient cognitions further complicates the effort. Houtman also stresses that there was no "generally accepted, systematically constructed theory of the origin, structure, and furnishing of the cosmos in all its parts" (Houtman, *Der Himmel im Alten Testament*, 283). Rather than see contradiction between descriptions, or import into Gen 1 the imagery from other passages, one must take each text for its own intention (pp. 314–15).

8. Janowski, "Das Biblische Weltbild," 8–12.

9. Houtman, *Der Himmel im Alten Testament*, 299–300. He notes approvingly (pp. 294–95) the earlier approach of Thorleif Boman, who argued that all cosmological language in the Hebrew Bible is "functional" in contrast to European expectations that such language be "visual" (Boman, *Hebrew Thought*, 175–83, esp. 181–82 for Gen 1). The conclusions of Boman differ somewhat from John H. Walton's functional

So there exists a cautionary trend in recent treatments by specialists in ancient Near Eastern cosmology who advocate less literal interpretations of textual and iconographic descriptions related to cosmography. For example, Keel and Schroer offer the following disavowal of literalistic portrayals:

> People in the ancient Near East did not conceive of the earth as a disk floating on the water with the firmament inverted over it like a bell jar, with the stars hanging from it . . . The textbook images that keep being reprinted of the "ancient Near Eastern world picture" are based on typical modern misunderstandings that fail to take into account the religious components of ancient Near Eastern conceptions and representations . . . Ancient Near Eastern images are conceptual not photographic.[10]

In order to illustrate the methodological problem, they compare such portraits to an Egyptian statue of the crown prince sucking the breast of the goddess, whose image is primarily represented in the form of a tree. Given what we know from other images of this goddess, the tree-form must be interpreted metaphorically. They comment that images often "combine aspects of (empirical) experience of the world and worldly outlook."[11] The ancients unified the concrete image and the abstract. But we moderns insist on separating them.[12] So, it is often difficult to know the degree to which language or art refers to physical semblance or applies in a more restrictive, analogical manner. Wayne Horowitz offers a similar warning in the preface to his comprehensive treatment on Mesopotamian cosmography:

> Ancient Mesopotamian authors do not distinguish between cosmographic ideas drawn from direct observation of the physical world (for example, the movement of stars in the sky) and those not derived from direct observation (for example, the geography of the Heaven of Anu above the sky or the fantastic regions visited by Gilgamesh in Gilg. IX–X). The current evidence

---

approach (Walton, *Genesis 1 as Ancient Cosmology*). The latter argues for functional intent in Old Testament depictions but maintains that a mental map of ancient Near Easterners remains in the background from which such language is drawn. Boman gives no consideration to broader ancient Near Eastern cosmology.

10. Keel and Schroer, *Creation*, 78–79. See also concerns expressed in Cornelius, ("The Visual Representation," 196).

11. Keel and Schroer, *Creation*, 79–80.

12. Janowski, "Das Biblische Weltbild," 18–19.

simply does not allow us to know, for instance, if ancient readers of Gilgamesh really believed that they too could have visited Utnapištim by sailing across the cosmic sea and the "waters of death," or if a few, many, most, or all ancient readers understood the topographical material in Gilg. IX–X in metaphysical or mystical terms.[13]

Richard Averbeck also argues that ancient Near Eastern writers "make it their practice to express their speculations about world forces and their situation amid them by means of very sophisticated compilations of mythological motifs and patterns."[14] Consequently these literary works should not be judged by contemporary expectations of visual models for how the physical universe should be portrayed in literature. Contrary to such expectations, the ancients used analogical thinking, molding physical descriptions to symbolize their belief, much in the same manner as their ritual, which was analogical action—performance that engaged symbolically in the realities of the supernatural world.[15] Such reservations require that we proceed carefully in our conclusions about ancient cosmic geography.

Ancient "Science"

While ancient Near Eastern thinkers were prescientific in terms of modern knowledge, they were not irrational.[16] The ancient authors would have understood contradiction; no one could believe in a purely literal sense that the goddess Tiamat was simultaneously both the cosmic ocean and a dragon with skin and tail (Enuma Elish i 4–5; iv 135–140; v 59). They could also distinguish natural causes from supernatural causes. For

---

13. Horowitz, *Mesopotamian Cosmic Geography*, xiv–xv.

14. Averbeck, "Ancient Near Eastern Mythography," 331. The term "myth" has many legitimate uses, depending on the emphasis or methodological perspective of the one who employs it (Doty, *Mythography*, 21–22; Csapo, *Theories of Mythology*, 1). Averbeck's concern is to look beyond a simplistic contrast between reality (natural and human history) and fiction (myth) in order to allow ancient cultures the freedom to portray their beliefs about origins and theology in their own terms. For the confusion between "myth" and "reality," see the helpful discussion by Lowery (*Toward a Poetics of Genesis 1–11*, 35–51).

15. Averbeck, "Ancient Near Eastern Mythography," 332.

16. Lloyd argues the same for comparing ancient Greek and Chinese thought. Both employ a common logic but differ only in the degree to which logical processing was formalized in the abstract (Lloyd, *Ancient Worlds*, 50).

example, we have a letter from an ancient scholar responding to a query from the Assyrian king, Esarhaddon, regarding the nature of an illness he was suffering. The scholar reassures him that the illness is seasonal and would pass: "This is a seasonal disease; all the people who were sick are well (now)."[17] On a different occasion, however, an advisor writes, "It is the work of the gods."[18] In other words, in the first instance, the illness was not caused supernaturally and therefore did not need ritual intervention; but the second case necessitates exorcism, or at least special supplication to the gods, depending on the status of the agent causing the disease. The capacity to apply critical, rational thought is illustrated in another text that reports how Sennacherib isolated divination priests in separate rooms in order to prevent collusion on the results of their extispicy.[19]

From her examination of astronomical and divinatory texts, Francesca Rochberg has shown that scholars in the ancient Near East employed "empirical, inductive, deductive, and analogical" types of reasoning.[20] In that respect, their practices bore much in common with modern scientific method.[21] Earlier studies, such as the classic essays in *The Intellectual Adventure of Ancient Man*, focused almost exclusively on mythological texts and epic narrative; therefore, they missed divination texts in which ancient scholars engaged in direct observation of the phenomena of nature.[22] This skewed their judgment about the capacity for ancient peoples to think about what they observed in nature. Nevertheless, Rochberg agrees on the basis of the mythological traditions that the ancient Mesopotamians did not clearly differentiate "nature" from

---

17. Hunger, ed., *Astrological Reports*, p. 4, no. 1, lines 8–10. The same advice is seen in another letter—in Parpola, ed., *Letters from Assyrian and Babylonian Scholars*, p. 188, no. 236, line 11. See discussion in van der Toorn, *Sin and Sanction*, 67–69.

18. Parpola, ed., *Letters From Assyrian and Babylonian Scholars*, p. 192, no. 241, line r.2.

19. Livingstone, ed., *Court Poetry*, p. 77–79, no. 3, line 33.

20. Rochberg, *Before Nature*, 3. Benjamin Foster observes that technology and mathematics were without mythological underpinning (Foster, "On Speculative Thought," 100). On the other hand, medicine was situated between applied technology (herb lore, empirical practice) and myth (demon caused), albeit closer to the science pole of this dichotomy (Scurlock, "Divination between Religion and Science," 8–9).

21. Cf. Lloyd, *Ancient Worlds*, 21–23.

22. Rochberg, *Before Nature*, 9, 39–40, 53. See Frankfort et al., *The Intellectual Adventure*.

emanations or manifestations of divine beings.[23] Consequently, they did not study "nature" as an object for its own sake, as in modern science. The chief difference, then, is not found in different *cognitive processes* but in *cultural constructs* about nature.[24]

Mesopotamians studied astronomy because it revealed "signs" from the gods, whose messages were "written" in the sky, not because they were interested in the "laws of nature."[25] Interpretation went beyond empirical observations to the study of omen series for the purpose of prognostication. It extended to linguistic deductions based on the semantic and orthographic relationships between the cuneiform signs used for recording. These deductions could be highly speculative, venturing into the physically impossible, such as an appearance of the sun in the middle of the night.[26] Such exploration shows hermeneutical interest but not any concern for physical causes.[27] Like compiling astronomical omen series, cataloging plants and animals, which is sometimes cited as an example of ancient "science," also shows philological interests rather than pursuit of "nature." Such philological interest often leads to displaying contradictory organization features, taxonomically speaking. So, as Watson and Horowitz note, while the lists show "a natural impulse to categorize and explain," as in modern science, the Mesopotamian purpose was quite different.[28] Similarly, in the realm of mathematical astronomy, Mesopotamians could make precise predictions; however, these were subordinate to the concerns for prognostication, operating in a world where divine, not natural, causality was determinate.[29]

Like Mesopotamians, ancient Egyptians did not differentiate between "nature" and the essence of the gods. The physical universe unfolded and differentiated coessentially with the gods from the first creative deity whose exact identity varied with the particular temple tradition

---

23. Rochberg, *Before Nature*, 56.

24. Rochberg, "A Critique of the Cognitive-Historical Thesis," 24–25.

25. Rochberg, *The Heavenly Writing*, 1–2; Rochberg, *Before Nature*, 20–21. Cf. Lloyd, *Ancient Worlds*, 16–18.

26. Van de Mieroop, *Philosophy before the Greeks*, 115–16, 126–27.

27. Van de Mieroop, *Philosophy before the Greeks*, 188–90; Rochberg, *Before Nature*, 165–66.

28. Rita Watson and Horowitz, *Writing Science before the Greeks*, 164–65. Cf. Rochberg, *Before Nature*, 101.

29. Rochberg, *Before Nature*, 234, 245.

consulted.[30] As Allen notes, "the Egyptians lived in a universe composed not of things but of beings."[31] There is no evidence, either, that ancient Egyptians had any interest in natural causality in the abstract. Rather their interests were practical. Applied technology in building and metallurgy was prominent, and their astronomical knowledge served calendrical purposes but without the precision it received in Mesopotamia, at least until Ptolemaic times.[32] Rather than for prognostication, the use of stars for dividing the night was important only in funerary mythology.[33] Similar to the Mesopotamians, the Egyptians applied a complex of treatments, including drugs and ritual prayers. But as Weeks notes, "Experimental science and pursuit of theoretical knowledge for its own sake, such important parts of our culture, were not parts of theirs."[34] These differences between modern and ancient culture must be respected in our interpretations, understanding that their reflections on "nature" differed from ours according to the framework by which they organized and correlated their observations within their worldview. Their reflections on the universe in which they lived proceeded according to a different agenda from ours.

Even if their linguistic images and iconography were metaphorical, these need not have been completely disconnected from the physicality of visual observation. Ancient presentation of geography is an example of this complexity. Ancient maps were an effort to represent social perspectives ("conceptual terrain") but not with complete disregard for replicating actual geographical relationships.[35] Mythology and real-world accuracy could be integrated, as in the case of the Egyptian map of the Fayum, which mixes accurate cartography with mythology.[36] In this way, analogical representations can incorporate a complex mixture of symbolic images with elements drawn from the real world. *So, merely relegating mythological texts to analogical thinking is too simple.* We need to look for clues that might indicate when real-world representation was part of the

30. Compare the cosmogonies of Heliopolis (*COS* 1.5), Hermopolis (*COS* 1.6), and Memphis (*COS* 1.15).

31. Allen, *Genesis in Egypt*, 8.

32. Robins, "Mathematics, Astronomy, and Calendars," 1799, 1811–12; R. A. Parker, "Ancient Egyptian Astronomy," 51.

33. Neugebauer, *The Exact Sciences in Antiquity*, 80–89.

34. K. R. Weeks, "Medicine," 1789.

35. Rochberg, "The Expression of Terrestrial and Celestial Order," 14, 43.

36. O'Connor, "From Topography to Cosmos," 67–77.

construct. Just as we moderns still have unclear mental representations of many phenomena of our natural world, we can grant that they did as well; yet these were nonetheless representations to some degree of their empirical experiences.

Human Proclivity to Model the Physical World

The above discussion acknowledges that we must be careful to read ancient texts emically, that is, trying to view the meaning of text or art from the viewpoint of the ancients. This cautions against over-literalizing the physical references in mythological texts or ascribing explanatory meaning to texts in ways that parallel modern science's exploration of natural causality. As William Doty asserts, *"Myth is not unsophisticated science but sophisticated poetic enunciation of meaning and significance."*[37]

At the same time, it is difficult to imagine that the ancients did not entertain physical models of the universe and that aspects of these conceptions did not find expression in their texts or iconography. The human mind, even at a very young age, seeks both to categorize and to explain the world.[38] As Wellman and Gelman conclude: "Children and lay adults are nonscientists; nonetheless, their thinking appears to be framed by initial hypotheses or modes of construal that function for them as framework theories function for scientists."[39] To be sure, reasoning faculties mature from childhood to adulthood, so model construction has the capacity to be more sophisticated; but the point is that modeling is intrinsic to human cognition.[40] If very young children categorize and explain their

---

37. Doty, *Mythography*, 94 (italics original).

38. Rita Watson and Horowitz, *Writing Science before the Greeks*, 161–62.

39. Wellman and Gelman, "Cognitive Development," 370–71. Evidence indicates that children do not theorize the same way as adults; nevertheless, their impulse to make sense of their world operates from innate, core systems of knowledge (Carey and Spelke, "Science," 515–33). One of these core domains is "objects" together with the rules that seem to govern their interaction. This capacity becomes enhanced with age and acquisition of scientific knowledge, but it is not replaced, even after awareness of complexities of quantum mechanics (Carey and Spelke, "Science," 519–20). Wellman and Gelman conclude: "Infants and children rapidly acquire several framework theories of core domains—certain foundational understandings of the world that in turn frame conceptual acquisitions" (Wellman and Gelman, "Cognitive Development," 365).

40. The actual mental representations that such mental-model theorists depict for children have been called into question due to methodological problems (Nobes

world, this inclination to modelling is probably true to some extent for the average fieldworker or artisan in the ancient world. They may not have expended much of their mental resources to theorize about their physical world. Sperber argues that many intuitive beliefs arise from spontaneous inferential processes operating on perception without engaging in conscious deliberation.[41] But it is difficult to imagine that they never mentally constructed a physical model in order to make sense of their observations, even if they did so without purely natural causality.[42] How much more would elite and ancient scholars, who received education and studied the physical world intensely, have formed conceptual models.

Models among Prescientific Peoples

In addition to studies in cognitive science, anthropological studies of prescientific peoples are also relevant. Paul Seely summarizes the work of early anthropologists on the mental pictures of these peoples about their natural world.[43] The almost-universal mental model includes a solid sky:

> Other stories could be cited, but it is sufficiently clear that scientifically naive peoples around the world from the Pacific Islands to North America, from Siberia to Africa, have perceived the sky as a solid inverted bowl touching the earth at the horizon . . . that if they would travel far enough they could "touch the sky with one's fingers," that migrating birds live "on the other side of the celestial vault," that an arrow or lance could "fasten in the sky," that the sky can have "a hole in it," that at the horizon "the dome of the sky is too close to the earth to permit

and Panagiotaki, "Mental Models," 347–63). Culture plays a larger role in knowledge acquisition than individual intuition or observation (Nobes and Panagiotaki, "Mental Models," 349). But this research does not call into question the human capacity or penchant to model the world.

41. Sperber, "Intuitive and Reflective Beliefs," 78. I thank Christoph Unger for directing my attention to this article.

42. These arguments from cognitive psychology run counter to the intuitive opinion that peasant farmers did not construct mental models. See, for example, the view of Collins, based on C. S. Lewis's intuitive thought (C. J. Collins, *Reading Genesis Well*, 252).

43. Seely, "The Firmament and the Water Above-I," esp. 228–31; Seely, "The Firmament and the Water Above-II," esp. 31–32; Seely, "The Geographical Meaning of 'Earth,'" esp. 231–33.

navigation," that where the sky touches the earth you can "lean a pestle against it," or "climb up it," that the sky is "smooth and hard . . . of solid rock, . . . as thick as a house," that the sky can "fall down" and someday "will fall down crushing the earth."[44]

Although the notion of water above it is rare, the sky is positioned over a flat-disc earth surrounded by, if not floating on, the ocean, as Seely points out:

> Thus it is that all over the world we find the belief in the earth as a flat circular disc floating in the middle of a single circular sea.[45]

The evidence from ancient South Asian and East Asian societies (e.g., India, China, Japan) is the same.[46] Whether or not there are indications of such a view among the ancient Mesopotamians, Egyptians, and Israelites will be treated below; but the question here pertains to conceptions that have emerged among prescientific peoples excluding the world of the Bible.

Seely's presentation needs critical discussion. Much of his material is derived from the records of Lucien Lévy-Bruhl (original research published in 1910) or the reports in *The Mythology of All Races* (first published in 1916), representing an early generation of anthropologists and mythologists who studied these cultures firsthand or had access to testimony of the first encounters these peoples had with Western explorers and missionaries.[47] Several potential problems adhere to these early encounters. First, statements about natural-world models can be shaped by the form of interrogation, where the Western interviewer's questions lead toward the sort of answer one expects to receive. For example, one might ask a hypothetical question, such as "What would happen if you walked in a straight line until reaching the horizon?" The indigenous person may never have thought about this, and his or her answer could be a guess that was spontaneously conceived. It is possible that this discounts some of the observations recorded. Evans-Pritchard, reflecting a generation later upon these earlier studies, states that the observations of many early explorers and missionaries are unreliable, and some were

---

44. Seely, "The Firmament and the Water Above–1," 230–31.

45. Seely, "The Geographical Meaning of 'Earth,'" 241.

46. Seely, "The Firmament and the Water Above–1," 231–32; Seely, "The Geographical Meaning of 'Earth,'" 241–42.

47. Lévy-Bruhl, *Primitive Mentality*; Gray, *The Mythology of All Races*.

fabrications. Furthermore, by the mid-twentieth century, anthropologists generally rejected the biased distinction in mentality between the nonlogical, magical thoughts of primitive people and the abstract reasoning that characterizes modern people.[48]

However, Evans-Pritchard's comments pertain to religious reflection more generally, not the curious statements about cosmology. If one reads the reports, many of the statements contain wording that seems unlikely to be a response to leading questions; and the testimonies are so widespread and relatively consistent that they seem unlikely to be attributable to interviewer bias.[49] Descriptions point to the physical nature of their conceptions. In addition to the phrases summarized by Seely and quoted above, the material associations of these beliefs is striking. As Lewis reported, the Tahitians and Samoans believed "that the sun descends into the sea each evening and traverses a submarine passage during the night to arise in the east next morning. The Tahitians alleged that people on Borabora, farther west, had heard the hissing as the sun plunged into the ocean at sunset."[50] It is not important whether this allegation about people on Borabora is true or not; such an idea would not be in circulation unless the Tahitians believed it possible, thus revealing the materiality of their cosmology. Ancient Chinese ideas were not consistent but show evidence that the Chinese thought in terms beyond metaphorical. The *kai thien* cosmology regarded the heavens as a solid dome over the earth, which itself was conceived of as an inverted bowl. The striking feature is the precise measurement assigned to the distance between the solid heavens and earth.[51]

More sophisticated research, performed by present-day ethnoastronomers and archaeoastronomers, has confirmed some of the general

48. Evans-Pritchard, *Theories of Primitive Religion*, 6, 88.

49. Readers are encouraged to consult firsthand the reports in Lévy-Bruhl, *Primative Mentality*; and in the volumes of *The Mythology of All Races*, with page citations offered by Seely as a starting reference. The editor of this volume writes, "by thus taking a broad survey, and by considering primarily the simple facts—as presented chiefly by travelers, missionaries, and anthropologists—we may hope to escape some of the peculiar dangers which beset the study of mythology, especially preconceived theories and prejudices, and the risk of taking for aboriginal what is really borrowed and vice versa (Gray, ed., *The Mythology of All Races*, xiii). In other words, the observations reported are not completely without critical assessment.

50. Lewis, "Voyaging Stars," 144–45.

51. Needham, "Astronomy in Ancient and Medieval China," 81; Needham, "The Cosmology of Early China," 88.

conclusions of first-generation anthropologists. For example, Mayan tradition maintained a flat, square earth with groundwater draining into a cosmic ocean. Astral objects make a daily circuit by plunging into and re-emerging from this ocean. Several Mayan models existed for the heavens that incorporated a dome or layers of domes. And the realm under the earth's surface received visitation from the sun each night.[52] These traditions persisted in basic contour even after exposure to European religious traditions with which the earlier ideas became syncretized. The Shipiho of South America believe the sun moves in a daily cycle through the underworld, which together with other astronomical beliefs forms part of an integrated model for agricultural and hunting purposes.[53] The Hopis of the southwestern United States believed that the sun travels under ground in order to rise in the east, and that this is part of a complex *model* of cosmology, not merely language of phenomenological observation. Young concludes her study of the Hopis: "astronomical observation and practices are central to their interlocking spheres of religion, ceremonial practice, and world view."[54] So the early reports should not be discounted completely, nor can one speak of cosmological language as merely "observational." There is a natural propensity of people to construct *models* that help them understand and utilize the natural world around them.

A second criticism of these early studies comes from later anthropologists, who criticized the early generation for assuming a "primitive mind" and therefore interpreting comments from indigenous people literalistically rather than as intended metaphor. Barbara Sproul writes, "Holding literally to the claims of any particular myth, then, is a great error in that it mistakes myth's values for science's facts and results in the worst sort of religiosity."[55] Louis Herbert Gray, the editor of *The Mythology of All Races*, begs readers to bear sympathetically with the myths reported in order to glean a positive message. These ancient and primitive stories, he reminds us, do not satisfy the expectation of the "exact sciences."[56] But it is also the case that twentieth-century mythologists were trying to rescue myth by taking it out of the domain of the physical world where it is doomed by modern science.[57] This does as much injustice to what

52. Lamb, "Tzotzil Maya Cosmology," 165–67.
53. Roe, "Mythic Substitution," 196, 221.
54. M. J. Young, "Astronomy," 61.
55. Sproul, *Primal Myths*, 4.
56. Gray, *The Mythology of All Races*, 1:xi–xii.
57. Segal, *Theorizing about Myth*, 19–21; Segal, "The Modern Study of Myth," 758–59.

prescientific people believe as does overliteralizing their words. The examples cited above suggest that physicality or materiality was indeed part of the mental *models* held by prescientific people.

One criticism of Seely by Noel Weeks is that lack of consistency among prescientific peoples or in ancient cosmological descriptions should warn against projecting a supposedly common ancient Near Eastern view on the biblical text.[58] However, differences in detail do not negate the existence of some general features still shared in common. Campos reports how some people, working from mere observation, construct ad hoc explanations for the physical world; nevertheless, in spite of internal inconsistency, these are part of holistic models in their use.[59] It is the existence of a common, general world picture that makes it probable that ancient Near Easterners shared the same assumptions as more modern prescientific peoples. This is confirmed by the ancient texts themselves (discussed below), which support *basic* contours drawn by modern, graphic representations. This commonness of basic features weakens Poythress's critique of materialistic interpretations of ancient creation texts. One does not need to read these texts as "full-blown physicalistic cosmology" to interpret from them *some* representation of the ancient Near Eastern mental map of physical cosmology.[60] So anthropological evidence is not proof of things ancient, but it is useful heuristically when exploring what is possible or even likely to be true in ancient times.

A Balanced Assessment for the Ancient Near East

The considerations just discussed should caution against two extremes. On the one hand, modern scholars have overread ancient texts with a literalism that does not respect the sophistication that the ancients exercised in describing cosmology. In addition to allowing for analogical

---

58. N. K. Weeks, "Cosmology in Historical Context," esp. 285. This criticism of Seely's arguments does not address all of his evidence, whether anthropological or biblical. In fairness to Weeks, this would have necessitated multiple articles or a short monograph. An additional criticism by Weeks ("Cosmology in Historical Context," 291), the lack of a "comprehensive" model, is irrelevant. Models are rarely comprehensive and need not be for the individual perceptions to be demonstrably false. Similar limitations mark the more recent critiques of Seely by Randall Younker and Richard Davidson (Younker and Davidson, "The Myth of the Solid Heavenly Dome," 31–56).

59. Campos, "Búzios Island," 240–41.

60. So, Poythress's criticism of drawing *any* conclusions about their physical model is unreasonable (Poythress, "Three Modern Myths," 343, cf. 336).

(or metaphorical) language, we should also recognize that ancient descriptions are often unclear and inconsistent, especially regarding details of such things as the boundary between earth's limit and the heavens, the means of access to the underworld, or the relationship between the surface ocean, the fresh waters beneath the earth's surface, and the underworld realm. Therefore, it is hazardous to speculate about how the ancients imagined such interfaces. These boundary features of cosmic geography are most problematic for visual representations, since it is exactly these connecting points that are necessary to portray a holistic visualization in graphic form. Modern conclusions about such matters contribute to overliteralized presentation of ancient cosmology.

On the other hand, there are good reasons to expect, *a priori*, that the ancients did construct mental models of their cosmos and that these ideas would follow cognitions that are common to other pre-scientific peoples. Also, some ancient notions of cosmic geography were not *just* phenomenological or analogical, but were also false perceptions of physical reality. The following treatment endeavors to attend carefully to ancient textual and iconographic portraits, respecting the analogical (or metaphorical) nature of ancient thinking *but at the same time noting clues in narrative as well as ancient ritual*, often overlooked in discussion, that inform us about assumptions in the ancient world picture. There is no attempt here at a comprehensive treatment of ancient Near Eastern cosmography; rather, three important features will illustrate the discrepancy between ancient models and reality, thereby setting the groundwork for exploration of divine accommodation in Scripture.

Tripartite Universe (with a Realm under the Earth)

The partitioning of the universe into three realms is a consistent construct across the ancient Near East. Heaven was the divine realm; earth's surface provided the domain for humans and temple dwellings for deities; and the underworld lodged the deceased and was inhabited by chthonic deities (for Egyptians it was the place of passage for rebirth to afterlife). The most well-known Mesopotamian creation tradition, Enuma Elish (Tablet iv 135–146), describes Marduk splitting the cosmic sea-goddess, Tiamat, in order to make space for earth—three parts consisting of heavenly realm with waters (Anu's domain), atmospheric realm (Enlil's domain), and ocean waters around and in continuity in some manner with the freshwater abyss beneath (Ea's domain). Later, in Tablet v 53–66, one reads the creation of earth in the space of Enlil's domain.⁶¹ More commonly presented in lesser known texts is the simple separation of heaven and earth.⁶² In some Mesopotamian texts, heaven and earth are further subdivided into two or three levels each. For example, in this scheme, the upper earth is the inhabitable surface of the earth, while the middle earth is the freshwater abyss beneath the surface, and the lower earth the realm of underworld deities.⁶³

A similar division is found in the Anatolian (Hittite) context and, even more proximate to ancient Israel, in north Levantine traditions from Ugarit (likely congruous with Canaanite traditions). The Hittite Song of Ullikummi refers to a "copper saw" that was used by the creator gods to cut apart heaven and earth. Its use in the Song was to cut the foot off from a rebel god planted in the underworld. In the process a chthonic deity describes seeing the deceased in the realm under the earth.⁶⁴ A Hittite ritual confirms this structure by reference to the heavens and the underworld

---

61. Weeks denies that this describes a three-tiered universe, criticizing older translations that interpret the construction of Esharra as the earth in Enuma Elish iv 142–145 (N. K. Weeks, "Cosmology in Historical Context," 288). He is correct that the earth is not described in these particular lines. However, they do describe a three-tiered universe in that the domain constructed *between* the waters above and below is the realm of Enlil, who would preside over the earth yet to be constructed in that space (Enuma Elish v 53–66). Enlil's domain is situated between those of Anu in the heavens and Ea in the Apsu, made clear in Enuma Elish iv 146, i.e., three parts. Weeks also attempts to deconstruct the possibility of physical referentiality by noting the inconsistent portrait of boundaries between salt and fresh waters (N. K. Weeks, "Cosmology in Historical Context," 289; for texts relating to this ambiguity, see Horowitz, *Mesopotamian Cosmic Geography*, 131, 340). But the intermingling of fresh-water rivers and salty ocean in southern Mesopotamia provided the ancients with an analogous boundary in the underworld, however incomplete or vague their notions might have been. The conceptual inconsistencies between fresh and salt water associated with Tiamat was evidently no problem either, since not only does the heavenly ocean derived from Tiamat's body provide fresh water (Tablet v 47–52), but Tiamat's body parts are also comingled with freshwater sources of the Apsu for the Tigris and Euphrates (Tablet v 53–60). After all, this is supernatural work of a creator-god. See Tsumura (*The Earth and the Waters*, 60–62) for further discussion on the semantic ambiguity of the Akkadian term, *tamtum*, for both fresh and salt water.

62. Rochberg, "Mesopotamian Cosmology," 317–18; Lambert, *Babylonian Creation Myths*, 169–71. See discussion in chapter 1, pages 26–28, and esp. 30–32.

63. Horowitz, *Mesopotamian Cosmic Geography*, 8–19, 125–28. Horowitz notes that at the time of creation in Enuma Elish, there was no human death, so the underworld was not yet inhabited by the deceased.

64. The Song of Ullikummi (Hoffner, *Hittite Myths*, no. 19 §§60–65; cf. B. J. Collins, *The Hittites*, 191).

as two divine realms distinct from the surface of the earth.⁶⁵ Ugaritic stories do not present a creation account, but extant texts refer to the three realms of heaven–earth–underworld. For example, in the Baal Epic, the hero Baal suffers defeat at the hands of Mot, the god of the underworld; and he must leave the divine council in heaven to descend into the realm of the dead under the surface of the earth, while earth itself suffers in his absence.⁶⁶ More prominent than in Mesopotamian tradition, however, is the place of the sea, represented in the cosmological division of heaven–sea–underworld that corresponds to the three prominent deities in the Baal Epic—Baal, Yamm, and Mot, respectively.⁶⁷ This special emphasis on the sea is due to Ugarit's maritime culture.⁶⁸

This geographical structure is taken for granted in stories that are not directly cosmological (as in creation accounts). In other words, cosmic geography is only incidentally mentioned in the course of the story. This dissociates geographical cognitions from myth in a way that reveals real-world assumptions. If the story is to cohere with expectations of how "life works," then some physical reality must be attributed to descriptions in the narrative for the story to "work." This is illustrated in the Gilgamesh Epic. Gilgamesh's friend Enkidu has a nightmare that portends his death. He describes in some detail the realities that await him in the underworld.⁶⁹ Like all dreams, this must conform in some measure to reality as understood by the dreamer. Even as deities came "down" from heaven above to dwell in shrines on mountaintops or ziggurats, underworld beings came "up" from below. Cracks in the earth reached to the underworld realm. In the source titled Gilgamesh and the Netherworld, Gilgamesh contacts his deceased friend through a hole in the ground from which Enkidu's ghost emerges.⁷⁰ The assumption that

---

65. B. J. Collins, *The Hittites*, 192. For text see Otten and Siegelova, "Die Hethitischen Gulš-Gottheiten," 32–38.

66. *KTU* 1.5, lines iv 1–v 17 (S. B. Parker, ed., *Ugaritic Narrative Poetry*, 146–48). Mot opens his mouth with one lip toward the heaven and one lip toward the earth, through which Baal descends to the underworld (*KTU* 1.5, lines ii 2–6 [S. B. Parker, ed., *Ugaritic Narrative Poetry*, 143, lines ii 2–6]). El anticipates restoration of earth when Baal returns to its surface (*KTU* 1.6, lines iii 4–21).

67. Del Olmo Lete, *Canaanite Religion*, 47–48.

68. Del Olmo Lete, *Canaanite Religion*, 53–54.

69. Epic of Gilgamesh, vii 162–208 (in George, trans., *The Epic of Gilgamesh*, 59–61).

70. Bilgamesh and the Netherworld, xii 86–87 (in George, trans., *The Epic of Gilgamesh*, 194; cf. Horowitz, *Mesopotamian Cosmic Geography*, 360).

demons could "pass through openings in the earth's surface" underlies incantations.[71] Continual food offerings to ancestors buried under houses or in underground tombs implies access from the realm of the dead below.[72] It is hard to make sense of these practices without some function in the physical reality of these people.

Egyptian conceptions of the netherworld are complex. What they thought transpired after death varied considerably, particular over time. One tradition, primarily early, describes postdeath events in the Duat (earthly regions at the horizon; sometimes translated "netherworld"); but it attaches the deceased person's progress to the return of the sun in the eastern horizon through the hidden inner body of the sky-goddess, Nut.[73] This is not an underworld. However, another tradition describes the existence of an inverted world of the dead that mirrors the surface of earth inhabited by the living.[74] Even as cosmic waters exist above the sky, these waters have a counterpart beneath the earth where one can "descend." The mirroring of these waters is expressed in the hieroglyphic determinatives for the waters above and below.[75] In this conception, the sun sets and rises in the Duat, but the Duat constitutes an interface between the visible horizon and the underworld to which the sun journeys at sunset.[76] Egyptologists give titles such as "Twelve Caves" and "Book of Caverns" to certain New Kingdom burial texts and iconography, drawing from language in the texts appropriate to an underworld.[77] The emergence of the role of the earth-god, Geb, in these texts also suggests an

---

71. Horowitz, *Mesopotamian Cosmic Geography*, 360–61. For general discussion regarding the properties of the underworld, see Horowitz, *Mesopotamian Cosmic Geography*, 348–62

72. For description of the Mesopotamian funerary cult, including the use of pipes in the ground, see Scurlock, "Death and the Afterlife," 3:1888–89. Similar pipes have been claimed for tombs at Ugarit, but this interpretation of the archaeological evidence has been overturned (Pitard, "The 'Libation Installations," 20–37). The Akkadian word, *apu* (B), can describe a "pit" for presentation of food to the deceased (*CAD* 1/2: 201), and similar pits were dug to access the underworld realm in Hittite ritual (B. J. Collins, *The Hittites*, 169–70).

73. See Lesko, "Ancient Egyptian Cosmogonies," 118–20; Hornung, *The Ancient Egyptian Books of the Afterlife*, 5–6, 11; Dijk, "Paradise," 309–11.

74. Allen, "The World of Ancient Egyptian Thought," 76.

75. Allen, *Genesis in Egypt*, 4.

76. Allen, *Genesis in Egypt*, 6–7.

77. E.g., the use of the Egyptian *qereret*, "cave," in descriptions of the journey (Hornung, *The Ancient Egyptian Books of the Afterlife*, 54, 84–85).

underworld location, as do many of the descriptions, such as "cauldrons" where the condemned are burned.[78] Magical incantations were necessary for the deceased to avoid experiencing the underworld in upside-down fashion, as though walking along the underside of the earth in reverse position. The deceased are equipped with incantations against snakes, which shows that their conception of the underworld corresponded to a real location beneath the earth's surface.[79] New Kingdom texts also begin incorporating these same underworld images into the older celestial motifs.[80] Artwork on coffin lids and in burial chambers depicts this three-tiered universe most clearly, sometimes combining iconography and text.[81] Figure 2 depicts the sky-goddess, Nut, arching over the reclined visage of the earth-god, Geb, with the god of the underworld, Osiris, partly emerging from under the earth at the Duat.

FIGURE 2: EGYPTIAN CREATION

E. A. Wallis Budge, *The Gods of the Egyptians*, vol. 2 (1904), facing p. 95. The Louvre.

---

78. E.g., Hornung, *The Ancient Egyptian Books of the Afterlife*, 63–64, 88–89, 97, 116, 149.

79. See COS 1.21:32 (cf. Lesko, "Ancient Egyptian Cosmogonies," 120–21).

80. Hornung, *The Ancient Egyptian Books of the Afterlife*, 112.

81. Cf. Cornelius, "The Visual Representation," 196–97 and p. 212, fig. 2; Keel and Schroer, *Creation*, 80–81 and p. 79, fig. 81. See also the text in COS 1.1:5–6 for captions that describe parts of such iconography.

The Egyptian descriptions and incantations, like the Mesopotamian materials discussed earlier, make sense only if some degree of physicality can be ascribed to their mental constructs.

Geocentrism (with a Flat Earth)

As far as is known, the idea that earth orbits the sun was first set forth by a Greek astronomer and mathematician, Aristarchus of Samos (c. 310 BCE—230 BCE).[82] But the idea did not displace the prevailing notion of geocentrism until Copernicus offered substantial mathematical support that eventually overturned the Ptolemaic model in the sixteenth and seventeenth centuries. Even the idea of a spherical earth, as far as is known, was first set forth in Greek science.[83] One would expect ancient Near Easterners to share a pre-Copernican model as well as the idea that the earth is flat, and this cognition is confirmed by both textual and iconographic evidence. Language of the sun descending on the western horizon and ascending in the east is not purely phenomenological. It was part of a complex schema that imagined the sun visiting the underworld at night. For example, one early Mesopotamian hymn declares:

> [Shamash, the sun God], imposing light, he makes his rounds,
> Keeping watch over the land by day and by night,
> The lands of Ea [Ea's domain is the Apsu beneath the earth].[84]

The Shamash Hymn speaks of the sun-god traversing the seas into the underworld where the gods rejoice when he makes his appearance and shows his radiance in "the deep" (*apsu*).[85]

A frequently printed image is the Sun-God Tablet (see fig. 3):[86]

---

82. Lindberg, *The Beginnings of Western Science*, 95–96.

83. Plato proposed a spherical earth surrounded by a spherical heavens (Lindberg, *The Beginnings of Western Science*, 41).

84. The Valorous Sun, lines 13–15 (in Foster, *Before the Muses*, 50).

85. Shamash Hymn, lines 27–42 (in Lambert, *Babylonian Wisdom Literature*, 128–29 [line 37]; see Foster, *Before the Muses*, 629).

86. For a recent and exhaustive study, see Woods, "The Sun-God Tablet," 23–103.

64 OLD TESTAMENT COSMOLOGY & DIVINE ACCOMMODATION

FIGURE 3: BABYLONIAN SUN-GOD TABLET

Kim Walton, taken at the British Museum. Used with permission.

On this tablet, iconography and text combine to show the sun-god in relation to the underworld waters (named in one of the captions as the Apsu).[87] The wavy lines are often wrongly interpreted as the "heavenly ocean."[88] However, the Akkadian term *apsu* is not used for any waters other than the deep ocean, the Abyss of the underworld god, Ea, or things

---

87. ZU.AB in line 1 of Caption II (above canopy) (Woods, "The Sun-God Tablet," 83).

88. This began with the initial publication of the tablet by L. W. King (*Babylonian Boundary Stones*, 121 n. 2) and has been followed by most since. E.g., Cornelius, "The Visual Representation," 198, 215; Wright, *The Early History of Heaven*, 36–37; Batto, *In the Beginning*, 9; Greenwood, *Scripture and Cosmology*, 61.

related to these, such as temple water basins.[89] Interpreted correctly, the iconography depicts Shamash emerging from his activity in the underworld waters at sunrise, reinforcing the standard tripartite cosmic divisions in Mesopotamian thought.[90] This portrayal is deeply metaphorical and theological, but it reinforces the belief a realm exists beneath the earth through which the sun moves during the night, and through which the planets and stars make their daytime journey.

The travels of Gilgamesh to the farthermost reaches of the earth take him to mountain ranges on east and west: they are depicted as unique vantage points from which to observe the sun rising and setting.[91] The assumption underlying this cognition is that the earth is fixed, and one needs to travel to the horizon for special access to the activity of the sun as it commences and ends its daily journey:

> To far-off regions unknown and for uncoun[ted] leagues You have persevered, O Shamash, what you went by day you returned by night . . . there is none who does such wearisome toil but you.[92]

The Egyptian beliefs about the underworld were noted above. This is relevant to the question of solar motion in the same way that it is in the Mesopotamian framework. In both cultures, astral objects were conceived as agents in motion, but this motion is not merely a phenomenal observation on the part of human perception; rather it occurs in a realm beneath earth's surface that is the locus of divine activity and part of a larger schema of real, populated places with physical relationships to one another.

Related to the question of geocentrism are ancient perceptions about the physical shape of the earth. The Babylonian World Map offers what we might today call an aerial view of the earth, drawn as a single,

---

89. See *CAD* 1/2:194-97.

90. For example, bull-man figures open the doors of sunrise for Shamash, and a serpent-canopy that arches over Shamash is associated with the serpentine boat of the Apsu, which glyphic art often uses to portray Shamash's journey through the underworld at night. This underworld, Apsu-serpent motif is also common on *kudurru* markers, a class of iconographical-textual artifacts to which the Shamash tablet is related. Stars appear in the waters, corresponding to their proper night time abode in the underworld after Shamash rises (Woods, "The Sun-God Tablet," 57, 71, 77-80).

91. Horowitz, *Mesopotamian Cosmic Geography*, 97-98.

92. Shamash Hymn, lines 43-45 (Foster, *Before the Muses*, 629; see Horowitz, *Mesopotamian Cosmic Geography*, 333-34).

circular continent with ocean flowing around it as an outer circle. Beyond the ocean are regions represented by triangles emanating from the ocean (see fig. 4).[93]

FIGURE 4: BABYLONIAN WORLD MAP

John H. Walton, taken at the British Museum. Used with permission.

These regions are likely islands, but in any event, the text ascribes to them exotic and mythological creatures and legendary inhabitants.[94]

93. Horowitz, *Mesopotamian Cosmic Geography*, 20–42.

94. Horowitz, *Mesopotamian Cosmic Geography*, 35–36; cf. Millard, "Cartography," 111. This comports to some degree with the mid-first-millennium-BCE Greek concept of Oceanus (Horowitz, *Mesopotamian Cosmic Geography*, 40–41).

The details do not represent geographical relationships as moderns would inscribe on a map but project geopolitical ideology of the ancient mapmakers.[95] Nevertheless, the general idea of a continental mass, ostensibly surrounded by water, suggests the limits of their world in that it functions to portray the global rule of the monarch (even if only imaginary ideologically). David O'Connor shows that Egyptian maps could "render topography with relative accuracy," at the same time suffusing it with mythological significance.[96] A similar construct is reflected in the story of Etana's flight to the heavens. The hero's view of earth and sea is reported at various altitudes above the earth. At a height just before the world disappears from view, the text describes the sea encircling the land like a boundary ditch.[97] The Egyptians appear to have shared this general idea, since one of the Egyptian terms for the sea, *shen-wer*, means "great encircler," perhaps a precursor to the Greek *okeanos*.[98] A corresponding image is the creator-god emerging from the cosmic waters and "floating" like a seed at the beginning of creation.[99] Another image of this event is the emergence of the primeval hillocks, the first land.[100] These texts suggest but do not in themselves prove that the ancients thought of the

---

95. Beate Pongratz-Leisten shows how texts and images with cosmological reference function as political statements (Pongratz-Leisten, "*Mental Map*," 261–79). Thus, the Babylonian World Map offers a geographical presentation that does not necessarily correspond to what we would consider "reality"; rather, it mixes real-space perception ("mental map") with "world view" to form a "culture-landscape" (276). Cf. Rochberg, "The Expression of Terrestrial and Celestial Order," 33–34.

96. O'Connor, "From Topography to Cosmos," 77.

97. Etana, III/A, lines 31–41 (in Foster, *Before the Muses*, 551; Horowitz, *Mesopotamian Cosmic Geography*, 62–63). Weeks interprets the "boundary ditch" image in Etana as necessitating another land mass on the other side of the ocean, hence the world was not really perceived as a single continent surrounded by water (N. K. Weeks, "Cosmology in Historical Context," 286). However, this is in direct contradiction to the interpretation of Horowitz whom he cites. Horowitz writes, "This couplet [with description of the irrigation ditch] seems to explain that the sea encircles the land just as canals and boundary ditches often surrounded fields and gardens" (Horowitz, *Mesopotamian Cosmic Geography*, 63). Horowitz notes that the limited width of a boundary ditch represents the limits of the cosmic ocean as observed from Etana's height above the earth, not that it entails another land mass on the other side (62). In other words, the other side of the boundary ditch is the end of the world.

98. Lesko, "Ancient Egyptian Cosmogonies," 117.

99. Seely, "The Geographical Meaning of 'Earth,'" 243. See CT 714 vi 343k–344d in *COS* 1:2 or Allen, *Genesis in Egypt*, 13.

100. See PT 600 in *COS* 1.4:7. Cf. Hoffmeier, "Some Thoughts on Genesis 1 & 2," 46; Allen, *Genesis in Egypt*, 10, 13–14.

earth as a flat disk floating on water. But one text in particular supports this interpretation. The account of Marduk's creative work in the Eridu Genesis uses the metaphor of a "raft" for the earth over the waters that originally covered all the world: "Marduk tied together a raft on the surface of the waters, He created dirt and heaped it on the raft."[101] In any metaphor, some aspects of the source image (a raft) are transferred to the target referent (earth). The clarifying description that Marduk heaped dirt on bundled reeds negates the material transfer from the metaphor. A raft in the southern marshes of Mesopotamia could be constructed from reeds, but that aspect is not applied to the target. Rather, the structural relationship between a raft and the water upon which it floats is the fundamental concept being conveyed. It is difficult to imagine in what sense this is metaphorical without a corresponding physical model being described. This text also corresponds to the creation account in Enuma Elish in which Marduk "built the earth over the waters."[102]

It needs to be stressed that background assumptions of a geocentric universe and flat earth are necessary to make sense of the geographical schema as a whole. As Horowitz summarizes, "All of the available evidence agrees that the earth's surface ends at the horizon, the place where heaven and earth meet [and] that the earth's surface was thought to be basically circular in shape."[103] We do not need to understand the details of how the ancients might have explained the interface between various regions of their universe (for example, between the sky–earth–underworld; or between the saltwater Apsu and the freshwater Apsu). They likely did not have an explanation. Yet failure to account for every facet of their model does not discount the physical reality of what they generalized. To a limited degree, they did have a *theory*, which is that the sun is the manifestation of a personal agent, the god Shamash (Mesopotamia) or Re (Egypt), and that *he* moves under independent power across the surface of the earth during the day and through the underworld at night. Their model of the natural world was metaphorical and theological; however, this also does not discount that the ancients did conceptualize the

---

101. Marduk, Creator of the World, lines 17–18 (in Foster, *Before the Muses*, 488; in Lambert, *Babylonian Creation Myths*, 372–73).

102. Enuma Elish vii 83 (in Horowitz, *Mesopotamian Cosmic Geography*, 129, 132). Cf. the hymnic line, "You balance the disk of the world in the midst of heaven (for) the circle of the lands" (Shamash Hymn, line 22; in Lambert, *Babylonian Wisdom Literature*, 126; in Foster, *Before the Muses*, 628).

103. Horowitz, *Mesopotamian Cosmic Geography*, 330 and 334.

physical structure of their universe, and traces of these assumptions are revealed incidentally in text and iconography.

Cosmic Ocean (behind a Solid Sky?)

The ancients understood that a correlation existed between clouds and rain. However, clouds were not the only feature associated with water above the earth. Some texts, both Mesopotamian and Egyptian, suggest that they conceived of water in mass at the limits of the heavens. Best-known is the account in Enuma Elish, which presents Marduk's first act of creation when he splits in half the deep-sea goddess, Tiamat:

> Bēl rested, surveying the corpse,
> In order to divide the lump by a clever scheme.
> He split her into two like a dried fish:
> One half of her he set up and stretched out as the heavens.
> He stretched the skin and appointed a watch
> With the instruction not to let her waters escape.[104]

This heavenly body of water mirrors the body of fresh water below it in clamshell fashion. As cautioned above, the ancients did not likely imagine that a dragon skin held back part of the ocean overhead, any more than one should expect literal consistency between the image of the goddess as watery expanse and as sea-dragon. And it is possible that the account simply presents the provision of atmospheric moisture and rain in symbolic imagery. However, Enuma Elish offers evidence that in *this* tradition at least, the physical structure of the heavens incorporates a reservoir of water. It describes clouds as the *staging* of waters drawn from a cosmic sea before it falls to earth:

> The foam which Tiāmat [. . .
> Marduk fashion [. . .
> He gathered it together and made it into clouds.
> The raging of the winds, violent rainstorms,
> The billowing of mist—the accumulation of her spittle—
> He appointed for himself and took them in his hand.[105]

104. Enuma Elish iv 135–140 (in Lambert, *Babylonian Creation Myths*, 94–95).

105. Enuma Elish v 47–52 (in Lambert, *Babylonian Creation Myths*, 100–101). Horowitz offers the translation "clouds" in line 49, but based on a conjectured reading of the text available to him (Horowitz, *Mesopotamian Cosmic Geography*, 117–18).

Marduk draws from Tiamat's waters, then collects and rolls them into clouds to make rain. This is not a one-time event; rather, Marduk establishes the ongoing meteorological system that continues to operate on the basis described in the text, even as he puts into place the other resources described in the context.

It must be admitted that Enuma Elish is the only Mesopotamian text that explicitly describes a *reservoir* of water in the heavens. However, several less direct lines of evidence point to this same cognition. One ancient Mesopotamian commentary interprets the etymology of "heaven" (*šame*) as "(composed) of water" (*ša me*).[106] It must be stressed that this is not a *modern* etymology, rather a commentary by an *ancient* scholar living in the original context. However, this need not necessitate a *reservoir*. Indeed the same word (*šame*) is related to a common term for precipitation.[107] However, other Mesopotamian texts suggest that morning dew comes from stars in the sky at night, which function as teats to release water from above (i.e., a water-laden reservoir).[108] But this, too, must be used with caution since elsewhere the metaphor of "breasts" is parallel to "clouds."[109]

A similar idea is conveyed by the Egyptian portrait of the sky-goddess Nut holding back the infinite waters (see fig. 2). This interpretation of iconography is confirmed by textual captions, indicating that waters were above her, that is, above heaven where the stars appear.[110] In both

---

Philippe Talon follows the same intuition ("*nuages*," Talon, *The Standard Babylonian Creation Myth*, 58, 96). However, Lambert's collation (Lambert, *Babylonian Creation Myths*, 100) from more manuscripts offers a clearer reading, *erpe*[*ti*]. The word translated "rain" in line 50 (*kaṣaṣu*) is rare (cf. Lambert, *Babylonian Creation Myths*, 478, notes on lines 50–52). Nevertheless, the source (Tiamat's spittle/venom) and other meteorological phenomena in these lines makes the concept of cloud formation from the heavenly waters and some form of precipitation very likely.

106. Horowitz, *Mesopotamian Cosmic Geography*, 224, 262; Lambert, *Babylonian Creation Myths*, 171.

107. Horowitz, *Mesopotamian Cosmic Geography*, 262.

108. Horowitz, *Mesopotamian Cosmic Geography*, 243–44, 262.

109. Horowitz, *Mesopotamian Cosmic Geography*, 263.

110. Allen, *Genesis in Egypt*, 4–5 and pl. 1; Allen, "The World of Ancient Egyptian Thought," 76; Hornung, *The Ancient Egyptian Books of the Afterlife*, 114 and fig. 64. The book of Nut describes the space outside Nut's body as "darkness" and "ocean" (*COS* 1.1:5–6). James Allen notes that the particular word for "ocean" (*qbḥw*, "cool waters"; cf. Faulkner, *A Concise Dictionary of Middle Egyptian*, 278) denotes waters upon which boats navigate as well as being a word for "sky." The Egyptians merely speculated as to what lies outside the known universe (Allen, *Genesis in Egypt*, 3–4); but the idea of

Enuma Elish and Egyptian tradition, the waters above constitute the primeval, cosmic ocean held in check through supernatural action. In the first case, Marduk appoints "a watch" over the interface created from Tiamat's "skin."[111] In Egyptian cosmology, the god of atmosphere, Shu, supports the sky-goddess, Nut—sometimes assisted by the eight primordial gods.[112] As noted in discussion of the underworld, these Mesopotamian and Egyptian texts involve complex schemas. The imagery pertains not merely to atmospheric functions of the water cycle. The images are embedded in mental constructs of the universe as a whole. Only the assumption that a potentially destructive reservoir of water exists in the physical structure of the heavens makes sense of the necessity for divine agency to keep it in check.[113]

In spite of the current trend in scholarship to assert the contrary, the ancients may have conceived of heaven as having a two-dimensional (perhaps even solid) interface, although not necessarily in the shape of a dome.[114] We deduce this not from the mineralogical terms used for the "floor" of heaven, which are symbolic materials.[115] More suggestive is the description of fixed stars being "etched" in permanent places on the surface of the heavens that rotated together every twenty-four hours. Gods and people lived *ina libbi* ("in the midst") of their regions, but the stars were drawn *ina muhhi* ("on the surface") of the lowest heaven.[116] This contrast in prepositions makes the best sense if heaven is structured in part with a two-dimensional interface. In addition, the ancients knew that some objects such as meteorites literally came from heaven, which they conceived as stones fallen from the barrier above.[117] Whatever held back the heavenly ocean may not have been dragon skin, but it consisted of material-like properties, a dam that not only held back water but also blocked the human gaze into the heavenly realm.

---

cosmic waters corresponds to their creation accounts.

111. Enuma Elish iv 139 (in Lambert, *Babylonian Creation Myths*, 95).

112. Allen, *Genesis in Egypt*, plate 3.

113. One could suggest that the ancients understood vapor as an invisible reservoir, but this seems highly unlikely.

114. Allen doubts that this interface was solid in Egyptian cosmology (Allen, *Genesis in Egypt*, 5).

115. Horowitz, *Mesopotamian Cosmic Geography*, 9–15, 263.

116. Horowitz, *Mesopotamian Cosmic Geography*, 14–15.

117. Horowitz, *Mesopotamian Cosmic Geography*, 263; Hoffmeier, "Some Thoughts on Genesis 1 & 2," 45; Lesko, "Ancient Egyptian Cosmogonies," 117.

In summary, this array of descriptions suggests that there is more going on than mere analogical thinking. The ancients' vocabulary was metaphorical, but this does not necessarily preclude the transfer of the image's physical aspects. These metaphors incorporated notions of physical reality in the natural world, consisting of a three-tiered universe; a flat-earth, geocentric astronomical scheme; and probably a watery reservoir in the heavens held in check by a two-dimensional (and less probably a solid) interface.

Israel's Shared Cosmic Assumptions

Ancient Israel shared many of the same assumptions as its neighbors regarding cosmic geography. This is evident in the Old Testament language of the cosmos, and it is unsurprising due to the geographical and temporal proximity of Israel to Mesopotamian and Egyptian traditions and even texts, as noted in chapter 1. However, this shared world picture has more to do with inhabiting the same cultural stream and less to do with any dependence on specific ancient Near Eastern traditions. Like the above discussion of ancient Near Eastern constructs, the following discussion does not come close to exhaustive treatment. Rather, the focus is on general cosmic structures that can be more securely validated by incidental details, particularly those appearing in *narrative* texts.

Tripartite Universe (with a Realm under the Earth)

One frequent schema of cosmic geography in the Old Testament divides the universe into three parts: heaven–earth–sea (*yam*, Exod 20:11).[118] Closely associated with the sea is the "abyss" (*tehom*, Ps 135:6). This term is also used alongside heaven and earth (Prov 3:19–20; Ps 148:1, 7) and may include the underworld.[119] Corresponding to "heaven–earth–sea" are creatures of these respective domains (birds, animals, fish; Zeph 1:3).[120] But one also finds the same categories of the cosmos (heaven–earth–underworld) that are prominent in the broader ancient Near Eastern world (Amos 9:2–3).[121]

---

118. Also, Pss 69:34 (Heb. 35); 96:11; 146:6; Neh 9:6; Jonah 1:9 (dry land).
119. Cf. Tsumura, *The Earth and the Waters*, 73–75.
120. Greenwood, *Scripture and Cosmology*, 86.
121. Also, Job 11:8–9; 26:5–6; Ps 139:8–9; and probably Exod 20:4 (Deut 5:8), if

Aside from distinctions in terminology, there is also strong evidence of the cosmic regions, heaven and underworld, in narrative descriptions. The heavens are "above" the earth's surface, described in physical-spatial terms in several passages. For example, when Israel's elders *ascend* the mountain to commune with God, they gaze at him above, through the sapphire-blue ceiling of heaven upon which God's feet rest (Exod 24:10). Similarly, Elisha views Elijah's *ascent* to heaven on the chariot of fire (2 Kgs 2:11). An underworld also exists in the cosmic geography of ancient Israelites. An example not commonly discussed is the Korahite *descent* into Sheol through a crack that opened in the earth (Num 16:31–34; "they went down . . . alive into Sheol").[122] Like Exod 24:11 and 2 Kgs 2:11, what is particularly important here is the narrative description of an experience that makes sense only if it corresponds to Israel's expectations about the structure of the physical universe. The vision of Samuel arising out of the earth (1 Sam 28:13) implies the same mental map.[123] It does not matter whether Samuel actually came back from the dead, or whether the experience was only visionary. For the experience or the narrative report to have cognitive effect, the description needed to cohere with real-world expectations. Ancient Israelites believed that a geographical realm of the dead existed below the surface of the earth.

Geocentricity (with a Flat Earth?)

Apart from theological considerations about any divine properties of the sun, the ancient Israelites conceived of solar motion in same manner as their contemporaries—not necessarily as a *personal* agent but as an object in motion.[124] While the word sometimes used to denote "sunrise" can

---

the phrase "in the earth beneath" corresponds to a subterranean realm that includes chthonic deities and the dead. For a maximal argument, see Wright, *The Early History of Heaven*, 53–54. See discussion below for counterarguments to the schema of a subterranean ocean.

122. For discussion of Sheol, particularly as a place, see P. S. Johnston, *Shades of Sheol*, esp. 70–77.

123. The possibility that necromancy involved digging a pit in the ground to access the realm of the dead, similar to Mesopotamian custom, further reinforces this (see Albertz and Schmitt, *Family and Household Religion*, 470). Although for the interpretation that the Hebrew 'ot refers to an ancestor statue rather than a pit, see Hays (*A Covenant With Death*, 170–74).

124. It is beyond the scope of this discussion to engage the question of orthodox Israelite faith versus the many other currents that existed alongside it.

emphasize its "shining light" (*zrḥ*; 2 Sam 3:24),¹²⁵ it is sometimes coupled with words of motion. For example, the sun travels a twenty-four-hour circuit, rising in the morning (*zrḥ*) and going [down] in the evening (*boʾ*; "to come, go"; Eccl 1:5). God's journey from the south (*boʾ*) is semantically parallel to his "dawning" (*zrḥ*; Deut 33:2). In both cases, an assumption about actual motion is associated with "dawning." But other descriptions of sunrise use a verb of motion. For example, the sun "had gone (*yṣʾ*) up over the earth" (Gen 19:23). The sun travels out of its chamber as a sound would travel across the earth (*yṣʾ*; Ps 19:4–5). In this psalm, the metaphor for God's pervasive glory is senseless without the notion of extending motion. God's command can stop the sun (Job 9:7).¹²⁶ When the sun sets, it "goes" [down] (*boʾ*; Deut 16:6). Solar motion was part of the encyclopedic entry about the sun rising, moving across the sky, setting, and traveling its circuit toward morning sunrise. Modern interpreters often dismiss this as merely "phenomenological" or "operational" use of language. The problem with this is that we moderns regard such language as phenomenological or operational, but the ancients did not. The motion of astral objects relative to the earth is part of an ancient schema of how objects in the real world relate and interact. As noted above, in their own way the ancients *did theorize* about these questions and constructed mental maps of cosmic geography. These mental maps may have been accurate enough for operational, calendar needs; but as physical models they were false. Orthodox Old Testament theology denied divine properties for the sun, but ancient Israelites, similar to their neighbors, likely assumed an operational model of the sun's daily cycle relative to a fixed earth. This likelihood is confirmed by Eccl 1:5, where a return path for the sun implies its motion within a physical model of astronomical relationships.¹²⁷

125. Also, 2 Kgs 3:22; cf. Isa 58:10, like noonday.

126. Josh 10:12–13 was a primary text used against heliocentrism, but the interpretation of this text is complicated by the possibility that the language denotes an omen rather than describes solar motion, or that it is simply divine warrior imagery (cf. Hab 3:11).

127. Poythress ("Three Modern Myths," 324–28) minimizes the problem by appeal to the fact that no human, even modern, has an absolute vantage point for observation. Rather, in consideration of the theory of general relativity, both earth and sun are in motion. Whether general relativity is the correct theory to apply here is not important; Poythress's point is that there is no absolute reference point for *motion*, and that is correct. However, for the ancients, they believed the earth was such a point (as did Western intellectuals until the Copernican revolution when the reference point shifted to the sun). So the *model* of the universe, *how* the ancients conceived of this

Did the ancient Israelites conceive of the earth as flat? Language such as "four corners" or "edges of the earth" (Isa 11:12) likely refers to compass orientation, not a physical description of the earth as though it had corners. The same expression refers to compass orientation in Mesopotamia.[128] However, in some Old Testament uses, the term "edge" suggests a geographical end to the earth at the horizon (Deut 13:7; Ps 19:4 [Heb. 5]). This might only be making the rhetorical point that something is "a long way away" (e.g., Deut 28:49, 64). However, this figure of speech is meaningful in this hyperbolic sense only because there is an ultimate geographical edge. Indeed, in Ps 19:4, the extreme edges of the earth are *not* hyperbolic in the poet's mind, since God's word extends to the most literal geographical extent, a place where the sun appears and disappears. Along this line of thought, Kyle Greenwood's elaboration of Seely's argument from Dan 4:11 bears some weight. The vision of a tree from which one can see the edges of the earth is sensible given an incidental assumption that the earth is flat.[129] This language is pure metaphor *only*

---

motion, and their mental representation is what matters in this discussion. Their models consisted of an encyclopedic range of ideas that are related to the motion they describe. Poythress maintains that even our modern, scientific models are not wholly accurate, and we need to grant to the ancients the right to use working models (in contrast to *theoretical* models) in their manner of speech without the culpability of error (even as we grant for modern working models). However, there is a difference between working models that are *valid approximations* for the real world and working models that are false. In the case of ancient cognitions, their *model* was false, not approximate, even if their *perception* of relative motion was accurate and serviceable. Poythress correctly notes that the most important question is what manner the text of Scripture might affirm such false assumptions; that is, whether *biblical authors and their texts theorize* in their informative intention (Poythress, "Three Modern Myths," 327). This is the subject of the next chapter.

Speaking of the terms for the sun's motion, Collins maintains that "there is no passage in which the portrayal corresponds to an actual physical model . . . conventionality serves the purpose of ready reference without being concerned with a physical model" (C. J. Collins, *Reading Genesis Well*, 251–52). The individual terms are "fairly bland," as he suggests, but Eccl 1:5 as a whole verse pair suggests a model of motion that makes best sense in the context of the cosmic geography similar to Israel's neighbors.

128. Horowitz, *Mesopotamian Cosmic Geography*, 204–7, 324–25; Greenwood, *Scripture and Cosmology*, 78.

129. Greenwood, *Scripture and Cosmology*, 75–76. Cf. Seely, "The Geographical Meaning of 'Earth,'" 238. The many examples of kings having dominion to the ends of the earth are hyperbolic, to be sure, but the vision of the tree is particularly revealing about cognitive assumptions. The same is true regarding the comparison of the earth to a blanket (or garment) in Job 38:13 (Seely, "The Geographical Meaning of 'Earth,'" 239).

for someone who is aware that the earth is spherical. As already noted, the cognition of a spherical earth is unattested before Greek science.[130]

While the language of supporting "pillars" (1 Sam 2:8; Job 9:6; Ps 75:3) is likely metaphorical (like "pillars of heaven," Job 26:11),[131] the *need* for support to stabilize the earth, whether purely supernatural or by some geophysical structure speculated by the ancients, is related to another notion that the earth is underlaid by a cosmic sea. There is debate as to whether the word "deep" (*tehom*) in the Old Testament ever refers to a subterranean ocean as a body of water. It may simply be a reference to the deep surface ocean or a vague notion of groundwater. Houtman argues that it is not so much a "place" but rather a designation for the "power of water" in its universality and many forms, both favorable and hostile.[132] He acknowledges that texts which speak of the earth "upon" (*'al*) the waters (Ps 24:2; 136:6) might mean that God's power holds it there firmly in place. But he suggests an alternative: that the earth is "higher than" the seas, citing uses of the proposition *'al* to mean "beside waters" (Gen 16:7).[133] C. John Collins adds that the "waters under the earth" in Exod 20:4 (Deut 5:8) should be understood in this manner, since commentary on this text in Deut 4:18 refers to fish in these waters.[134] However, fish images are known to represent supernatural beings, some of whom are related to the god Ea, whose domain is the subterranean abyss.[135] So, in this case, the fish images represent chthonic deities. Furthermore, the construction in Ps 136:6 more likely denotes spreading (*raqa'*) the

---

130. Our modern idiom "ends of the earth" is used by convention from ancient literary tradition even though those using it understand that the earth is spherical. However, the ancients did not.

131. Compare the pillars visualized on a Mesopotamian *kudurru* (boundary marker), illustrated with discussion in Cornelius, "The Visual Representation," 198, 214, fig. 4; and in Keel and Schroer, *Creation*, 81–82, fig. 84.

132. Houtman, *Der Himmel im Alten Testament*, 269.

133. Also, Exod 14:2, 9; Num 24:6; Ps 1:3. Houtman notes that the collocation of the verb "founded" (*ysd*) with "upon" (*'al*) simply means "grounded" in a metaphorical sense (Pss 24:2; 104:5) (Houtman, *Der Himmel im Alten Testament*, 270). Seely insists that this imagery requires the sense of "set something upon a foundation base" (Seely, "The Geographical Meaning of 'Earth,'" 251). The resolution of the difference depends on what aspects of the image of foundation-work are intended to be transferred to the target, the creation of earth.

134. C. J. Collins, *Genesis 1–4*, 264; C. J. Collins, *Reading Genesis Well*, 248.

135. E.g., the *apkallu* (see Greenfield, "Apkallu," 72–74).

earth over top of water, as Seely has argued using the collocation of a synonymous verb (*radad*) with '*al* in 1 Kgs 6:32.¹³⁶

In several passages, the abyss (*tehom*) is the subterranean source for groundwater (Prov 8:24; Ezek 31:3-5). But it also appears in Ps 135:6 alongside the common word for ocean (*yam*), possibly suggesting coextension between surface ocean (*yam*) and the abyss (*tehom*) that extends below the earth. This is reinforced by the parallelism in the passage between the words "heaven/earth" and "sea/abyss," where heavens are over the surface (earth/sea) even as the abyss descends below them. Furthermore, Job 38:16-17 might locate the abyss in proximity to the underworld realm of the dead, as in Mesopotamian cosmic geography (cf. Jonah 2:2-6).¹³⁷ While it overliteralizes the evidence to say that the earth "floats" on the abyss, these texts nevertheless seem to describe a mental map that is consistent in general contours with a flat earth surrounded on all sides and beneath by waters.

Cosmic Ocean (behind a Solid Sky?)

The ancient Israelites knew that rain was associated with cloud formation (1 Kgs 18:43-45).¹³⁸ Averbeck has demonstrated that the phrase, "windows of the heavens" through which rain falls (Gen 7:11; 8:2; Mal 3:10) is metaphorical for clouds. He points to the Ugaritic story of Baal's palace construction, which includes the placement of a "window," identified in semantic parallelism with the word for clouds. The "window" allows the storm-god, Baal, to water the earth with rain:¹³⁹

> let a window opening be opened in the house
> a window in the midst of the palace
> So let a break be opened in the clouds . . .

---

136. Seely, "The Geographical Meaning of 'Earth,'" 251. Seely's examples of collocation between the verb "to found" (*yasad*) with '*al* likewise show positioning over something, which is what the metaphor of foundation suggests.

137. Further, see Cornelius, "The Visual Representation," 200; Greenwood, *Scripture and Cosmology*, 97-98, although some passages cited could be read differently.

138. Also, Job 38:34; Ps 135:7; Prov 25:14. Poythress's discussion is cogent insofar as demonstrating the Israelites' understanding of clouds and rain (Poythress, "Rain Water versus a Heavenly Sea," 184-89).

139. Averbeck, "The Three 'Daughters' of Ba'al," 238-45.

> He [the builder] opened a window
> opening in the house a window
> In the midst of the palace. Baal opened
> a rift in the clouds.[140]

Like the image of "pillars" for the earth and heavens, "the windows of the heavens" is a figure of speech, not intended by the ancients to be understood in a physical-structural manner.

How, then, does one understand Gen 1:7 regarding the separation of waters above the "firmament/expanse" (*raqia'*)? A good case can be made that this too is metaphorical, related to language of "windows/clouds" from which these waters flow as rain. Averbeck argues that the fundamental concerns of the first three days of Gen 1 match those of the Baal Epic—specifically, the agricultural need for light, rain from clouds, and the growth of vegetation on dry land (represented in the Baal Epic by Baal's three daughters). Thus, the "waters above" in Gen 1:7 corresponds to the clouds and rain.[141] Poythress uses an argument from relevance to support the meaning of "clouds" in Gen 1:7.[142] He maintains that a heavenly ocean would have had no relevance to ancient Israel, neither in their agricultural interests nor in their associations with divine Providence. The weight of these arguments depends *in part* on how one regards the accessibility and hierarchy of assumptions brought forward by the utterances of Gen 1. Do the mental reflexes of the ideal Israelite reader more naturally gravitate to categories similar to those expressed in the Baal Epic, or would associations with cosmology reflected in the Mesopotamian tradition (Enuma Elish) or Egyptian creation accounts have been more dominant?

---

140. *CAT* 1.4 vii 17–19, 25–28, quoted from Averbeck, "The Three 'Daughters' of Ba'al," 240. Cf. S. B. Parker, ed., *Ugaritic Narrative Poetry*, 136.

141. Averbeck, "The Three 'Daughters' of Ba'al," 245. Younker and Davidson argue that Prov 8:28 uses the word for "clouds" (*šahaq*) in reference to the waters above (counterpart to the "deep" (*tehom*) (Younker and Davidson, "The Myth of the Solid Heavenly Dome," 52). While this word denotes clouds in some uses (e.g., Ps 77:17 [Heb. 18]; Job 38:37), it is not the dominant use. Most uses are imprecise as to whether it is "clouds" or "skies" more generally, and some uses are not appropriate to "clouds" at all (e.g., Ps 89:6 [Heb. 7], 37 [Heb. 38]; Job 37:18). Indeed, Prov 3:20, which is parallel to Prov 8:28, *cannot* be clouds, since even the ancients knew that dew can fall on a cloudless night (cf. "heavens" drop dew in Deut 33:28). The use in Prov 8:28 is best understood as a general reference to the sky, without specifically explicating the *raqia'* in Gen 1:6–8.

142. Poythress, "Rain Water versus a Heavenly Sea," 189–91.

The close similarity between the language of Gen 1 and the language in both Mesopotamian and Egyptian creation traditions was discussed in chapter 1. Regarding the association between Gen 1:7 and either the Baal Epic or Enuma Elish, it strikes me as most significant that only in Gen 1:7 and Enuma Elish iv 135–46 does one find such explicit language of a creator deity dividing the cosmic ocean into an upper, heavenly realm and a lower, subterranean realm. The rareness of this motif increases the possibility that the two traditions are related.[143] Of course, if one regards the description in Enuma Elish as metaphor, then this supports a metaphorical interpretation for Gen 1:7 as well. But, as argued above, the author of Enuma Elish most likely imagined a physical structure of the cosmos that included a heavenly reservoir of water. It will be argued in chapter 4 that allusion to the Enuma Elish tradition was intentional in order to efficiently stake a theological counterclaim.

Yet more telling in my judgment is the construction of prepositions in Gen 1:7 as well as consideration of the changes in prepositions that govern various objects related to the "firmament/expanse" (*raqia'*) in Gen 1.[144] The assignment of prepositions is particularly clear: water was "*above* with respect to" (*me'al + le*) the *raqia'*, which is parallel in grammatical construction to the description in Ezek 1:25 that denotes a position on top of the *raqia'*. This description contrasts with waters "*below* with respect to" (*mittaḥat + le*) the *raqia'*. The latter combination denotes an object underneath something (Judg 3:16). Hence waters are positionally *above* the firmament/expanse, not a part of it.[145] Reinforcing this impression, and by contrast, God placed astral objects "in" (*be*)

---

143. On the basis of a thirteenth-century (or earlier) date for the composition of Genesis, it has been argued that Genesis could not echo Enuma Elish, which likely originated in the twelfth century (e.g., N. K. Weeks, "Cosmology in Historical Context," 287). On the dating of Enuma Elish, see Lambert, *Babylonian Creation Myths*, 439–44. However, traditions ascribing aspects of creation to Marduk are earlier, including a conflict motif involving the blood of another slain god (see UET VI 398, line 2–9; Lambert, *Babylonian Creation Myths*, 313). Known textual sources for other motifs in Enuma Elish (e.g., Anzu, Atrahasis) date earlier. The rise of Marduk to supremacy in the Middle Babylonian period, which is the primary evidence for dating its composition, is not an essential component to the existence of earlier traditions about Marduk in circulation before an early composition of Genesis. Therefore, the argument is not strong.

144. This paragraph sets aside for the moment questions about the nature of the *raqia'*, whether two-dimensional (solid or otherwise) or three-dimensional (i.e., "expanse" composed of atmosphere and heaven).

145. Seely, "The Firmament and the Water Above-2," 41–42.

the firmament/expanse (Gen 1:14-15), and let the birds fly across the "surface" (i.e., "in front of; ʾal-pene) the firmament/expanse (Gen 1:20). From the vantage point of an earth observer, birds fly in front of the expanse (i.e., at low altitude), relatively speaking. But it is the contrast between the astral objects and the waters that is most telling. The astral objects are either fixed on the surface of the *raqiaʿ* (if it is imagined as a two-dimensional interface) or moving in the space of the "expanse" of *raqiaʿ* (if it is imagined as three-dimensional space above the earth). The placement of the waters "above" the *raqiaʿ*, in either case, precludes the possibility that these waters are the clouds.[146] Clouds are below the sun, moon, and stars, since they block their view; but the waters are described as above the place where these objects are fixed. This interpretation is also consistent with the creation of the *raqiaʿ*, which is situated between these waters and the earth. Whether interface or expanse, Gen 1 speaks of a body of water above the heavens. Even Houtman, who argues against a heavenly water mass for Ps 148:4, affirms the inescapability of this interpretation for Gen 1:7.[147]

A corresponding relationship is described in Ps 148:1-4, where the astral objects and associated angelic host reside in heaven and highest heaven, but the waters are located even above (*meʿal*) these. The presentation is staircase parallelism: heavens > heavens of heavens > waters above. Attempts to interpret Ps 148:4 as "waters [that descend] from above," in the fashion of a rain curtain, fail to recognize that when the word *meʿal* refers to objects descending, it is invariably associated with a verb of motion.[148] This analysis of the preposition, *meʿal*, in both Gen 1 and Ps 148 suggests a mental map where water exists beyond the atmosphere (i.e.,

---

146. As noted in chapter 1, this observation did not escape Luther and was decisive in his interpretation that the waters could not be clouds.

147. Houtman, *Der Himmel im Alten Testament*, 264, 268.

148. Houtman argues that the compound preposition here retains the full force of each component, i.e., "from above" (Houtman, *Der Himmel im Alten Testament*, 266; citing GKC §119d). His chief supporting example of *meʿal* with heavens, Ps 108:4 (Heb. 5), is weak. Ps 108:5 extols the superlative nature of God's love, i.e., "above [higher than] the heavens" (not that his love descends from the heavens). This corresponds to the parallel verse member that places God's faithfulness at similar heights (not that God's faithfulness is directionally oriented; cf. Pss 36:5 [Heb. 6]; 57:10 [Heb. 11]). The parallel text in Ps 57:10 makes clear through the addition of the preposition *ʿad* ("up to") that any idea of "down from" is excluded. For examples of *meʿal* where motion "from above" is indicated with collocated verbs of motion, see Gen 24:64; 1 Sam 4:18.

clouds), a notion difficult to conceptualize apart from a reservoir, as suggested from broader ancient Near Eastern cosmology.

There is a related question, whether the *raqiaʿ* should be interpreted as a two-dimensional interface (reflected in the translation "firmament") or a three-dimensional space above the earth that incorporates both atmosphere and astral realm (reflected in the translation "expanse"). As noted above, the ancient Near Eastern data offers some evidence for the notion of a two-dimensional interface, perhaps even solid. The Old Testament, likewise, offers some support for this in the description of the elders' vision of heaven (Exod 24:10) and Ezekiel's vision of the *raqiaʿ* (Ezek 1:22). Since only special privilege enables humans to gaze *through* to see the God above, some sort of interface is being described. While a floor of some kind is envisioned, the language should not be pressed materially.[149] Alternatively, consideration of the descriptions in Gen 1 itself is inconclusive. On the one hand, Gen 1:8 equates the *raqiaʿ* with the heavens (*šamayim*; also parallel in Ps 19:1 [Heb. 2]). This supports the translation "expanse," since it is the domain of birds and divine beings (Deut 4:17; Pss 11:4; 148:1-2; cf. 150:1).[150] But metonymy can account for flexibility of meaning, where "heavens" becomes the general-use word that *incorporates* the part that is called *raqiaʿ*. The conclusion of Wright nuances the polyvalence of the word: "This 'firmament' (*raqiaʿ*) is part of the heavenly structure whether it is the equivalent of *šamayim* ("heaven/sky") or is what separates it from the earth."[151] Like many ancient Near Eastern descriptions of cosmology, it is best to recognize that the language is vague and to focus instead on the question of the general concept. In other words, whether one posits for *raqiaʿ* a solid firmament, an ill-defined interface, or some more vague notion of "expanse" that incorporates both atmosphere and astral realm, it remains likely that the ancients, including the Israelites, assumed that a reservoir of water

---

149. Both passages are explicit in the use of simile. Younker and Davidson correctly observe that in Ezek 1:22, the *raqiaʿ* is not said to be made of crystal but only has the "gleam of crystal" (Younker and Davidson, "The Myth of the Solid Heavenly Dome," 48).

150. N. K. Weeks, "Cosmology in Historical Context," 291-92.

151. Wright, *The Early History of Heaven*, 55. While stressing the "physicalistic" side of the biblical language, he argues that the descriptions of heaven involve mixed metaphors, and that only a general model is possible to sketch (Wright, *The Early History of Heaven*, 58, 88-89). Even the descriptions of various "heavens" lack consistency and should caution against overly specific structural notions (Stadelmann, *The Hebrew Conception of the World*, 41).

existed beyond the vast domains above their heads. Its shape and continuity with the boundaries of the cosmic abyss and the horizon are not defined. But such specific details need not have been speculated by the ancients themselves or understood by us to discern a general mental map of cosmic waters.

Conclusions

Prescientific Mental Models of the Cosmos

Ancient cognitions about the physical universe were constructed from phenomenological perceptions similar in several ways to other prescientific peoples. But these perceptions were not purely operational for the agricultural needs of society; rather, the ancients constructed *models* of relationships between objects in the cosmos that were integrated with theological beliefs that made sense with these physical models. While not scientific in the modern sense, nevertheless, these models constitute a theory about how the natural world operates, even if these models are not fully developed in a holistic manner.

Basic Contours of Ancient Near Eastern Cosmography

While metaphorical and theologically symbolic language was used by the ancients to convey their belief systems, certain shared assumptions are discernible from the iconographical and textual evidence: (1) a three-tiered universe (with a physical, underworld realm); (2) an earth-sun system wherein the sun moved around a flat earth that is fixed in relation to a subterranean body of water; and (3) an extension of cosmic waters (a reservoir) beyond the atmosphere into the heavenly realm. These conclusions are not only derived from direct statements in ancient texts or iconography; they are also supported from incidental details in narrative and narratival poetry. These incidental details point to assumptions embedded in the cognitive environment in such a way that they must have been believed in order for the narratives to make sense to the ancient audience. Therefore, these assumptions about cosmology cannot be relegated to pure metaphor or symbol.

The Need for a Doctrine of Accommodation

Attempts to deny or minimize the problem of ancient assumptions and models by appealing to operational language or to lack of theorizing in the culture are not adequate. In the history of interpretation, Jewish and Christian scholars invoked the notion of divine accommodation to account for language *and* content that was deemed problematic. The next chapter surveys this history. In chapter 4, I apply relevance theory to consider in what manner, if any, are these problematic cognitive assumptions explicated or implicated by the text.

3

Divine Accommodation in Historical Perspective

What Is Divine Accommodation?

Broadly speaking, "accommodation" refers to the manner by which God manifests his presence or intervenes in time and space in order to facilitate finite, human understanding. Sometimes the word "condescension" is used, highlighting the fact that God has "come down" to the level or capacity of humanity to make himself understood.[1] The incarnation of the Son of God is the most extraordinary example. God took on human nature to make his gracious attributes *personally experienced* by humankind (John 1:14–18). Since God's interventions include his spoken word, divine disclosure is also *linguistic*. All Scripture is an accommodation by the mere fact that God speaks to people in languages that are linguistically and culturally conditioned. The choice of Hebrew or Greek, for example, necessarily limits the range of verbal expression; and since natural languages do not exist independent of cultural context, the use of those languages necessarily invokes the encyclopedic ranges of ideas attached to those languages, as discussed

---

1. Benin, *The Footprints of God*, xiv–xv; Sunshine, "Accommodation Historically Considered," 238. The synonymous Latin verbs *accommodare* and *attemperare* mean "to adjust" or "to adapt" to something in an appropriate manner. The Greek Fathers used *katabainō* and *sunkatabainō* in the sense of "descend," as to another's social level. That the Latin and Greek terms do share semantic overlap in the sense of "adaptation," see Huijgen, *Divine Accommodation in John Calvin's Theology*, 58, 65, 71, 76–77.

in previous chapters. So linguistic and cultural accommodation are not easily disentangled.

Although theologians throughout church history used the idea of accommodation in the linguistic sense for the words of Scripture, greater attention in the ancient and medieval church was given to the manner in which God revealed *his presence* or the *nature* of his instructions for life and worship. But in the Enlightenment, European thinkers began giving more consideration to cultural differences between themselves and the original authors of Scripture. Because this included cosmological views, application of accommodation was also accompanied by an expansion of concordant interpretations in the face of developments in natural science. In other words, Christian scholars sought to bring the biblical language into alignment with what emerging science was discovering. As will be argued, a lack of clarity about how biblical language interacts with cultural assumptions, cosmological or otherwise, has led to controversy among interpreters over linguistic accommodation and cultural accommodation.

The following survey is far from complete; rather, it offers a representative sample of theologians in order to illustrate how the concept of accommodation has been applied throughout the history of interpretation. Since cosmology is of chief interest, this survey also attempts to correlate the use of accommodation with interpretations of Gen 1.

Accommodation in the Ancient Church

Early Church Fathers

Embroiled in debates between Christians and Jews, the early church fathers endeavored to explain how it is that God changed the nature of his regulations and worship from the Old Testament to the New Testament. One solution was to suggest a punitive function of the law. So, for Justin (c. 100–c. 165) and Irenaeus (c. 130–c. 200), the ethical instruction of the Old Testament remained unchanged for the Christian church, but the ritual aspects of Mosaic law were regarded as accommodation to the ancient Israelite, cultural context so as to restrain the evil impulses of God's stubborn people.[2] For Tertullian (c. 155/160–c. 240), Athanasius (c. 297–373), and Theodoret (393–466), God's toleration of sacrifice was

---

2. Benin, *The Footprints of God*, 3–6.

necessary because of Jewish ignorance and ingratitude, and the need to regulate the propensity toward idolatry.³

Other church fathers held a less punitive view of the Mosaic law and emphasized its pedagogical nature—a cultural adaptation for more effective communication. In the words of Benin, Eusebius (c. 260–339/340) and Augustine (354–430) viewed Judaism as "a religion adjusted to the needs of a different society and culture than the Roman one."⁴ Gregory of Nazianzus (329–389) and others employed a medical metaphor to describe God's accommodation: God accommodates to human beings just as a physician prescribes different medications depending on the patient and the condition being treated. The shift between Old and New Covenants was gradual, like a mother transitioning her child from breast milk, to soft food, to solids.⁵ In a similar manner, ancient Jewish sages spoke of the Torah's institution of sacrifice as a father adapting his instruction to children; the sacrificial system was like poor-quality food from which a nobleman must be weaned over time while sitting at a king's table.⁶ The Babylonian Talmud affirms that "The words of Torah are in the language of the sons of man."⁷

By far the greatest challenge for the church fathers, however, was not to explain the shift from Judaism to Christianity, but to account for the incarnation, especially in the face of gnostics, educated pagans, and Arians.⁸ Here the pedagogical model was found to be most useful, and none of the church fathers surpassed John Chrysostom (347–407) in this regard. Chrysostom argued that God proportioned the truth of revelation to the capacity of human weakness to bear.⁹ It is in the context of pedagogical thinking that the church fathers' view of accommodation in Scripture is best understood.

In the Alexandrian tradition of North Africa, Origen (c. 184–c. 254) used the pedagogical purpose of accommodation to explain why Scripture addresses different levels of truth corresponding to the body

---

3. Benin, *The Footprints of God*, 28, 71; Huijgen, *Divine Accommodation in John Calvin's Theology*, 59–60.

4. Benin, *The Footprints of God*, 22, 95–96.

5. Benin, *The Footprints of God*, 41, 48, 50–51.

6. Benin, *The Footprints of God*, 127–28.

7. Snobelen, "'In the Language of Men,'" 692 (*Berakhot* 31b; *Ketubot* 67b; *Yebamot* 71b).

8. Benin, *The Footprints of God*, 9, 25, 102.

9. Huijgen, *Divine Accommodation in John Calvin's Theology*, 75–77, 81.

(literal meaning), soul (moral sense), and spirit (theological truths). In practice, this manifests itself only in two levels: the literal and the deeper meanings. The literal sense offered to the uneducated and initiates an understandable meaning appropriate to their maturity level; but the goal was to train them up in higher levels of understanding.[10] For Origen, problems in the literal meaning of the text drove readers to search for a figurative meaning.[11] On occasion, however, he would go to great length in order to explain how a literal interpretation is possible. For example, he squared the measurements of Noah's ark in order to allow adequate size to fit the animal types known to him.[12] But with particular regard to the reading of creation texts, he thought that the contradictions on the surface reading of Gen 1 and 2 were intended to press readers beyond a simplistic literalism. Gen 1 taught mysteries through a "semblance of history and not through actual events."[13] Origen was not alone in the Alexandrian tradition to deny the reality of a literal six-day creation. Didymus (c. 313–398) and Athanasius followed suit, favoring an instantaneous creation presented in a figurative manner in the biblical text for the benefit of spiritual lessons.[14] The concern to protect instantaneous creation would become an established interpretation through the writing of Augustine (see below).

The theologians of the Antiochene tradition in the eastern Mediterranean also drew on the pedagogical nature of accommodation, especially championing the idea that God unfolded truth progressively through different "economies" from Old Testament to New. It is this stream of thought that came to full expression in Chrysostom, mentioned above. Their hermeneutic emphasized the historical meaning of Scripture in reaction to the *excesses* in allegorical interpretation.[15] But they did not oppose allegory itself, since the Antiochene fathers also read the same threefold level of meaning that Origen set forth.[16] The differences arose because of emphasis either upon rhetorical readings of Scripture (in the

---

10. F. Young, "Alexandrian and Antiochene Exegesis," 335; Vogt, "Origen of Alexandria," 546; Huijgen, *Divine Accommodation in John Calvin's Theology*, 64.

11. Vogt, "Origen of Alexandria," 547.

12. F. Young, "Alexandrian and Antiochene Exegesis," 336.

13. *On First Principles*, 4.3, cited in A. J. Brown, *The Days of Creation*, 29. Cf. Vogt, "Origen of Alexandria," 547.

14. A. J. Brown, *The Days of Creation*, 30–31.

15. Benin, *The Footprints of God*, 57.

16. Allert, *Early Christian Readings*, 125–26, 181–84, 194, 197.

Antiochene tradition) or upon philosophical readings of the Bible (in the Alexandrian tradition).[17]

Consequently, the Antiochene school understood the six days of creation as a chronological sequence of six normal days. The orderliness of the creation account served to teach more precisely about the ways of God, who could have created instantly but chose instead to do so in a six-day fashion as instruction for the human workweek. This application of accommodation for pedagogical reasons presages the later reasoning of John Calvin. Among the Syriac Fathers as well, the literal understanding of Gen 1 stood in contrast to Alexandrian allegorizing. But within the Antiochene tradition, a more complicated voice was also heard. The reading of Gregory of Nyssa (c. 335—c. 395) did not follow a chronological sequence but rather a logical one that attended to questions of ontology over chronology for the days of Gen 1. In this he anticipated the emphasis on differentiation (days 1–3) and adornment (days 4–6) of creation that prevailed in medieval exegesis.[18] This would eventuate in the "paneling" view of days 1–3/4–6 frequently seen in literary approaches today. It is not that the Antiochene Fathers failed to draw typological interpretations, but their use of Scripture remained rooted in the more historical sense of the text. Their concern was to protect both history *and* the capacity of the authors of Scripture to use rhetorical art.[19] In other words, they were not opposed to recognizing literary artistry in the text. Indeed, in the view of all the church fathers, the literal included figurative language.[20]

Augustine

Augustine (354–430) was the bridge between the ancient church and all medieval interpretation that followed. As noted above, along with Eusebius, Augustine argued that God spoke through his word to diverse audiences; and the Jewish culture of the Old Testament was not the Roman culture of the church. Therefore, the unfolding of the

---

17. Allert, *Early Christian Readings*, 136–37.

18. A. J. Brown, *The Days of Creation*, 33–35.

19. F. Young, "Alexandrian and Antiochene Exegesis," 345–48; Vogt, "Origen of Alexandria," 159–63.

20. Kannengiesser, "The Literal Meaning of Scripture," 173–74.

divine plan necessitated different "economies" of instruction.[21] Indeed, his early commentary work on Genesis viewed the days of Gen 1 as figurative for successive stages in human history.[22] Similarly, he employed the medical metaphor: that God would prescribe different medicine to heal the ailments of a diverse human race. However, his use of the technical language of accommodation was sparse in comparison to his forerunners.[23] Even so, in broad strokes, Augustine viewed Scripture on analogy to the incarnation where God's Word (John 1:1, 14) "descends to the discrete bits of sound that we make."[24] Humans must respond with similar humility. His lasting legacy on hermeneutics stemmed not only from his masterful synthesis of the patristic exegesis before him but also from his passionate insistence on the inner process of humbly responding to Scripture.[25]

In his apologetic for the Christian faith, Augustine showed a strong concern for the interpretation of Genesis and its implications for a Christian doctrine of creation. He insisted on an instantaneous creation, where the days of Gen 1 were literary recurrences of the one moment ("day") when God spoke everything into being, an idea he borrowed from Ambrose (c. 339–397).[26] In Augustine's view, this protected the transcendence of God against excess anthropomorphism.[27] His efforts at both figurative and literal interpretation of Genesis also defended Christianity against adherents of his former faith, Manicheanism, who believed in the eternality of matter and the inferiority of Old Testament cosmology.[28] In addition, it also helped explain chronological difficulties in the text, such as the creation of plants before the sun; a problem alleviated if everything appeared on one instantaneous "day." The literary interpretation, then, avoided contradiction and served a pedagogical purpose: "If you cannot yet understand it [i.e., instantaneous creation], you should leave the

---

21. Benin, *The Footprints of God*, 94–98; Huijgen, *Divine Accommodation in John Calvin's Theology*, 86–87.

22. *Against the Manicheans* 1.23 (Augustine, *Against the Manichees*, 83–88; cf. A. J. Brown, *The Days of Creation*, 45).

23. Huijgen, *Divine Accommodation in John Calvin's Theology*, 88.

24. Norris, "Augustine," 405–6, citing Augustine on Ps 103.

25. Kannengiesser, "Augustine of Hippo (354–430)," 1149.

26. A. J. Brown, *The Days of Creation*, 50.

27. Kannengiesser, "Augustine of Hippo (354–430)," 1167–68.

28. Greene-McCreight, *Ad Litteram*, 32–35; Howell, "Natural Knowledge and Textual Meaning," 119–20.

matter for the consideration of those who can; and, since Scripture does not abandon you in your infirmity, but with a mother's love accompanies your slower steps, you will make progress.[29] This pedagogical purpose appears elsewhere when Augustine refers to the word choice of Gen 1:1 as "a manner that is accommodated to unlearned readers and hearers."[30]

Augustine also apologized for Christians who held embarrassingly inaccurate views of cosmology (such as a flat earth), because their comments created an unnecessary obstacle to the gospel:[31]

> Now, it is a disgraceful and dangerous thing for an infidel to hear a Christian, presumably giving the meaning of Holy Scripture, talking nonsense on these topics; and we should take all means to prevent such an embarrassing situation, in which people show up vast ignorance in a Christian and laugh it to scorn. The shame is not so much that an ignorant individual is derided, but that people outside the household of faith think our sacred writers held such opinions, and, to the great loss of those for whose salvation we toil, the writers of our Scripture are criticized and rejected as unlearned men . . . Reckless and incompetent expounders of Holy Scripture bring untold trouble and sorrow on their wiser brethren when they are caught in one of their mischievous false opinions and are taken to task by those who are not bound by the authority of our sacred books.[32]

In this, he strove to demonstrate that Scripture was consistent with the current thinking about cosmology in his day.[33] Referring to those who mock biblical language about cosmology, he wrote: "When they are able, from reliable evidence, to prove some fact of physical science, we shall show that it is not contrary to our Scripture."[34] This comment falls

---

29. *The Literal Meaning of Genesis* 5.3.6; cf. 4.33.52 (Augustine, *The Literal Meaning of Genesis*, 150; cf. Greene-McCreight, *Ad Litteram*, 60-61; A. J. Brown, *The Days of Creation*, 49, 51).

30. *The Literal Meaning of Genesis* 1.14.28 (Augustine, *The Literal Meaning of Genesis*, 35-36).

31. Snobelen, "'In the Language of Men,'" 696; Sunshine, "Accommodation Historically Considered," 244-45.

32. *The Literal Meaning of Genesis* 1.19.39 (Augustine, *The Literal Meaning of Genesis*, 42-43).

33. Norris, "Augustine," 395; Howell, "Natural Knowledge and Textual Meaning," 125-26.

34. *The Literal Meaning of Genesis* 1.21.41 (Augustine, *The Literal Meaning of Genesis*, 45).

in the context of wrestling with *interpretive options for Gen 1*, not the reconsideration of the science. Both must be true, and the Christian must be careful not to attribute to Scripture a truth it is not teaching.[35] For example, he conceded the possibility that the sun was in fact smaller than some stars, but he explained that it only appeared larger due to relative distance (from a human perspective), thereby alleviating the difficulty of Gen 1:16.[36] When interpreting "literally," Augustine looked for a meaning that was "obvious to everyone from the testimony of the senses."[37] The plain, literal sense, however, might blur at times into what might be considered a more figurative meaning, as in the case of the creation of "light," which Augustine conceived as including the angels, whose gaze at either the Creator or his creatures referred to morning and evening, respectively.[38] At the same time, he considered the possibility that no good response to a certain criticism of Scripture might be forthcoming—in which case he urged steadfastness in holding to the faith: "either we shall have some ability to demonstrate that it is absolutely false, or at least we ourselves will hold it so without any shadow of a doubt."[39] What is important to observe in all this is how Augustine allowed both his philosophical theology on the one hand, and his understanding of the natural world (i.e., "science") on the other, to guide his interpretative enterprise.[40] Furthermore, when faced with competing options for interpretation, with humility he warned against holding to one view too firmly, lest in the light of further research it be shown false and so undermine faith.[41]

---

35. Howell, "Natural Knowledge and Textual Meaning," 128, 132–33.

36. *The Literal Meaning of Genesis* 2.16.33–34 (Augustine, *The Literal Meaning of Genesis*, 69–70; Snobelen, "'In the Language of Men,'" 697).

37. *The Literal Meaning of Genesis* 2.9.22 (Augustine, *The Literal Meaning of Genesis*, 60).

38. Greene-McCreight, *Ad Litteram*, 44.

39. *The Literal Meaning of Genesis* 1.21.41 (Augustine, *The Literal Meaning of Genesis*, 45).

40. For examples, see Greene-McCreight, *Ad Litteram*, 73–80. Cf. Howell, "Natural Knowledge and Textual Meaning," 141, 143–44.

41. *The Literal Meaning of Genesis* 1.18.37 (Augustine, *The Literal Meaning of Genesis*, 41).

Accommodation in the Medieval Church and Renaissance

Medieval Church

Both Jewish and Christian scholarship continued to make use of the idea of accommodation as divine pedagogy. Rabbinic exegetes wrestled with anthropomorphic language and the meaning of sacrifice in the absence of the temple, utilizing the pedagogical aspect of accommodation in a variety of ways.[42] Similarly, as Christian interpretation expanded the possibilities of spiritual meaning in the text, accommodation helped explain how there might be different levels of meaning for commoners and more sophisticated interpreters.[43] But advances in Hebrew grammar and lexicography during the earlier Middle Ages gave rise to renewed emphasis on literal interpretation among the rabbis.[44] This emphasis on literal interpretation would in turn exert an important influence on developments within Christian Scholasticism as well.[45] Corresponding to this, in the later Middle Ages there was a renewed interest in the Greek classical tradition, which resulted in a more rationalistic and systematic approach to all fields of knowledge, including the literal-historical reading of texts.[46] Moving beyond the literal to the spiritual sense remained important to medieval exegetes; however, by the later Middle Ages, the theological message of the Bible was found to be rooted more and more in the literal meaning of its words.[47]

This growing emphasis during the Middle Ages on literal meaning reinforced the dominant interpretation of the days of Gen 1 as natural, historically sequential days. Augustine was so highly respected that all interpreters needed to take his views as the starting point for discussion, but the majority limited his insistence on instantaneous creation to the initial matter of Gen 1:1.[48] At the same time, some voices both early and later in the Middle Ages continued to view the days of Gen 1 in a

---

42. Benin, *The Footprints of God*, 140–41, 148–51, 176. Cf. Funkenstein, *Theology and the Scientific Imagination*, 222–23.

43. Benin, *The Footprints of God*, 178; Sunshine, "Accommodation Historically Considered," 247–48.

44. Harris, "Medieval Jewish Biblical Exegesis," 141–44; Reventlow, *History of Biblical Interpretation*, 220, 224–25.

45. Reventlow, *History of Biblical Interpretation*, 245–48.

46. Ocker, "Scholastic Interpretation," 255, 262–65.

47. Ocker, "Scholastic Interpretation," 266–68.

48. A. J. Brown, *The Days of Creation*, 102.

purely figurative manner. In the early period, Augustine was followed by Archbishop Theodore (d. 690), Abbot Hadrian (d. 709), and Eriugena (c. 810—c. 877), although the latter combined the instantaneous-creation view for all six days with an unorthodox notion of emanation of the divine essence.[49] Peter Abelard (1079-1142), representing an important minority of medieval Scholastics who followed Augustine with a more Platonic philosophy, understood the days of Gen 1 as a literary accommodation for the uninformed.[50] Peter Lombard (c. 1095-1169) drew upon the instantaneous view of Augustine for his comments on creation of humanity, interpreting the "days" as merely an analogy in order for God to speak intelligibly to ignorant people. However, this was a seeming inconsistency with his preference to restrict instantaneous creation to initial matter. In this he reaffirmed the common medieval interpretation of the first three days as a work of "distinction" and the second three days as a work of "adorning."[51] Not only is this a medieval precursor to modern interpretation (as the views of Gregory of Nyssa were an ancient precursor to the medieval view), but ideas of physical progression and development were proposed by many medieval interpreters, who understood the initial creation of Gen 1:1 as the commencement of a series of natural processes that automatically unfolded into various forms.[52]

Renaissance

In language reminiscent of the church fathers, Erasmus (1466-1536) illustrates the continuity across the centuries in the use of accommodation, in his case between the Middle Ages and the Reformation:

> Divine wisdom speaks to us in baby-talk and like a loving mother accommodates its words to our state of infancy. It offers milk to tiny infants in Christ, and herbs to the sick. But you must hasten to grow so that you may receive solid food. It lowers itself to your lowliness, but you on your part must rise to its sublimity.[53]

---

49. A. J. Brown, *The Days of Creation*, 61-66.
50. A. J. Brown, *The Days of Creation*, 72-75.
51. A. J. Brown, *The Days of Creation*, 68-70.
52. A. J. Brown, *The Days of Creation*, 76-77.
53. *Enchiridion* (Holb.33.33-34.1) cited in Huijgen, *Divine Accommodation in John Calvin's Theology*, 95.

In this, Erasmus follows church tradition in speaking of accommodation as a way of bridging God's transcendence in revelation. In a similar way, Jesus "adapted the uncomplicated language and imagery of the parables to the capacity of the multitudes."[54]

The growing interest in literal interpretation, which as noted above began to expand in the late Middle Ages, shows its continued influence. But this was not without consideration for literary style. An important and influential English humanist, John Colet (c. 1466–1519), represents a stream of interpretation in the English Renaissance. Regarding accommodation, he referred to Moses as a "poet," who adapted the analogy of a human workweek for pedagogical purposes to help the Jews observe Sabbath rest:

> And he does this in such a way, in my opinion, that we may perceive him to have had regard to popular conceptions, and to the uneducated multitude whom he taught . . . And he does this after the manner of some popular poet, that he may the better study [i.e., adapt himself to] the spirit of simple-minded rustics; imagining a succession of events, and works, and times, such as could by no means find place with so great an Artificer.[55]

> [Moses fixed creation in six days] that by imitating God, whom poet-like he imagined to have worked six days and rested on the seventh, the people might be led to rest on every seventh day, and to the contemplation and worship of God. No doubt he was satisfied with this number seven, in which to include both the works and the rest that ended them, from the perfectness of that number . . . For it is certain that he would never have fixed upon that number of days, were it not to incite the people to imitation, by setting before them a pattern, so to speak, in this wise and useful invention; to the intent that they should put an end to their daily occupations every six days, and spend the seventh in an exalted contemplation of God.[56]

In a later letter, Colet compares the poetic manner of Moses's speech in Gen 1 to the accommodative manner of the incarnation.[57] Colet's view,

---

54. Huijgen, *Divine Accommodation in John Calvin's Theology*, 100.

55. Colet, *Letters to Radulphus*, 8–10. I thank C. John Collins for making available to me this edition of Colet's letter to Radulphus. For fuller discussion of Colet, see C. J. Collins, *Reading Genesis Well*, 148–52. Cf. Baroway, "The Bible as Poetry," 462; Benin, *The Footprints of God*, 192; and A. J. Brown, *The Days of Creation*, 98–99.

56. Colet, *Letters to Radulphus*, 23–24.

57. Colet, *Letters to Radulphus*, 27–28.

articulated well before the Enlightenment, anticipates by five hundred years the modern interpretation that the days of Gen 1 are a literary device built on analogy to the seven-day pattern already understood by the Israelites.

Accommodation in the Reformation and the Age of Science

Emergence of Literal Interpretation

Throughout the history of interpretation, the "literal sense" of Scripture, that is, the historical-contextual meaning which included figures of speech, had always been the assumed starting point. It was from here that allegorical meanings unfolded, because it was the words of the text that pointed to deeper meaning. However, the growing medieval and Renaissance move to attend to authorial intent and the literal sense of Scripture blossomed in the Reformation, and this shifted the focus of interest to history.[58] This precipitated a new expectation that the Bible would speak more comprehensively not only about history but also science. Even in the Renaissance, a new genre called "mirror literature" attempted to place encyclopedic knowledge within the categories of the days of creation.[59] As scientific discoveries expanded, scholars endeavored to place this new knowledge in a sacred framework. Harrison states, "The Bible thus came to compete with secular writings on their own ground, although its superiority to all competitors was at this [early] time widely granted."[60] As will be shown, this resulted in two contrasting approaches to interpretation. As interpreters looked more closely at the biblical text for information relating to emerging science, some drew upon the doctrine of accommodation to allow harmonization between the language of the text and science as they knew it. Biblical authority was actually bolstered when concord could be shown.[61] But with the rise of rationalism, a second approach developed. The notion of accommodation became a tool to set aside the authority of the biblical text wherever it conflicted with truth derived by human reason, which included natural philosophy (i.e., science).

58. Harrison, *The Bible*, 122–29.
59. A. J. Brown, *The Days of Creation*, 137.
60. Harrison, *The Bible*, 126.
61. A. J. Brown, *The Days of Creation*, 132.

Luther

Luther (1483–1546) did not articulate his thoughts about accommodation to the degree of his younger contemporary, Calvin. But he spoke of the Scripture's need to use anthropomorphic imagery to speak of God in an understandable manner, that is, for pedagogical purpose. For example, in his commentary on Gen 6:6, he defended such imagery by comparing it to a parent addressing a child, "It is for this reason that God lowers Himself to the level of our weak comprehension and presents Himself to us in images, in coverings, as it were, in simplicity adapted to a child."[62] He applied the same notion to the creation account in general.[63]

The literal approach that developed in the medieval period among Jewish and Christian interpreters, especially as expressed in the writings of Nicholas Lyra (c. 1270–1340), gradually attracted Martin Luther (1483–1546).[64] He wrote, "In Scripture we should let the words retain their natural force, just as they read, and give no other interpretation unless a clear article of faith compels otherwise."[65] He was embedded in the Aristotelian natural philosophy of his day, so he interpreted the language of Genesis through these categories of geocentric astronomy.[66] At times he explains that his intellect fails in his ability to make scientific correlations, such as his understanding of the "waters" above the "firmament." But he offers the common opinion of interpreters that these waters are an icy layer to keep the spheres orbiting the earth cool in their motion.[67] This illustrates his commitment to a literal concordism between the text of Genesis and the science of his day. He did not think this was necessarily the explicit intention of the "teaching of Moses," but that astronomers could make a sensible contribution to understanding the realities behind the text: "Therefore this division of the spheres is not the teaching of Moses or of Holy Scripture; but it was thought out by

---

62. *Lectures on Genesis* (Gen 6:6) (Luther, *Lectures on Genesis Chapters 6–14*, 45).

63. *Lectures on Genesis* (Gen 1:1) (Luther, *Lectures on Genesis Chapters 1–5*, 14).

64. Benin, *The Footprints of God*, 185–87.

65. Written in the context of discussing the Lord's Supper; *Confessions Concerning Christ's Supper* (Luther, *Word and Sacrament III*, 270). Thus, his literal hermeneutic pressed for consubstantiation.

66. See his explicit affirmation of Aristotle at Gen 1:6 (Luther, *Lectures on Genesis Chapters 1–5*, 26–27). Further, see Mattox, "Cosmology," 297–99.

67. *Lectures on Genesis* (Gen 1:6) (Luther, *Lectures on Genesis Chapters 1–5*, 28, 31).

learned men for the purpose of teaching, something which we ought to recognize as being of great benefit."[68]

Recognizing the astronomical debates of his day, Luther refused to commit Scripture to an explanation regarding the relationship between astronomical objects and the light perceived from them:

> But Moses makes the difference and calls the sun and the moon the larger lights. The fact that the astronomers debate about the size of these bodies really has nothing to do with this passage. But this has something to do with the passage, that we observe that Scripture so designates these bodies, not on the basis of the magnitude of their masses but on the basis of the magnitude of their light.[69]

In effect, Luther was working with a notion of accommodation that explains Scripture as speaking in observational language. For the ultimate realities of physics, he deferred to the astronomers of his day:

> But I am giving no consideration to these ideas, for the astronomers are the experts from whom it is most convenient to get what may be discussed about these subjects . . . For me it is enough that in those bodies, which are so elegant and necessary for our life, we recognize both the goodness of God and His power . . . These are views which are proper to our profession; that is, they are theological, and they have power to instill confidence in our hearts.[70]

Even though Luther made his best effort to correlate Scripture with natural philosophy, he maintained that the Bible and scientists were employing different language for different purposes:

> Therefore just as a philosopher employs his own terms, so the Holy Spirit, too, employs His. An astronomer, therefore, does right when he uses the terms "spheres," "apsides," and "epicycles"; they belong to his profession and enable him to teach others with greater ease. By way of contrast, the Holy Spirit and Holy Scriptures know nothing about those designations and call the

---

68. *Lectures on Genesis* (Gen 1:6) (Luther, *Lectures on Genesis Chapters 1–5*, 31).

69. *Lectures on Genesis* (Gen 1:14) (Luther, *Lectures on Genesis Chapters 1–5*, 40). This exact use of accommodation in similar wording is already employed by the medieval Rabbi Abraham ibn Ezra (1089–c. 1167) (see discussion and quotation in Funkenstein, *Theology and the Scientific Imagination*, 216).

70. *Lectures on Genesis* (Gen 1:14) (Luther, *Lectures on Genesis Chapters 1–5*, 41).

entire area above "heaven." Nor should an astronomer find fault with this; let each of the two speak in his own terminology.[71]

Luther probably never imagined that science could contradict Scripture; rather the interpreter needed to acknowledge that the Bible was not addressing questions of natural philosophy directly. At the same time, Luther maintained that human reason was incapable of arriving at perfect knowledge in matters of science.[72] He read Gen 1 as a creation spanning six natural days, albeit in a manner consistent (in concord) with the associations one might predict for one who held to an Aristotelian astronomy.

Calvin

Pedagogy was the basic framework for how John Calvin (1509–1564) viewed revelation, and accommodation served a central function within it. Changes in human history necessitated different adaptations of truth; and also, by the Holy Spirit God tailors lessons appropriate to different individuals.[73] So, in order to account for the changes in God's administration between the two Testaments, he uses the metaphor of a farmer who labors differently in various agricultural seasons, or a father who adjusts his household instruction depending on the age of his children, or a physician who changes medications depending on the condition:

> I reply that God ought not to be considered changeable merely because he accommodated diverse forms to different ages, as he knows would be expedient for each. If a farmer sets certain tasks for his household in the winter, other tasks for the summer, we shall not on this account accuse him of inconsistency, or think that he departs from the proper rule of agriculture, which accords with the continuous order of nature. In like manner, if a householder instructs, rules, and guides, his children one way in infancy, another way in youth, and still another in young manhood, we shall not on this account call him fickle and say that he abandons his purpose . . . If a physician cures a young man of disease in the best way, but uses another sort of remedy on

---

71. *Lectures on Genesis* (Gen 1:14) (Luther, *Lectures on Genesis Chapters 1–5*, 47–48).

72. *Lectures on Genesis* (Gen 1:14) (Luther, *Lectures on Genesis Chapters 1–5*, 42).

73. Benin, *The Footprints of God*, 191–92; Huijgen, *Divine Accommodation in John Calvin's Theology*, 382–83.

the same person when he is old, shall we then say that he has rejected the method of cure that had pleased him before.[74]

One of the most repeated comments by Calvin on accommodation comes in the context of explaining the necessity of the incarnation:

> For who even of slight intelligence does not understand that, as nurses commonly do with infants, God is wont in a measure to "lisp" in speaking to us? Thus such forms of speaking do not so much express clearly what God is like as accommodate the knowledge of him to our slight capacity.[75]

Just as God reveals his nature or actions, so God similarly accommodates in speaking his word. For example, in reference to why the creation of angels is left out of the creation account in Gen 1, he explains, "To be sure, Moses accommodating himself to the rudeness of the common folk, mentions in the history of the Creation no other works of God than those which show themselves to our own eyes."[76]

Yet, as encompassing as his view of accommodation was, Calvin did not address the tension of Scripture versus emerging science directly; rather, he simply explained the text as an accommodation to human perception, both in terms of the manner of God's creative activity as well as the language God used to describe it. Following the late medieval and Renaissance trend to read textual sources in their original languages, Calvin employed his humanist training for a sharp focus on the plain sense of the Bible.[77] He was acutely concerned with the historical references of Genesis and took pains to identify them, as for example, the exact location of the rivers in Gen 2.[78]

The six days of Gen 1 are not a mere *literary* device (as seen above in Colet) to present God's creation as a six-day process in order to instruct humanity concerning the work/Sabbath cycle. Rather, Calvin wrote, "Let us rather conclude that God himself took the space of six days, for the purpose of accommodating his work to the capacity of men."[79]

---

74. *Institutes of the Christian Religion* 2.11.13–14 (Calvin, *Institutes*).
75. *Institutes of the Christian Religion* 1.13.1 (Calvin, *Institutes*).
76. *Institutes of the Christian Religion* 1.14.3 (Calvin, *Institutes*).
77. Calvin's attention to philological detail is demonstrated in Greene-McCreight, *Ad Litteram*, 107–11.
78. Greene-McCreight, *Ad Litteram*, 127, 131–32.
79. *Commentaries on the Book of Genesis* (Gen 1:5) (Calvin, *Genesis*, 1:78).

Calvin's commentary on Gen 1:6 illustrates well his method to utilize common sense reason. Regarding the separation of waters on Day 2, Calvin writes:

> For it appears opposed to common sense, and quite incredible, that there should be waters above the heaven. Hence some resort to allegory, and philosophize concerning angels; but quite beside the purpose. For, to my mind, this is a certain principle, that nothing is here treated of but the visible form of the world. He who would learn astronomy, and other recondite arts, let him go elsewhere . . . I conclude, that the waters here meant are such as the rude and unlearned may perceive.[80]

He continues with an explanation that these heavenly waters are the clouds and rain. More detailed discussion of the heavenly waters is found in Calvin's commentary on Ps 148:4. This passage also illustrates his use of rational observation for understanding cosmological texts. While tacitly acknowledging the common view of his day that there are layers of spheres above the earth composed of the four elements, he argues that the "waters above the heavens" must be rain:

> As under the name of *the heavens* he [the psalmist] comprehends the air, or at least all the space from the middle region of the air upwards, he calls rains, *the waters above the heavens*. There is no foundation for the conjecture which some have made, that there are waters deposited above the four elements; and when the Psalmist speaks of these waters as being above, he clearly points at the descent of rain. It is adhering too strictly to the letter of the words employed, to conceive as if there were some sea up in the heavens, where the waters were permanently deposited; for we know that Moses and the Prophets ordinarily speak in a popular style, suited to the lowest apprehension. It would be absurd, then, to seek to reduce what they say to the rules of philosophy; as, for example, in the passage before us, the Psalmist notes the marvellous fact that God holds the waters suspended in the air, because it seems contrary to nature that they should mount aloft, and also, that though fluid they should hang in vacant space.[81]

---

80. *Commentaries on the Book of Genesis* (Gen 1:6) (Calvin, *Genesis*, 1:79–80).

81. *Commentary on the Book of Psalms* (Ps 148:3) (Calvin, *Psalms*, 5:305). Similar are Calvin's comments on Ps 136:7.

Using accommodation in the same way as Augustine, Calvin explains the "great luminaries" of Gen 1:16 as an appeal to common perception:

> Moses makes two great luminaries; but astronomers prove, by conclusive reasons, that the star of Saturn, which, on account of its great distance, appears the least of all, is greater than the moon. Here lies the difference; Moses wrote in a popular style things which, without instruction, all ordinary persons, endued with common sense, are able to understand; but astronomers investigate with great labor whatever the sagacity of the human mind can comprehend . . . [In contrast, Moses] was ordained a teacher as well of the unlearned and rude as of the learned, he could not otherwise fulfil his office than by descending to this grosser method of instruction. . . . Moses, therefore, rather adapts his discourse to common usage.[82]

In using popular style, Moses stands in contrasts to astronomers, who speak more extensively and precisely in matters of natural philosophy. Calvin believed that Moses knew the scientific reality behind the language with which he wrote but that he chose to speak more plainly

> For as it became a theologian, he had respect for *us* rather than the *stars*. Nor, in truth, was he ignorant of the fact, that the moon had not sufficient brightness to enlighten the earth, unless it borrowed from the sun; but he deemed it enough to declare what we all may plainly perceive, that the moon is a dispenser of light to us.[83]

Several Enlightenment scientists would echo similar sentiments as Calvin—that Moses knew natural philosophy but spoke to commoners— in their defense of Copernican astronomy.[84] Most famous is Galileo, who quotes Cardinal Baronio in a letter to the Grand Duchess Christina: "The intention of the Holy Ghost is to teach us how one goes to heaven, not how heaven goes."[85] They continued to expound Scripture in concordant

---

82. *Commentaries on the Book of Genesis* (Gen 1:16) (Calvin, *Genesis*, 1:86–87). Similar comments are echoed for Ps 136:7—"The Holy Spirit had no intention to teach astronomy . . . [but] would rather speak childishly than unintelligibly to the humble and unlearned" (Calvin, *Genesis*, 5:184–85).

83. *Commentaries on the Book of Genesis* (Gen 1:15) (Calvin, *Genesis*, 1:85–86).

84. Benin, *The Footprints of God*, 195–96; Harrison, *The Bible*, 132–33; Snobelen, "'In the Language of Men,'" 713 (Galileo), 717 (Campanella).

85. *Letter to the Grand Duchess Christina* in Galileo, *Discoveries and Opinions of*

terms; however, while Luther had been rooted in Aristotelian astronomy, these later scholars sought to show how Moses understood Copernican astronomy, nuggets of truth waiting to be rediscovered by Enlightenment scientists.[86]

During the post-Reformation period, this view of the sacred authors' knowledge about nature would eventually change, even among the orthodox. In discussing the view of Jean-Alphones Turretin (1671–1737), Klauber and Sunshine write, "Since Scripture is accommodated to the level of man's understanding, it would make sense that it would not provide more advanced scientific knowledge than was generally available at the time when it was written."[87] This position characterizes not only Cartesian rationalists, but also nineteenth-century conservatives such as the Old Princetonians.

It is important to note that at a theoretical level, Calvin saw no necessary conflicts between the Bible and science; the debates of the

---

Galileo, 186. This echoes Calvin's comment regarding Gen 1:6 cited above. Galileo states his doctrine of accommodation also in very Calvin-like terms: "These propositions [anthropological language and references to natural science] uttered by the Holy Ghost were set down in that manner by the sacred scribes in order to accommodate them to the capacities of the common people, who are rude and unlearned" (Galileo, *Discoveries and Opinions of Galileo*, 181). Galileo is clear in a number of places that "the Bible cannot err" and "the holy Bible can never speak untruth"; rather, when there is apparent conflict between the Bible and science, the problem resided in an improper interpretation of Scripture (Galileo, *Discoveries and Opinions of Galileo*, 179–81). Like Calvin, Galileo believed the authors of Scripture knew the truth of natural science but only spoke to matters of salvation (Galileo, *Discoveries and Opinions of Galileo*, 184–85). Also, science is rightfully employed in clarifying the text: "having arrived at any certainties in physics, we ought to utilize these as the most appropriate aids in the true exposition of the Bible and in the investigation of those meanings which are necessarily contained therein, for these must be concordant with demonstrated truths" (Galileo, *Discoveries and Opinions of Galileo*, 183). At the same time, Galileo exhibits more of the spirit of the Enlightenment than of Calvin by granting to science a methodological priority on any matters outside of salvation: "I think that in discussions of physical problems [i.e., science] we ought to begin not from the authority of scriptural passages, but from the sense experiences and necessary demonstrations" (Galileo, *Discoveries and Opinions of Galileo*, 182). He goes on to discuss his confidence that God has spoken truly in nature through the establishment of immutable laws as much as he has in Scripture by the Holy Spirit. By default, empirical demonstrations cannot be contradicted by the Bible. In such appearances, one's interpretation must give way via accommodative language. However, Galileo's commitment to the empirical method did not express itself in the extreme of the Dutch Cartesians (see below).

86. Snobelen, "'In the Language of Men,'" 725.

87. Klauber and Sunshine, "Jean-Alphones Turrettini," 19.

seventeenth century were beyond his time. Contrary to common misunderstanding, Huijgen writes, "Calvin did not address the Copernican world view, nor did he employ the idea of accommodation to demarcate the place of natural sciences . . . So, Calvin's concept of accommodation was drawn into a discussion for which it was not devised."[88] What Calvin does do is use the science of his day to help interpret Scripture when it serves that purpose; but he refrains from discussing any specific conflicts in the discussions of his day, rather he utilizes accommodation when the plain sense of the text seems at odds with the scientific belief.[89]

One noncosmological example of Calvin's use of accommodation is often overlooked in discussions, yet it is an important one to consider for this issue.[90] In his commentary on Ps 58:4, Calvin deliberates whether or not David imagined that magic actually works as a reality behind his metaphor—[his enemies are] "like a deaf viper that stops its ear, so that it does not hear the voice of charmers." After considering that snake charming might be the result of satanic activity, Calvin concludes instead:

> But we may avoid all occasion for such curious inquiry [i.e., satanic activity], by adopting the view already referred to, that David here borrows his comparison from a popular and prevailing error, and is to be merely supposed as saying, that no kind of serpent was imbued with greater craft than his enemies, not even the species (if such there were) which guards itself against enchantment.[91]

The "view already referred to" is Calvin's previous comment that, "we suppose David to speak in mere accommodation to mistaken,

---

88. Huijgen, *Divine Accommodation in John Calvin's Theology*, 374. See the important excursus in which Huijgen cogently defends this proposition against the common opinion today that Calvin explicitly challenged the Copernican model (pp. 222-24). However, as Huijgen notes, Calvin does allude to heliocentrism disparagingly in his *sermon* on 1 Cor 10:19-22. But Calvin's preaching targets the attitude of some who are espousing new theories more than a general criticism of science against Scripture. Similar conclusions can also be found in Greene-McCreight (*Ad Litteram*, 130-31, incl. notes 171-80).

89. Greene-McCreight, *Ad Litteram*, 131.

90. This accommodation to human error is noted in Hooykaas "Calvin and Copernicus," 141; Benin, *The Footprints of God*, 195-96; and Balserak, *Divinity Compromised*, 48.

91. *Commentary on the Book of Psalms* (Ps 58:4) (Calvin, *Psalms*, 2:373)—The crucial sentence is: *Davidem ex communi errore similitudinem hanc esse mutuatum* (Baum, et al., *Ioannis Calvini Opera*, 561). The phrase, *ex communi errore*, translated "popular and prevailing error" might be rendered "common misconception."

though generally received opinion. He would certainly seem, however, to insinuate that serpents can be fascinated by enchantment; and I can see no harm in granting it."[92]

There are actually two potential problems in this verse. The first, which Calvin recognizes, is the question whether magic actually effects snake charming; the second, of which Calvin seems unaware, is whether snakes actually hear when they in fact do not even have ears. This example of accommodation will be examined more fully in the next chapter. It is important to note here that Calvin used accommodation to explain how David played upon an erroneous assumption in the popular culture of his day in order to make a rhetorical point, namely, the nature of snakes as deadly and cunning.

Socinus

It has been argued that the writings of Faustus Socinus (1539–1604) mark the beginning of a new trend in the seventeenth century. Rather than conceive of accommodation in Scripture as adaptation to the humble limits of human observation (accommodation in manner of speech), Socinus maintained that at times such language was a concession to error on the part of the human author (accommodation in content of truth).[93]

Without doubting that Socinus was unorthodox on many matters, this understanding of Socinus is based upon a questionable interpretation of his view on inspiration. It is beyond the scope of this survey to adequately deal with the sources, which are rare and largely untranslated. However, since his view has become an important part of the discourse on the history of accommodation, the following is an attempt to reconsider Socinus's view from what is available in English translation. Hopefully, it is sufficient to point to the need for more thorough reexamination of the primary sources.

A more sympathetic reading of Socinus shows that his view of Scripture was *similar* in nuance to the view espoused by many inerrantist biblical scholars today. Regarding the assertion that Socinus ascribed error to apostolic interpretation of the Old Testament, on close reading

---

92. *Commentary on the Book of Psalms* (Ps 58:4) (Calvin, *Psalms*, 2:372).

93. Sunshine, "Accommodation in Calvin and Socinus"; Klauber and Sunshine, "Jean-Alphones Turrettini," 13–14; Lee, "Accommodation," 336–37; Lee, "Biblical Accommodation and Authority," 5–7, 238–41; Sunshine, "Accommodation Historically Considered," 257–58.

of his statement, he regarded the apostolic use of the Old Testament as a form of what today is called *sensus plenior*, not erroneous violations of the plain sense of the Old Testament.[94] He did concede, reluctantly, that in minor matters of history the New Testament may *appear* to be in error.[95] As an example of what he means by this, he cites Chrysostom's commentary on Matthew where Chrysostom argues that any differences between the evangelists are "trivial." In modern discussion, these are differences resolved by many inerrantists through redaction criticism. At one place he defined "doctrine" as "things indispensably to be done or believed."[96] This suggests to some that his particular definition of doctrine allowed for a large margin of error in the text on matters falling outside this narrow view.[97] But in reading his apology on the authority of Scripture, at every turn Socinus seems eager to point out the reliability of the New Testament, and that, *if* there be found some small corruption in the New Testament, it is of "no consequence."[98] He regarded historical and doctrinal parts of the Bible to be inseparable and mutually dependent.[99] Likewise, for the Old Testament, Moses wrote reliably of things long before his time, including creation, because they were divinely revealed to him.[100] If one believes the New Testament, then, he argues that the same fidelity must be extended to the Old Testament.[101]

In his break from traditional orthodoxy, Socinus relied on his rational faculties to *interpret* the text. However, the extent of Socinus's commitment to a rationalistic method needs to be put into perspective.

---

94. Old Testament statements relating to Christ are "at least in some part, of another meaning from what the letter of the Old Testament seems to impart; and such too, as without the revelation of the New, nobody could even have suspected anything of" (Socinus, *An Argument*, 26).

95. "Moreover, the repugnancies or diversities [of Scripture], whether real or in appearance, are in points of small moment relating to history" (Socinus, *An Argument*, 21).

96. Socinus, *An Argument*, 142.

97. Sunshine, "Accommodation in Calvin and Socinus."54-55; Klauber and Sunshine, "Jean-Alphones Turrettini," 13.

98. "It has been said already, that no such thing [i.e., corruption] is to be found there, or such as is of no consequence; and therefore unfit to create even a suspicion of any corruption truly so called, and which really depraves either doctrine or history" (Socinus, *An Argument*, 49).

99. Socinus, *An Argument*, 13.

100. Socinus, *An Argument*, 67-68.

101. Socinus, *An Argument*, 72, 143.

Socinus proclaimed his willingness "to believe things and facts, however difficult or surprising in their nature, or otherwise in appearance impossible."[102] This is not the statement of a thoroughgoing rationalist. His rationalism does not differ from unorthodox (e.g., non-Trinitarian) argumentation that had been employed for centuries, arguments based in part on personal senses of what is reasonable. Rational faculties have always been used for theological formulation by both the unorthodox as well as the orthodox and in their respective interpretations of Scripture. Consider, for example, the use of reason in Calvin's interpretation of cosmological texts noted in the above discussion. Overall, considering the apologetic nature of Socinus's *An Argument for the Authority of Holy Scripture* (i.e., he makes concessions for the sake of establishing a minimal foundation for biblical authority), his method of argumentation anticipates in many ways what can be found today among some conservative apologists.

In one significant instance, Socinus's application of accommodation shows an expansion from how it had been traditionally used, a point correctly set forth by Klauber, Sunshine, and Lee.[103] Since Socinus did not believe in a conscious intermediate state or in eternal torment for the unrighteous, he defended his interpretation of passages that were problematic for his denial. As the capstone of his efforts, he cites Jesus' parable of Lazarus:

> For whoever is thrown into Gehenna, from him, indeed, that celestial life is taken and he is completely punished. It is to be noted, however, that Christ and the Apostles insofar as possible accommodated themselves in the opinions of men which at the time largely prevailed, as clearly the parable of Dives and Lazarus [Luke 16:20–31] sufficiently teaches. For that someone should be in hell and tortured, another to be in the bosom of Abraham, etc., are obviously fictitious and similar to those which the poets write concerning Ixion, Sisyphus, Tantalus.[104]
>
> So much then concerning the state of the dead before the Last Day. One should deal cautiously with this matter, just even as Christ himself and the Apostles accommodated themselves to

---

102. Socinus, *An Argument*, 115.

103. Sunshine, "Accommodation in Calvin and Socinus," 68–69; Klauber and Sunshine, "Jean-Alphones Turrettini," 14; Lee, "Accommodation," 336–37; Sunshine, "Accommodation Historically Considered," 258.

104. Socinus, "Epitome," 105.

the level of the people as the parable of Lazarus [Luke 16:20ff.] and the rich man teaches. This was not the time to perturb the Jews, as even now is not the time, although Jesus sometimes speaks thus in order that it be sufficiently clear that he will resuscitate only the faithful, John 6[:38–39, 40, 54]. And Paul [Phil 3:10–11] most clearly proclaims that he labors in order that he "may, if possible, attain the resurrection." Thus, in the meantime, certain things may be said that even indicate this thing [general resurrection] to men, until at length age matures and men are able to accustom themselves to these ways of talking [about the state and destiny of the unrighteous dead].¹⁰⁵

In Socinus's view, Luke 16 presents a concession by Jesus to the common, albeit erroneous, belief of his contemporaries in a general resurrection. Jesus used the illustration in the parable because it served his point to condemn the Pharisees.¹⁰⁶ Socinus's method differs from Calvin's comments on Ps 58:4 only in degree, however. His application of accommodation touched on potential matters of doctrine whereas Calvin's did not. But from our contemporary theological vantage point, one might take the same posture as Socinus toward the possibility that in this parable Jesus endorsed intercompartmental communication within the intermediate state. Potentially, this approach could be used to explain away any interpretation of Scripture that one finds objectionable on other grounds (whether reason or apparent conflict with other biblical texts).

It is difficult to determine the extent to which later Scholastic use of accommodation can be traced to Socinus's actual view. The rationalistic element of Socinus's theological method became more pronounced, and later views became attributed to him that perhaps were not originally his (hence "Socinians").¹⁰⁷ In any event, the cogency of my interpretation of Socinus does not change the conclusion—by the end of the seventeenth century, the view that accommodation incorporated errors of the culture from the biblical world was widespread.¹⁰⁸

105. Socinus, "Epitome," 121–22.

106. It is not accurate to suggest, as does Lee ("Accommodation," 337), that Socinus denied the bodily resurrection altogether, rather just of the unrighteous. What Socinus does is use accommodation to account for a text that might on the surface offer contradictory witness to his theological interpretation. In principle, accommodation has always worked in this manner—for example, to explain anthropomorphic language that contradicts the theology that God has no body or spatial limits.

107. Ogonowski, "Faustus Socinus," 207–9.

108. Lee, "Accommodation," 337; Lee, "Biblical Accommodation and Authority," 161; Sunshine, "Accommodation Historically Considered," 259.

René Descartes and Dutch Cartesians

More clearly than Socinus, the articulation of accommodation by Descartes (1596–1650) and Christophor Wittich (1625–1687) shows the growing confidence in human reason to stand in judgment not only over traditional *interpretations* of Scripture (as in Socinus) but also over *Scripture itself* as a possible source of truth. As Huijgen notes, for Descartes "Scriptural expressions that are 'accommodated to the people's understanding contain only some truth; God could even, for pedagogical purposes, use a lie.'"[109] Similarly, Wittich wrote that Scripture "speaks according to the people's erroneous opinion."[110] In response to criticism from more orthodox scholars, Wittich argued that the "scope" of the Bible was not scientific but limited to matters of salvation. This distinguished the theological message of Scripture from other matters in which it merely endorses popular misconceptions.[111] A sharp separation emerged in domains of truth—philosophy on all matters accessible by reason (e.g., science) and Scripture on matters that transcend the "power of the human mind."[112] Among rationalists, the traditional use of accommodation as language *adapted* to the limited capacity of human understanding expanded to include *adoption* of culturally conditioned values, which in turn are subject to philosophical evaluation.[113]

Spinoza

For Baruch Spinoza (1632–1677), faith and philosophy were radically separated. The former was a matter of morals and piety only, the latter the domain of all human knowledge, including *spiritual* truth:

---

109. Huijgen, *Divine Accommodation in John Calvin's Theology*, 30 n. 92.

110. Cited in Huijgen, *Divine Accommodation in John Calvin's Theology*, 30; also Lee, "Accommodation," 337.

111. Huijgen, *Divine Accommodation in John Calvin's Theology*, 30; Lee, "Accommodation," 30.

112. Lee ("Accommodation," 337) citing Balthasar Bekker (1634–1698). See also Huijgen, *Divine Accommodation in John Calvin's Theology*, 31. This is similar to the separation of domains in Galileo (cf. A. J. Brown, *The Days of Creation*, 129); however, Galileo maintained higher regard for the ultimate truthfulness of Scripture (see above discussion of Calvin and Galileo).

113. Muller, *Post-Reformation Reformed Dogmatics*, 2:305–6.

> So now the point we set out to prove has been made abundantly clear, namely, that God adapted his revelations to the understanding and beliefs of the prophets, who may well have been ignorant of matters that have no bearing on charity and moral conduct but concern philosophical speculation, and were in fact ignorant of them, holding conflicting beliefs. Therefore knowledge of science and matters spiritual should by no means be expected of them. So we conclude that we must believe the prophets only with regard to the purpose and substance of the revelation; in all else one is free to believe as one will.[114]

> It now remains for me finally to show that between faith and theology on the one side and philosophy on the other there is no relation and no affinity . . . The aim of philosophy is, quite simply, truth, while the aim of faith, as we have abundantly shown, is nothing other than obedience and piety.[115]

Since Scripture does not come by human reason but only by prophetic "imagination," this opens the appropriation of Scripture to the individual's moral conscience and the right of private judgment:

> Up to this point our object has been to separate philosophy from theology and to show that the latter allows freedom to philosophise for every individual.[116]

> Therefore, as the sovereign right to free opinion belongs to every man even in matters of religion . . . there also belongs to every man the sovereign right and supreme authority to judge freely with regard to religion, and consequently to explain it and interpret it himself.[117]

In view of this individual right to respond to religion and to Scripture as one chooses, Spinoza applies the notion of "accommodation."[118] For Spinoza, accommodation meant that the primitive authors could not transcend the worldview of their age. So rather than simply a pedagogical tool to help the common person understand truth, Scripture

---

114. Spinoza, *Theological-Political Treatise* 2, pp. 32–33. As examples of what he means by "spiritual," Spinoza cites free will and the existence of angels.
115. Spinoza, *Theological-Political Treatise* 14, pp. 164.
116. Spinoza, *Theological-Political Treatise* 16 , pp. 173.
117. Spinoza, *Theological-Political Treatise* 7, pp. 103.
118. Spinoza, *Theological-Political Treatise* 7, pp. 103–4.

interpretation became a right that saw individuals choose which texts and meanings should be accommodated to personal faith. Spinoza writes, "Just as Scripture was once adapted to the understanding of the people of that time, in the same way anyone may now adapt it to his own beliefs if he feels that this will enable him to obey God with heartier will in those matters that pertain to justice and charity."[119]

As Huijgen notes, this freed human reason from biblical authority altogether by placing it over revelation.[120] Thus, the function of accommodation shifted in the seventeenth century—from an explanation for how revelation adapted to limited human understanding to an explanation for how human rationale determines what qualifies as truth in Scripture.[121] Most seventeenth- and eighteenth-century scholars did not utilize accommodation to bracket out biblical revelation to the degree employed by some Dutch Cartesians and Spinoza. However, since no clear criteria existed for determining when accommodation applied and when it did not, in practice accommodation marginalized an increasing number of texts. Or, in different terms, accommodation became an "ever regressive principle" that forced Scripture into irrelevancy in relation to natural science.[122] This trend came to dominate continental scholarship in the eighteenth century and eventually British and North American scholarship as well in the late nineteenth century.

Accommodation and the Refinement of Scientific Concordism

As some interpreters were excluding the Bible as a source for natural science, other interpreters were working methodologically in the opposite direction. The attempt to correlate the language of Genesis with science is seen in the commentaries of Martin Luther and to a lessor extent John Calvin. Both employed natural philosophy, as they knew it, to illuminate difficult references in the text containing language that had been adapted to uneducated people. In the seventeenth century, however, the appropriation of accommodation led to a new interpretive goal. As Harrison writes, "the text provoked scientific and cosmological

---

119. Spinoza, *Theological-Political Treatise* 14, pp. 158.

120. Huijgen, *Divine Accommodation in John Calvin's Theology*, 32; to whom I am indebted for leads on Spinoza throughout.

121. Huijgen, *Divine Accommodation in John Calvin's Theology*, 375.

122. Huijgen, *Divine Accommodation in John Calvin's Theology*, 375.

questions."¹²³ So, rather than just an adaptation of scientific realities to the common understanding of Scripture, Scripture was thought to contain hidden meaning, missed by uneducated readers but rediscovered by the help of emerging science. Thus, the Bible holds deeper, scientific meaning in a way reminiscent of allegorical interpretation where the text contains deeper, spiritual meaning.¹²⁴ So while some scholars simply dismissed the biblical record as erroneous, making accommodation practically irrelevant, others took up the challenge to write natural history by reading more *into* the accommodated biblical account.¹²⁵ The question was not *whether* the Bible teaches science, but to what *degree*.¹²⁶

One influential thinker was Thomas Burnet (1635–1715), whose two-volume *Sacred Theory of the Earth* (1681 and 1689) illustrates the blending of accommodation theory with a commitment to engage emerging physics.¹²⁷ Burnet believed that Gen 1 described the earth only from the viewpoint of Moses at the time he wrote the account—hence Genesis does not yield an account of the creation of primitive earth. According to Burnet, Gen 1 is "a description of the present form of the earth, which was its form then when Moses wrote": Gen 1 presents "only [an] ideal, accommodated to the present terraqueous form of the earth."¹²⁸ For Burnet the *original* earth was a perfect sphere, smooth like an eggshell (an ideal form not depicted by Moses); yet, interpreting in concordant fashion, there were subterranean waters beneath the crust, since God had "founded it upon the seas" (Ps 24:2; 136:6; Prov 8:27). The present form of the world emerged during the deluge when this perfect crust of the earth was broken up by the gushing forth of these subterraneal waters (Gen 7:11).¹²⁹

Burnet's mixture of approaches received private affirmation in correspondence from Isaac Newton (1642–1727).¹³⁰ However, Newton

---

123. Harrison, *The Bible*, 129.

124. Harris, "Medieval Jewish Biblical Exegesis," 135–38.

125. Cf. A. J. Brown, *The Days of Creation*, 168–69.

126. Harris, "Medieval Jewish Biblical Exegesis," 140–41.

127. An early attempt to correlate natural history with the Bible in a *geographically regional* scope is that of Dane Nicolaus Steno (1638–1686) (see A. J. Brown, *The Days of Creation*, 151–52).

128. English adapted from the original dialect cited by A. J. Brown, *The Days of Creation*, 153.

129. Harris, "Medieval Jewish Biblical Exegesis," 142–43.

130. Harris, "Medieval Jewish Biblical Exegesis," 143.

himself adhered to the need to follow the six-day pattern of Gen 1 more closely, even if he advocated a day-age understanding of the first three days: "As to Moses I do not think his description of the creation either philosophical or feigned, but that he described realities in a language artificially adapted to the sense of the vulgar."[131] For Newton, this involved a gradual increase in earth's rotational rate so that the "days" in Gen 1 were originally much longer. Brown concludes, "In being willing to alter the duration of the creation days, while maintaining their historical reality, Newton distinguishes his approach from the purely ideal ones of Burnet or Henry More and so represents a key pioneer of the 'day-age' approach."[132]

Like Burnet, William Whiston (1667–1752), in his *New Theory of the Earth* (1696), utilized accommodation in viewing Gen 1 as observational language from the viewpoint of someone standing on earth; but unlike Burnet, he exhibited scientific concordism, sticking rather closely the natural order of events: the earth was originally a comet that God stabilized in orbit around the sun, after which time the atmosphere settled to create its crust, the oceans condensed, and the atmosphere cleared sufficiently by the fourth day to allow the sun and moon to appear. Like Newton, Whiston allowed for a change in the earth's rotation so that a "day" was initially a year in length.[133] As scientific learning expanded in the eighteenth century, new knowledge gave evidence of an earth that was much older than anyone had previously imagined. The well-established notion of accommodation, particularly in the form of "day-age" theory, facilitated acceptance of this: one such theory was Georges Buffon's (1707–1788) argument that the earth was approximately seventy-five thousand years old.[134] Even before Buffon's theory, Anton Lazzaro Moro (1687–1764) was unsatisfied that the flood could account for the complexities of geological observation, and he advocated a day-age model that harmonized geological epochs with figurative days in Genesis.[135] In this way, interpretation began to adjust to deep time.

---

131. English adapted from the original dialect cited by A. J. Brown, *The Days of Creation*, 154.

132. A. J. Brown, *The Days of Creation*, 155.

133. A. J. Brown, *The Days of Creation*, 164–65.

134. McCalla, *The Creationist Debate*, 56–57; A. J. Brown, *The Days of Creation*, 208–9.

135. A. J. Brown, *The Days of Creation*, 187–88.

Another important approach to harmonization arose through reconsideration of the place of the angels at the time of creation. In order to account for the fall of angels, as well as the burgeoning knowledge about extinct fossil forms, the idea arose that between the original creation of Gen 1:1 and the chaotic state of the planet in Gen 1:2 an indeterminable length of time elapsed—hence the origins of the ruin-restitution hypothesis, or "gap theory."[136] This interpretive move offered the advantage of maintaining both an old earth as well as a literal six-day (re-)creation, and as such, it was only partially concordant in comparison to the day-age efforts current at the time.

Brown observes that by 1800, the "mantle of authority had shifted to human reason."[137] Genesis commentaries needed the support of science for credibility, but not the other way around. The developments of science into the nineteenth century only added to the difficulties to harmonize the Bible with science in a concordant manner.[138] The use of accommodation expanded, and concordism of the day-age variety or adherence to the semiconcordant gap theory became common. There were also voices resisting these currents. Some maintained that geology failed to demonstrate deep time, and they criticized attempts to harmonize Scripture with an old-earth model.[139] Others, especially on the European continent, continued an approach that separated science from the Bible entirely, attempting to rescue the respective value of both.[140] While this position is normally identified with higher criticism, Brown describes some as adhering to a "'believing non-concordism', a rejection of the concordist enterprise that stemmed neither from scepticism nor from a strict literalism."[141] By the end of the nineteenth century, the basic positions on accommodation relating to science and the Bible had been staked: (1) young earth with interpretation of science to deny deep time;

---

136. A. J. Brown, *The Days of Creation*, 195–96.

137. A. J. Brown, *The Days of Creation*, 169. Buffon's words in 1778 offer insight into current thinking: "Why then exclaim so strongly about this borrowing of time [i.e., day-age] that we only take to the degree that we are forced to it by the demonstrative knowledge of the phenomena of nature?" (*Les époques de la nature* [1:62], cited in A. J. Brown, *The Days of Creation*, 208.

138. For discussion of these complex developments, see D. A. Young, *The Biblical Flood*, 65–168; Cameron, *Biblical Higher Criticism*, 290–324; McCalla, *The Creationist Debate*, 55–67; A. J. Brown, *The Days of Creation*, 219–79.

139. A. J. Brown, *The Days of Creation*, 259–64.

140. Cameron, *Biblical Higher Criticism*, 303–7.

141. A. J. Brown, *The Days of Creation*, 254–59. The quote is on page 255.

(2) old earth with some model of scientific concord; (3) old earth with no effort to find scientific concord, utilizing a purely literary reading of Genesis.

Accommodation among Late Nineteenth-Century Conservatives

Because of the importance of late nineteenth-century, conservative theologians (especially Old Princetonians) in contemporary debates regarding accommodation and the veracity of Scripture, there is value in summarizing the views of representative figures.[142] The most programmatic figure of Old Princeton was Charles Hodge (1797–1878). In wrestling with the challenges of nineteenth-century science to the Mosaic account of creation, Hodge stated: "The language of the Bible . . . is framed in accordance with the common usage of men," and he quotes Calvin that "Moses accommodated himself to the ignorance of common people," so what is presented in the history of creation is only language of appearance.[143] He differentiated between what the writers of Scripture "thought or believed and what they teach."[144] So, as an example, he maintained that it is not a question of whether the writers of Scripture believed that the earth was the center of the solar system; rather, did they teach this?[145]

Hodge accepted the old-earth consensus of geology in his day, and he reconciled this with Gen 1 using a day-age approach, which he favored over the gap theory. Methodologically, he writes,

> It is of course admitted that, taking this account by itself, it would be most natural to understand the word ["day"] in its ordinary sense; but if that sense brings the Mosaic account into conflict with facts, and another sense avoids such conflict, then it is obligatory on us to adopt the other.[146]

---

142. The Dutch Reformed tradition, represented by Herman Bavinck, is also important; but Bavinck's view on accommodation does not differ from the Princeton tradition (contrary to Rogers and McKim, discussed below). See Bavinck, *In the Beginning*, 120–21; Bavinck, *Reformed Dogmatics*, 1:445–46

143. Hodge, *Systematic Theology*, 1:569–70, cf. 1:170–71.

144. Hodge, *Systematic Theology*, 1:170.

145. Hodge, *Systematic Theology*, 1:169.

146. Hodge, *Systematic Theology*, 1:570–71.

Hodge observed, "The Church has been forced more than once to alter her interpretation of the Bible to accommodate the discoveries of science"; yet, in his view it has in each case helped verify that the Bible is divinely inspired.[147]

While arguing that the primary task of the Bible is not to teach astronomy and geology, Hodge maintained that Scripture is true whenever it does address such matters: "[Plenary inspiration] is not confined to moral and religious truths, but extends to the statements of facts, whether scientific, historical, or geographical."[148] But he was careful not to extend accommodation beyond language use to matters of theological substance, such as the existence of angels and demons.[149] Criticizing rationalism's dismissal of the supernatural, he describes its position: "It was granted by some that Christ and the Apostles did teach the church doctrines, but this, it was said, was done only by way of accommodation to the prejudices, superstitions, or modes of thought of the men of that generation."[150]

While Hodge criticized Darwinism because it left out God's design, he was nevertheless willing to respect that some interpreters could harmonize in their minds a theistic model of evolution and the Bible.[151]

Another stalwart of Old Princeton, Archibald Alexander Hodge (1823–1886), expressed his view in the following way:

> [The authors of Scripture] use the language and idiom proper to their nation and class. They adopt the *usus loquendi* [usage of language] of terms current among their people, without committing themselves to the philosophical ideas in which the usage originated . . . Like all purely literary men of every age, they describe the order and the facts of nature according to their appearances, and not as related to their abstract law or cause.[152]

---

147. Hodge, *Systematic Theology*, 1:573–74. Quoting Hodge on the unity of the human race ("the church . . . is willing that the Bible should be interpreted under the guidance of the facts of science"), Mark Noll observes that Hodge differentiated between "fact" and "theory" (Noll, *The Princeton Theology*, 143). An old earth was "fact" but evolution was only "theory."

148. Hodge, *Systematic Theology*, 1:163.

149. Hodge, *Systematic Theology*, 1:639, 1:646, 2:118.

150. Hodge, *Systematic Theology*, 3:196.

151. Noll, *The Princeton Theology*, 145–52, esp. 151; Gundlach, *Process and Providence*, 124–26.

152. Hodge, *Outlines of Theology*, 72.

This statement underscores his belief that the authors of Scripture used common language of observation for speaking about nature, not attempting to convey theory about laws and causes of nature. A. A. Hodge accepted both the "gradual progression" of the physical earth over deep time as well as the successive changes in life from "elementary to the more complex."[153] While details of geological history were not yet worked out in concord with the Genesis account, he affirmed a general harmony. He believed that once science matured, it would be seen in closer concord; at the same time, "Sometimes it is the views of the theologian which are amended into harmony with perfected and demonstrated science" (he cites the Copernican system as an example).[154] His conciliatory comments regarding the compatibility of evolution with Christian theism were very influential, at least among northern Presbyterians, although he was personally far from being convinced of the cogency of the science and so maintained essentially the same position as his father, Charles Hodge.[155]

Bridging the twentieth century, the last great Princetonian, Benjamin Breckinridge Warfield (1851–1921), wrote concerning the apostle Paul:

> A presumption may be held to lie also that he shared the ordinary opinions of his day in certain matters lying outside the scope of his teachings, as, for example, with reference to the form of the earth, or its relation to the sun; and, it is not inconceivable that the form of his language when incidentally adverting to such matters, might occasionally play into the hands of such a presumption.[156]

Applying the notion of accommodation as broadly as to the apostle's lifestyle (1 Cor 9:22), Warfield differentiated between accommodation to human prejudice and affirmation of error: "It is one thing to adapt the teaching of truth to the stage of receptivity of the learner; it is another thing to adopt the errors of the time as the very matter to be taught."[157] In his application of accommodation, then, Warfield follows suit with

---

153. Hodge, *Outlines of Theology*, 245.

154. Hodge, *Outlines of Theology*, 246–47.

155. Gundlach, *Process and Providence*, 162–63, 166.

156. Warfield, "The Real Problem of Inspiration," 197.

157. Warfield, "The Real Problem of Inspiration," 195. See the careful interpretive use of this quote in Silva, "Old Princeton, Westminster, and Inerrancy," 68.

his predecessors. Concerning evolution, he saw no *necessary* conflict between the Bible and the theory of evolution as a mechanism of divine action:

> The most important of these subsidiary questions [i.e., questions secondary to the fact of divine creation] has concerned the method of the divine procedure in creating man ... 'evolution' cannot act as a substitute for creation, but at best can supply only a theory of the method of divine providence.[158]

He himself regarded evolution as "scientific speculation" or "speculative biology"; and his overriding concern was to guard the unity of the human race, which, he argued, did have serious theological and ethical consequences.[159]

Although not among the Princetonians, William G. T. Shedd (1820-1894) was another influential theologian of the "Old School" (i.e., conservatives) whose work remains among nineteenth-century classics. His statements are included here because they are particularly clear on the matters concerning accommodation and cosmology. Shedd wrote that the human author of Scripture was preserved by divine guidance from "misconception and error upon the *subject* of which he treats."[160] Addressing claims of conflict between the Bible and natural sciences, he maintained, "The inspired writers were permitted to employ astronomy and physics of the people and age to which they themselves belonged, because the true astronomy and physics would have been unintelligible."[161]

Quoting Frances Bacon's *Advancement of Learning*, Shedd affirms, "The scope or purpose of the Spirit of God is not to express matters of nature in the scriptures otherwise than in passage, and for application to man's capacity, and to matters moral or divine."[162] In other words, natural science is not the subject of Scripture, and when language related to science is used, it is accommodated to the capacity of the audience and subordinate to other informative intentions. So, he notes that biblical language on "physics ... contains no pantheism or polytheism"

---

158. Warfield, "On the Antiquity," 238.
159. Warfield, "On the Antiquity," 254-56. Cf. Gundlach, *Process and Providence*, 241-42.
160. Shedd, *Dogmatic Theology*, 1:103 (italics original).
161. Shedd, *Dogmatic Theology*, 1:104.
162. Shedd, *Dogmatic Theology*, 1:105.

(matters of theological import).¹⁶³ At the same time, Shedd argues that "physical science is to some extent taught by revelation and recorded by inspiration. It is erroneous to say that the Bible commits itself to no physics whatever."¹⁶⁴ He explains himself by commenting on the opening chapters of Genesis: "Moses does not represent a cosmogony like that of Assyria, or Egypt, or India, or Greece and Rome."¹⁶⁵ Especially important to this contrast with "heathen" cosmologies are the manner in which Genesis teaches creation ex nihilo, the independence of God from the universe, God's omnipotence, and the contrast in general order of creation in Genesis compared to "heathen cosmogonies." He argues that the order of events in Genesis is counterintuitive (e.g., creation of light and plants happens before creation of the sun); therefore, it must be divinely revealed. The Genesis order, he maintains, is in general concord with science as known in his day.¹⁶⁶

One final example of "Old School" theologians is Augustus Hopkins Strong (1836–1921), who is particularly important for purposes of this monograph because his explanation of accommodation foreshadows the application of relevance theory by eighty years. In the context of his discussion of Scripture on "Errors in Matters of Science," he applies accommodation in customary terms: "What is charged as such (i.e., error) is simply truth presented in popular and impressive forms." In the next sentence he uses the phrase "phenomenological language."¹⁶⁷ In his next paragraph, however, Shedd draws on several other thinkers to formulate the issue in terms consistent with the principle of optimal relevance:

> The Scripture writers unconsciously observe Herbert Spencer's principle of style: Economy of the reader's or hearer's attention,—the *more energy is expended* upon the form the less there remains to grapple with substance (Essays, 1–47). Wendt, Teaching of Jesus, 1:130, brings out the principle of Jesus' style: "The greatest clearness in the smallest compass."¹⁶⁸

Strong offers several examples, but then he expands on the important distinction between observation and interpretation of natural events: "It

---

163. Shedd, *Dogmatic Theology*, 1:103.
164. Shedd, *Dogmatic Theology*, 1:105.
165. Shedd, *Dogmatic Theology*, 1:106.
166. Shedd, *Dogmatic Theology*, 1:106–8.
167. Strong, *Systematic Theology*, 1:223.
168. Strong, *Systematic Theology*, 1:223 (italics added).

is not necessary to a proper view of inspiration to suppose that the human authors of Scripture had in mind the proper scientific interpretation of the natural events they recorded. It is enough that this was in the mind of the inspiring Spirit."[169]

Concerning seventeenth-century thought, Harrison observes, "The conclusion which most exegetes wanted to avoid was one which suggested that Moses was expert in theological matters, but totally ignorant in the field of physical science, for this conclusion would impugn the whole authority of scripture."[170] At some point in the modern period, this sentiment changed even among conservative theologians; there was a shift from Calvin's view, that super-endowed human authors accommodated an ignorant audience, to the view that God accommodated both the human authors and their audience. Like Charles Hodge and Warfield, Strong attributed no special knowledge to the human authors of Scripture beyond the intended substance of their teaching. Perhaps because the Princetonians placed the locus of inspiration in the *text* of Scripture, this presented no problem.

Contemporary Discussion
(Late Twentieth and Twenty-First Centuries)

Accommodation in Linguistic Form and Cultural Context

Accommodation has become an important issue in recent discussions surrounding the evangelical doctrine of Scripture. Considerable controversy arose with the publication of Rogers and McKim's *The Authority and Interpretation of the Bible*.[171] They argued that accommodation throughout church history shows subordination of linguistic "form" in the Bible (i.e., linguistic style, manner of speech) to "function" (i.e., to communicate the content of its saving message).[172] This allowed for unintentional human error in matters unrelated to primary message of Scripture without compromising biblical authority.[173] In their understanding, this was the Augustinian-Calvinist approach followed by

169. Strong, *Systematic Theology*, 1:223.
170. Harrison, *The Bible*, 133; cf. 137–38.
171. Rogers and McKim, *The Authority and Interpretation of the Bible*.
172. Rogers and McKim, *The Authority and Interpretation of the Bible*, 98–99.
173. Rogers and McKim, *The Authority and Interpretation of the Bible*, 111–13, 126.

some post-Reformation rationalists, as exemplified by Wittich: here the distinction between content and form enables the interpreter to preserve the veracity of the Bible's message in spite of some mistaken thoughts of the writers. By focusing on the proper scope of biblical revelation and its accommodative language, Wittich avoided the conflict between Scripture and emerging science.[174] In their opinion, it was the Old Princetonians who popularized a view of accommodation that denied the culturally conditioned aspects of Scripture which might contain error.[175] Rogers and McKim write:

> [The Dutch-Reformed tradition that opposed Hodge and Warfield] reaffirmed a Reformed tradition that found authority in the saving content, not the supernatural form of Scripture . . . They accented God's accommodated method of communicating with humankind. The Bible was understood to speak in ordinary language about salvation, not technical terminology about science.[176]

Rogers and McKim extended accommodation beyond technical language, however, to include value-laden content from the cultural milieu:

> God had condescended to use imperfect human forms of communication to accomplish God's perfect, divine function of bringing salvation. The gospel message, not the cultural context or the linguistic forms, was understood to be normative for later readers of the Bible. The Bible was infallible in achieving its saving purpose.[177]

What is important to observe in this quote is the inclusion of both linguistic form *and* cultural context in the discussion.

Woodbridge objected, arguing that Rogers and McKim misrepresented the historical evidence on many points.[178] Calvin's doctrine of accommodation, while allowing the rudimentary nature of the biblical language, did *not* admit to error in detail or content.[179] Also

---

174. Rogers and McKim, *The Authority and Interpretation of the Bible*, 171, 188.

175. Rogers and McKim, *The Authority and Interpretation of the Bible*, 341–42, 457–59.

176. Rogers and McKim, *The Authority and Interpretation of the Bible*, 399.

177. Rogers and McKim, *The Authority and Interpretation of the Bible*, 126.

178. Woodbridge, *Biblical Authority*.

179. Woodbridge, *Biblical Authority*, 57–63; Balserak, *Divinity Compromised*, 163–68.

central to Rogers and McKim's argument is a mistaken understanding of post-Reformation scholastics that undergirds their critique of the Old Princetonians.[180] Rogers and McKim present a view that it was scholastics such as Wittich, not the Old Princetonians, who followed the Augustinian-Reformed tradition, whereas in reality the opposite is true. The reading of Reformation and post-Reformation scholars presented in this chapter concurs with Woodbridge's assessment. So, Rogers and McKim's attempt to redefine the traditional view of accommodation and its relationship to the truthfulness of Scripture is very problematic. Nonetheless, the argument over the proper understanding of accommodation in cultural content continues to play out.[181]

Aside from historical judgments, which stack against Rogers and McKim, consideration of their argument highlights important questions: First, how is accommodation related to the scope of revelation and authorial intent? Second, how does the Bible's linguistic form relate to the cultural context of its utterances? To repeat what was stated at the opening of this chapter, since natural languages do not exist independent of cultural context, the use of those languages necessarily invokes the encyclopedic ranges of ideas attached to those languages. So linguistic and cultural accommodation are not easily disentangled. These questions present abiding difficulties for all parties in the debate and furnish the backdrop for discussion in the next chapter.

Negative and Positive Accommodation

In addition to the difference between accommodation in language (manner) and accommodation in content (matter), Hofmann, followed by Sunshine, differentiates between "negative" and "positive" accommodation regarding content.[182] The distinction draws on ancient

---

180. Muller, *Post-Reformation Reformed Dogmatics*, 2:100, 141, 305.

181. See, for example, snippets in Merrick and Garrett, eds., *Five Views on Biblical Inerrancy*, 159, 183, 266–70, 318.

182. Hofmann, "Accommodation," 1:22–24; Sunshine, "Accommodation Historically Considered," 260–61. Cf. Richardson and Gooch, "Accommodation Ethics," esp. 98–104. Note that these terms are used differently by Benin, for whom "positive accommodation" means Christian use of pagan ideas as a platform for dialogue (e.g., Paul in Athens) and "negative accommodation" means a polemic by Christian interpreters against the Jewish tradition (Benin, *The Footprints of God*, xv–xvi).

Greek philosophical discussion of pedagogy. Negative accommodation refers to a teacher who allows false assumptions to remain uncorrected in the mind of a pupil for the sake of helping them along the path of understanding. Hence the teacher tolerates "a certain amount of error for a time."[183] Positive accommodation refers to a teacher who "distinctly approves such erroneous ideas or consciously sets them forth as truth."[184] In the assessment of the Greek philosophers, the temporary nature and pedagogical value of negative accommodation justified its use. In contrast, positive accommodation was regarded as deceit and was morally censured.

The distinction between negative and positive accommodation is useful but has limited value when applied to biblical cosmology. First, negative accommodation serves for a limited period of time until more complete truth can be revealed. But in the progress of revelation, the Bible never clarifies any truth regarding cosmology. Second, Hofmann himself regarded cosmological language to be phenomenological (*manner* of speech), and therefore by definition not negative accommodation, which only pertains to accommodation of *content*.[185] Third, positive accommodation entails an *intention* to mislead, whether supplying erroneous ideas or endorsing existing error. This shifts the discussion back onto authorial intent. Even those who argue strongly that Scripture incorporates false cultural values do not regard this as intentional deceit. Rather, these cases involve partial inspiration whereby God through the human author sets forth truthful ideas, yet these truths are sometimes embedded in a context that also contains some false ideas. In the case of partial inspiration, it is the task of the interpreter to discern exactly what the divine author intends. For similar reasons, Huijgen expressed concern about the limitations of accommodation in general: "the idea of accommodation as a hermeneutical tool is in these cases imprecise. For when something is regarded as accommodated, it remains unclear what precisely is accommodated—the language, the imagery, or the matter at hand—, and by whom: by God, or by the Biblical author?"[186] For this reason, more careful examination of the interaction between language

---

183. Hofmann, "Accommodation," 23.
184. Hofmann, "Accommodation," 23.
185. Hofmann, "Accommodation," 23–24.
186. Huijgen, *Divine Accommodation in John Calvin's Theology*, 375–76.

and cultural context in recognition of the complexity of dual authorship is necessary.

Calvin's commentary on Ps 58:4 illustrates the complexity of the problem. Calvin believed that David used an erroneous assumption from the culture of his day to create a metaphor. Is this negative accommodation, because David was simply using the illustration of snake charming to create the metaphor? Or is this positive accommodation, because the construction of this metaphor encouraged a concept (the efficacy of magic) that David knew to be false? Another illustration is in 1 Sam 28, when God provided that Samuel return from the dead through a necromancer's pit. Is this negative accommodation, because God adapted a misunderstood spatial relationship between the land of the living and the land of the dead in order to create an effective prophetic proclamation? Or is this positive accommodation, because God created an experience that affirmed Sheol's location under the surface of the earth, a common but false cultural assumption? The boundaries between negative and positive are blurred, and one must consider more carefully the complexities of linguistic and cultural interaction in the text to ascertain the author's informative intention.

Conclusions

This chapter surveyed the history of the use of accommodation, emphasizing the significance for the church's interpretation of cosmological texts and their relationship to natural science. A number of lessons emerge from this historical overview.

Scope of Revelation and Scientific Concord

Beginning with the church fathers, interpreters used accommodation to clarify the pedagogical strategy of God's revelation across salvation history. But a commitment to scientific concordism emerged during the seventeenth-to-eighteenth-century struggle to maintain the Bible's relevance in an age when science was becoming the epistemological starting point of intellectual discourse.

Luther and Calvin were explicit that the intent of Scripture was not to teach natural science, and their employment of accommodation served to relieve Scripture of that task. But beginning in the seventeenth century, scholars expected Scripture to serve as a framework for comprehensive knowledge of the world, including the interests of natural science. Demonstrating scientific concord became a necessary task to prove the validity of the Bible. By the time of Old Princeton, an old earth was commonly accepted among educated conservatives, who continued the tradition of scientific concordism. Ironically, by insisting on scientific concordism, the orthodox provided rationalists the leverage to deny the truthfulness of the Bible not only in natural science but in matters unrelated to science as well.

Accommodation as Linguistic and Cultural

Beginning with the church fathers, accommodation was framed primarily in pedagogical terms and described the manner by which God adapted his message of salvation to limited human understanding. A shift in seventeenth-century rationalism expanded accommodation to biblical content that was perceived as so culturally relative that its authority became subordinate to individual judgment.

The church has always struggled with the problem of cultural accommodation, seen for example in its explanation for why God instituted and later abandoned the Old Testament law or the sacrificial system. Reformers employed the idea of accommodation to emphasize that the language of the Bible relating to natural science was merely observational, crafted for the uneducated, yet subordinate to its saving message. So accommodation was both linguistic and cultural. Post-Reformation rationalists used accommodation to grant to any individual the freedom to appropriate only those passages deemed helpful for moral development. A debate continues over the nature of accommodation as it pertains to matters of cultural and scientific content. However, language and the culture in which it is embedded are not easily disentangled. As will be shown in the next chapter, relevance theory offers categories for examining utterances and cognitive environment that more carefully divide informative intention from contextual assumptions that play no role in meaning.

A Complicated Tradition of Interpretation

Every would-be orthodox view on the interpretation of Genesis that is entertained today has precursors in pre-Enlightenment Christian exegesis.

In the context of modern debate, it is important to recognize that ancient and medieval theologians did alter their interpretations for "scientific" reasons. These interpreters also sensed some of the inconsistencies internal to the Genesis creation account, and this contributed to their proclivity to interpret the text figuratively according to the dictates of their *philosophical* reasoning. So knowledge of the physical universe, internal textual considerations, and philosophy all played a role in exegesis. Following from this, it is *not* accurate to say that until the Enlightenment, there was an untroubled consensus to read Gen 1 as six ordinary days. An unbroken stream of pre-Enlightenment exegesis of Gen 1 felt free to interpret the days as other than normal (although "day-age" models, strictly speaking, did not emerge until the age of science). It may not have been the *majority* opinion, but an *important minority* of influential theologians throughout the ancient and medieval period deviated from literal interpretation. Therefore, attributing nonliteral exegesis simply to the church's compromise with Enlightenment science does an injustice to complexities in the history of interpretation.

Literalism, Scientific Models, and Inerrancy

The term "literal" must be distinguished from both "literalism" and the language of "scientific models" if we are to respect both the authorial intent as well as the veracity of Scripture.

Theologians throughout history embraced accommodation to free the words of Scripture from enslavement to overly literal interpretation. Sometimes they ventured into speculative allegory, but Bible interpreters always regarded literal readings of Scripture to include figurative language. Confusion between literalism and inerrancy creates an unnecessary problem around the veracity of the biblical text.[187]

Nascent Relevance Theory

The history of accommodation shows that interpreters have always attended in their own way to audience theory, which is the premise for relevance theory.

---

187. Vanhoozer, "Augustinian Inerrancy," 218–23; Sunshine, "Accommodation Historically Considered," 263.

As early as Origen and Calvin, theologians understood that accommodation was necessary so as not to confuse the audience of Scripture with inaccessible linguistic forms and content that were beyond their cognitive abilities and distracted from the thrust of the Bible's message. This was most clearly stated by A. H. Strong, who expressed communication principles that foreshadow the idea of optimal relevance.

4

Accommodation and Relevance

Introduction

The fundamental problem with which the previous chapter left off is the difficulty defining exactly what "accommodation" entails. Is accommodation only in *manner* of linguistic style, or does it also involve matters of *content*? One conclusion was that it must include content in some measure, for natural languages do not exist independent of cultural context, so the use of words necessarily invokes the encyclopedic ranges of ideas attached to those words, which means that linguistic and cultural accommodation are not easily disentangled. Indeed, throughout the history of interpretation, theologians have wrestled with accommodation in regard to salvation history, whether it be the discontinuity between the Testaments or nature of the incarnation, both of which are matters of *content*. When accommodation entails some sort of concession to false notions, distinguishing negative accommodation from positive accommodation helps in principle, namely, that one does not want to attribute intentional deceit on the part of the biblical author, human or divine. But as was argued, the categories of negative and positive accommodation have limited value when applied to cosmological language.

Relevance theory suggests that we should approach the problem from a different angle by asking more precisely what assumptions in the cognitive environment a speaker or author intends to evoke in the communicative act as part of inferred meaning. Before applying relevance theory to problems of accommodation, several concepts beyond those introduced in chapter 1 need to be understood. First, it is important to understand the distinction between "explicated" and "implicated" meaning. Second, there is an important distinction between what is only implicit in the background of a text and what an author intentionally implicates in the informative intention. Finally, informative intention varies on a continuum between what is strongly and weakly communicated by an utterance.

Contextual Assumptions and Inferred Meaning

Explicated and Implicated Meaning

In examining the interaction between words of an utterance and their cognitive environment, relevance theorists make a distinction between "explicature" and "implicature." "Explicature" refers to the meaning of the actual language (code) used in an utterance after it has been disambiguated and enriched from context. "Implicature" refers to meaning that is inferred exclusively from context and not logically entailed by the linguistically encoded meaning of the utterance. Sperber and Wilson write, "a thought that is *explicitly* expressed must be in some kind of correspondence to the semantic representation of the sentence uttered, [but] those [thoughts] that are *implicitly* conveyed are under no such constraint."[1] These definitions should not be confused with the more common use of the words "explicit" and "implicit," where "explicit" usually means the precise wording of an utterance ("what is said") and all other meaning is implicit.[2] Rather, relevance theorists include implicit assumptions that are linked with the *language* of an utterance into their definition of

---

1. Sperber and Wilson, *Relevance* (1995 ed.), 11 (italics original; see a more technical discussion on page 182). The following technical definitions are offered by Carston: "explicature: an ostensively communicated assumption which is inferentially developed from one of the incomplete conceptual representations (logical forms) encoded by the utterance" (Carston, *Thoughts and Utterances*, 377, cf. 124; cf. Sperber and Wilson, "Pragmatics," 479). Conversely, "implicature: an ostensively communicated assumption which is not an explicature; that is, a communicated assumption which is derived solely via processes of pragmatic inference" (Carston, *Thoughts and Utterances*, 377, cf. 137; cf. Sperber and Wilson, "Pragmatics," 480).

2. The usage of these terms was introduced by Paul Grice, as noted in chapter 1, and is common in both everyday communication as well as in technical linguistics; but relevance theorists have refined the definitions as outlined in this section.

"explicature."³ The following example illustrates the distinction between explicated meaning (explicature) and implicated meaning (implicature).

Example: Explicature and Implicature
Sue walks into the office and states to her colleague, Bill:

> Sue: "I will have no trouble having the report on your desk by noon."

The words that Sue uttered encode a number of concepts; the meanings of some of these are contained in the bare dictionary meanings of her words; for example:

(a) Sue will send the report to Bill by *12:00 p.m.* ("noon").

(b) This task will *not be difficult* to complete ("no trouble").

Some explicated meaning is also inferred when Bill disambiguates and enriches Sue's words from the context that is mutually understood between them; for example:

(c) "the report" needs disambiguation (which report?), which Bill supplies from context

(d) "noon," in this context, is enriched by shared knowledge of the specific deadline.

So Sue explicates that it is not difficult for her to finish and send the report that Bill requires to Bill by roughly 12:00 p.m. on the same day of her utterance, thereby meeting the deadline.

However, the meaning is still not exhausted by what is explicated. Let's say that Sue and Bill also share an understanding that Bill has anxiety that the project will be completed on time. Even though Sue's *words* do not contain any meaning directly associated with Bill's anxiety, nevertheless, Sue's words indirectly address (implicate) Bill's anxiety due to the relevance of this in their shared understanding. So,

(e) Sue communicates to Bill that he need not be anxious.

This meaning is implicated, because it includes contextual understandings that exist independent of any specific words in Sue's utterance. Sue could have explicated this by adding the words, "So no

---

3. For the difference between what relevance theorists mean by the explicature/implicature distinction on the one hand and what post-Gricean linguists mean by the "what is said"/implicature distinction on the other, see Carston, "Relevance Theory," 633–34; Carston, "Word Meaning," 176–78.

worries." Bill would still need to enrich this statement from context by linking "worries" with his anxiety in this particular situation; but Sue's utterance would contain words that in this context logically link to Bill's anxiety; so relief from anxiety would be explicated, not simply implicated. This illustrates how meaning is inferred by disambiguating and enriching words in an utterance (explicating) and by linking the utterance to other relevant contextual assumptions (implicating). In view of the common use the terms "explicit" and "implicit," perhaps one can approximate the technical definitions in the following matter: everything contributing to "explicatures" is communicated explicitly (*whether tacit or overt*), and everything contributing to "implicatures" is implicitly communicated.

Implicit versus Explicated and Implicated Assumptions

The above example illustrates how many ideas necessary for comprehending an utterance are implicit. There is an important, technical distinction between assumptions that are only implicit in the cognitive environment and those particular assumptions that are implicated in the informative intent of a speaker or writer. This distinction is crucial for understanding the discussion about divine accommodation in this chapter as well as consideration of theological implications in chapter 5.

The following example illustrates this important distinction.[4] Imagine a situation in which Bill and Sue are looking for a way to gain a better view into the distance; and Sue exclaims, "There is a tree." Sue has implicated the assumption that one can climb a tree to gain a better vantage point. However, there are other conclusions one could infer from her statement. Since trees need water to survive, it is implicit that there is also a source of water. Bill could derive the implication that there is water, but it was not Sue's informative intent to implicate anything about water. Hence, the implicit assumption about water was not part of her meaning. Conversely, imagine that Sue and Bill are hiking in the desert and in need of a source of water. Sue exclaims, "There is a tree." Now, due to changed contextual relevance, the implicit assumption about water is implicated, not any advantage gained by climbing the tree.

---

4. This is adapted from Anne Furlong ("A Modest Proposal," 336–37). Furlong uses this to illustrate the difference between a mere object from which we might derive implications and a communicative act that involves human discourse. Objects are mute whereas humans speak with informative intentions. I have created changing contexts of relevance to illustrate my point regarding implicature.

Strong and Weak Communication

The notions of explicated and implicated meaning can be described by the *degree* to which a speaker relies on contextual assumptions and how *manifest* those assumptions are to speaker and audience. A speaker uses words to guide an audience's attention, to "make manifest" (or more manifest) those contextual features that are important to infer meaning. A speaker's words make manifest a set of assumptions, and it is the task of the listener to decide which subset of these assumptions the speaker intends for interpretation. So, in the above illustration involving Sue's words to Bill regarding the report deadline, her words made manifest a set of shared assumptions about a specific report, its deadline, and Bill's anxiety over it.

The more dependent an utterance is on contextual enrichment supplied by the audience, the weaker are the inferences. Conversely, the less dependent an utterance is on contextual links, the stronger will be the inferences.[5] But as Carston notes, "In cases of weakly communicated assumptions, the interpreter takes a large measure of responsibility for inferring them."[6] If a speaker says nothing to encourage an audience to

---

5. Although he does not use relevance theory, this supports Walton's notions of "high context" and "low context" dependent statements (Walton and Sandy, *The Lost World of Scripture*, 43–44).

6. Carston, *Thoughts and Utterances*, 381. Carston defines strong versus weak communication: "a communicated assumption ('explicature' or 'implicature') is strongly communicated when the 'informative intention' to make manifest that particular assumption is made highly mutually manifest; the degree of strength with which an assumption is communicated varies on a continuum through to cases of very weak communication, where there is some 'indeterminacy' regarding which specific assumptions within some conceptual range fall under the speaker's informative intention" (Carston, *Thoughts and Utterances*, 380–81; cf. Sperber and Wilson, *Relevance* (1995 ed.), 178–79). Sperber and Wilson write, "When the hearer's expectations of relevance can be satisfied by deriving any one of a range of roughly similar premises, the hearer also has to take some responsibility for the particular premises he supplies and the conclusions he derives from them" (Sperber and Wilson, "Pragmatics," 484). Elsewhere, Wilson and Sperber explain: "We have already argued that implicatures may vary in strength. The same is true of explicatures. The identification of an explicature involves a certain amount of inference. Since the inference process is non-demonstrative [not subject to strict rules of logical deduction for validity; see Carston, *Thoughts and Utterances*, 378] and draws on background knowledge, the hearer must take a certain degree of responsibility for how it comes out. How much responsibility he has to take varies from utterance to utterance: explicatures may be weaker or stronger, depending on the degree of indeterminacy introduced by the inferential aspect of comprehension" (Wilson and Sperber, "Truthfulness and

draw upon a potential contextual assumption, then the audience takes *full* responsibility for doing so.[7] One cannot hold the speaker responsible for incorrectly inferred meanings. This concept will become very important below, when examining the assumptions that an audience might draw upon in cases of accommodation.

Example: Strong and Weak Communication (Degree of Manifestness)

Returning to the example of Sue's utterance, the effectiveness of communication depends upon the degree to which certain assumptions were shared *manifestly* between them. Sue's "no trouble" might be relevant to Bill's state of anxiety for one of several reasons shared between them:

(a) Bill's confession of anxiety about *this* project in a previous conversation

(b) their shared experience in *past* projects

(c) an expression on Bill's face

Any of these could be contextually implicated in Sue's intention to relieve Bill of anxiety about the deadline. Yet, each implicit assumption might be ranked as stronger or weaker from (a) to (c). Assumption (a) is most manifest because it is part of their shared communication on this very project. Assumption (b) may be true if it is assumed that Bill is always anxious about deadlines. But this assumption might be false in *this* case. Assumption (c) might be right or wrong depending on the meaning of a subtle nonverbal expression made manifest by Bill as he looked at Sue earlier that morning.

The weakness of (c) is easily illustrated. For example, one can imagine a fourth interpretation: Bill may have concluded from the words "no trouble" that Sue could actually have the report on his desk by ten o'clock a.m. Instead of concluding that her words are reassuring him not to feel anxious, Bill concludes that Sue is asserting her right to pace her own work within certain reasonable limits (i.e., in relation to the noon deadline). This illustrates that even the disposition of a relationship between parties in the conversation can influence the communicative exchange.

Relevance," 77). For a clear and concise illustration of the explicature/implicature distinction as well as strong and weak inferences, see Green, "Relevance Theory and Theological Interpretation," 78–81.

7. Sperber and Wilson, *Relevance* (1995 ed.), 199.

The following graph attempts to illustrate the continuum in relative strength and weakness of inferred interpretation:

FIGURE 5: INFERRED INTERPRETATION

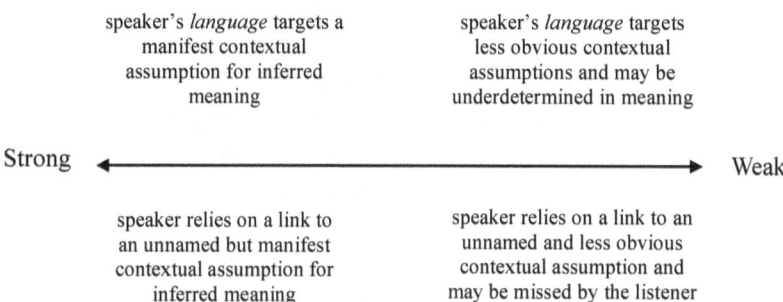

Inferred Premises and Conclusions

One of the ways that communication can be examined is by listing in a formal manner the contextual assumptions (premises) and the inferred meaning (conclusions). Ordinarily, people do not consciously construct a logical syllogism in their mind when interpreting an utterance. They intuitively use a loose sort of inferential reasoning.[8] However, for purposes of discussing how interpretation works, it can be useful to use an informal syllogism. In any given act of communication, identification of the right contextual assumptions is crucial in determining what a speaker is intending to communicate, because it is upon these assumptions that conclusions are drawn about intended meaning.

Example: Inferred Premises and Conclusions

Suppose Sue and Jack have the following exchange in the school library:

Sue: "Is Bill going to read Hilber's book?"

Jack: "Bill avoids linguistics."

---

8. Sperber and Wilson, *Relevance* (1995 ed.), esp. 69.

Contextual Assumption 1: Hilber's book is linguistic in approach.

Contextual Assumption 2: Bill regards linguistics as unhelpful.

Conclusion 1: Bill is not likely to read Hilber's book.

Conclusion 2: Bill would find Hilber's book unhelpful.

Contextual Assumption 1 is embedded in Sue's and Jack's encyclopedic knowledge of "Hilber's book." We might also say that Contextual Assumption 1 is *strongly implicated* in Jack's answer to Sue, since his utterance makes no sense in context unless it provides a premise for Sue to infer the answer to her question (Conclusion 1). If Assumption 1 is true, Bill's inferred Conclusion 1 is correctly warranted.

Contextual Assumption 2 is not logically entailed in Jack's words, "Bill avoids linguistics." This assumption, then, is not explicated, but it is potentially implicated. Sue might infer from this exchange that Bill would find Hilber's book unhelpful. But this would be a *weaker* assumption in the exchange between Jack and Sue, since it is not necessarily relevant to Sue's query. Perhaps Sue was not asking about the quality of Hilber's book . . . Let's say that she was only wondering if she might be able to sell her copy of Hilber's book to Bill. Consequently, she would not likely access Contextual Assumption 2 as a premise so as to draw any conclusion about the quality of Hilber's book. On the other hand, if Jack had said, "Bill avoids linguistics *for reasons we both know*," then he would have made Contextual Assumption 2 *highly manifest* in his utterance, strengthening its contribution to informative intention. Jack would be drawing attention to the reason Bill avoids linguistics and thereby implicating something about the quality of Hilber's book in Bill's mind.

What if Contextual Assumption 2 is false? After all, the reason for Bill's avoidance of linguistics might be other than his judgment about its helpfulness. Let's posit that when Sue and Jack see Bill frown at the mention of linguistics, it is because Bill's abusive father was a linguist, not because Bill regards linguistics as unhelpful. All along, Jack and Sue had been assuming something wrong about Bill regarding his posture toward linguistics. Fortunately for the success of this communicative event, Sue was not asking about the quality of Hilber's book, what Bill's attitude might be toward various kinds of disciplines (whether academic or in family), nor *why* Bill avoids linguistics. *What is important to note in this case is that a false assumption in the encyclopedic entry of a speaker and audience need not be explicated or implicated in the informative intention of an utterance.* This example is useful when examining false contextual assumptions in cosmological language of the Bible.

Example: 1 Cor 5:9–11

Paul's follow-up instructions to the Corinthians in 1 Cor 5:9–11 illustrate how an audience can fail to draw the correct inferences from a communication—in this case a previous letter with instructions regarding separation from sinners. While we cannot reconstruct the exact wording of Paul's previous letter (perhaps 1 Cor 5:9 paraphrases it), it is possible to determine the assumptions upon which the Corinthians based their actions, since Paul explicitly refers to these assumptions.

> I wrote to you in my letter not to associate with sexually immoral people—not at all referring to the immoral of this world, or the covetous and thieves, or idolaters, since you would then need to go out of the world. But now I am writing to you not to associate with anyone who identifies as a Christian who is sexually immoral or covetous, or is an idolater, a reviler, a drunkard, or a thief. Do not even eat with such a one (1 Cor 5:9–11).

Paul's corrective names two possible assumptions:

Contextual Assumption 1: dissociation pertains to people of these types *outside the church*

Contextual Assumption 2: dissociation pertains *only* to these types *inside the church*

Paul's previous letter evidently was not *strongly explicit* regarding those whom the Corinthians should discipline. The Corinthians had incorrectly inferred from Assumption 1 that Paul intended them to dissociate from non-Christians but to maintain fellowship with Christians who behave this way. Their misapplication of Paul's instruction occurred due to incorrect disambiguation, a mistake in the assumption necessary to correctly understand the explicature of his previous letter. The creation texts taken up below involve a similar problem of determining what contextual assumptions are necessary to interpret the author's meaning.

Summary

These examples illustrate the difference between explicated and implicated meaning (as distinct from assumptions that are only implicit), how contextual assumptions disambiguate and enrich the meaning of an utterance, the notion of responsibility for interpretation that a speaker or audience might bear, and how relevance acts as a filter in the selection of contextual assumptions. To summarize briefly, in any utterance, a speaker uses language that stimulates a set of potential assumptions in the cognitive environment. It is the task of the listener to decide which subset of these assumptions the speaker intended and then to draw appropriate inferences (i.e., to determine from the possible set of assumptions what is actually being explicated and implicated by the speaker).[9] Relevance serves as the guide to both parties of this communicative action.

Inspiration, Meaning, and Dual Authorship

The entire discussion on divine accommodation, whether historically considered or in contemporary debate, presupposes that the Bible is divinely inspired. The message written in *human* words has been believed by the church to be *divine* words as well (e.g., "I will be with your mouth," Exod 4:15; "says your God," Isa 40:1; "God spoke . . . by the prophets," Heb 1:1; "being carried by the Holy Spirit, men spoke from God," 2 Pet 1:21; "All Scripture is God-breathed," 2 Tim 3:16). Unless there is divine disclosure through the words of Scripture, there would be no question of divine accommodation to consider. This union of human and divine comes not through mechanical dictation, but by a more intimate process of superintendence by God's Spirit, such that the human voice retains the distinct individuality of each author even though signifying God's words as well.[10] As John Frame explains it, "God creates an *identity* between his own words and some human words, so that what the human words say, God says."[11] This locates inspiration in the *words of the text* of Scripture, what is traditionally called verbal inspiration.

Consideration of the *meaning* of a text requires additional discussion. As discussed above, "meaning" is informed by the contextual elements that are drawn upon by an utterance to create a cognitive effect on an audience. Communication involves an author making *manifest* a subset of contextual assumptions from the "encyclopedic entries" shared with an audience. This is more complicated with dual authorship, which posits

---

9. Sperber and Wilson, *Relevance* (1995 ed.), 179.

10. Warfield, "The Biblical Idea of Inspiration," 152–53.

11. Frame, *The Doctrine of the Word of God*, 82. This is the traditional understanding of inspiration; there are other constructs (e.g., Barthian) outside the scope of this work.

two different ranges of assumptions with respect to the divine author and the human authors. The divine author's knowledge is infinite and perfect whereas the human author's knowledge is limited and contextually conditioned. Some assumptions shared between the human author and audience and believed to be true are held by the divine author to be false. This is pertinent to the informative intention of cosmological texts and divine accommodation.

The traditional approach to accommodation in cosmology states that the divine author allowed observational language to be used by the human author on certain matters. The difficulty with this approach is that it too easily disregards some problematic assumptions that existed in the mind of the human author and were readily accessible in the communicative event (see chapter 2). Calvin and Warfield cautiously recognized that the human author's language might incidentally play on common assumptions of their day that were false.[12] As discussed in chapter 3, recognition of negative and positive accommodation does not offer an adequate refinement to this.

Relevance theory turns attention to *precisely those assumptions that were necessary to infer an author's intended meaning*. In terms of strong and weak explicatures and implicatures, we need to consider the degree to which certain words in an utterance encourage an audience to build premises for interpretive conclusions. Assumptions that are unnecessary (or only weakly related) as interpretive premises are not relevant to textual meaning. Alongside strongly implicated assumptions are weakly related assumptions, readily accessible but not contributing to proper interpretive conclusions. *Proper interpretation* recognizes only those assumptions that are necessary to infer intended meaning, regardless of what other contextual assumptions might be accessible in the mind of the author and audience.[13]

If the traditional view of accommodation generally underplays the existence of false assumptions implicit in the cognitive environment of the text, there is an alternative view that too quickly draws those false assumptions into the informative intention. Kenton Sparks writes:

---

12. See discussion in chapter 3 (above pages 103-4, 116-17), especially Calvin on Ps 58:4 and Warfield on the biblical author's language that "incidentally" shared in "the ordinary opinions of his day."

13. Collins describes this concept in the terms of speech-act theory: "The text as a social act, and not the whole array of things an author thought, is our access point to authorial intention" (C. J. Collins, *Reading Genesis Well*, 244).

Accommodation tells us that any errant views in Scripture stem, not from the character of our perfect God, but from his adoption in revelation of the finite and fallen perspectives of his human audience ... accommodation does not introduce errors into Scripture; it is instead a theological explanation for the presence of human errors in Scripture."[14]

Sparks offers a cosmological example of accommodation: "For instance, though the human author of Genesis may have intended to convey that there was a great body of water above the 'firmament' (see Gen. 1:6–8 RSV), the divine author will have intended this only in part."[15]

The phrase "in part" is too nondescript. Perhaps a more helpful approach is to examine which cognitive assumptions are explicated or implicated in meaning, their relative strength, and how they contribute to meaning. Some assumptions remain only implicit in the background and are not implicated at all; or they are only weakly related to the informative intention.

Poythress notes that a statement of truth cannot be built on "the false assumptions of the audience."[16] Arguing with categories similar to relevance theory, he writes further, "a person's freedom [to draw on erroneous assumptions] will depend on how serious the effects are of the erroneous beliefs, how close the beliefs are to truth or half-truth, and how much the straightening out or improving of the beliefs will be an aid to his cause rather than an *irrelevancy*.[17] The focus, then, is on those contex-

---

14. Sparks, *God's Word in Human Words*, 256.

15. Sparks, *God's Word in Human Words*, 202–3.

16. Poythress, "Adequacy of Language and Accommodation," 368. When reading Poythress's essay, it is important to understand that he defines "implication" in terms of logical entailment, and from this, he correctly concludes that all the implications of Scripture must be true (368). In my use of contemporary relevance theory, "explicature" and "implicature" are more restrictive components of what Poythress terms "implication." Furthermore, both explicature and implicature have varying degrees of strong or weak relationship to the actual words of an utterance. Degrees of strength is not part of Poythress's discussion.

17. Poythress, "Adequacy of Language and Accommodation," 369 (italics added). Collins expresses similar distinctions when he writes, "If the validity of the speaker's point depends on the truth value of the thing alluded to, then we may say that a good-faith communication implies that the speaker is also affirming the alluded part" (C. J. Collins, *Reading Genesis Well*, 91). Conversely, sometimes an author grants an assumption that is unnecessary to the truth of the informative intention as a matter of "*arguendo*" (C. J. Collins, *Reading Genesis Well*, 100). The concession, then, has a rhetorical function without interfering with the truth of the proposition to which the speaker commits (cf. C. J. Collins, *Reading Genesis Well*, 243–44).

tual assumptions that provide necessary premises for interpretation and how optimal relevance guides the most appropriate selection.

Accommodation and Relevance

Tomatoes as Vegetables? A Nonbiblical Example

A mundane illustration of accommodation and relevance is that of the grocer who locates tomatoes in the vegetable section of the supermarket even though the tomato is technically a fruit.[18] Granted, this is an action, not a verbal utterance; nevertheless, this action has communicative effect and depends on contextual assumptions to guide the would-be shopper, so it offers a valid illustration. Although many people know tomatoes are not vegetables, many others have never unlearned the misconception that tomatoes are vegetables. Placing tomatoes with vegetables plays along with this common, albeit erroneous, assumption. Furthermore, it reinforces this falsehood in the mind of the uninformed. Yet, no one would accuse the grocer of deception or error.[19] The placement of tomatoes with vegetables accommodates shoppers who naturally group tomatoes with other vegetables, even if it is actually a fruit. Even for the informed, the produce manager is merely organizing the food stock by adapting to culinary interests rather than by adhering to strict botanical categories. The grocer's organization draws on the most accessible assumptions linked to a grocery shopper's expectations of relevance. Anyone who constructs their botanical classifications according to the scheme in the produce department must accept full responsibility for inferring conclusions that are not part of the informative intention of the grocer. This illustration could be extended to Scripture's dual authorship in the following manner: The produce manager (Scripture's divine author) guides the stockperson (Scripture's human author) to place tomatoes for the shoppers (Scripture's audience) in the vegetable section. Both the stockperson and shoppers may share the false assumption that tomatoes are vegetables, but the produce manager's informative intention is not to convey botanical information. But placing tomatoes with vegetables in

---

18. Glucksberg uses this illustration in his rejection of "folk-theory" that gives priority to literal interpretation (Glucksberg, *Understanding Figurative Language*, 15); but it serves equally well to illustrate accommodation in relevance theory terms.

19. This is not merely an illustration of negative accommodation, since the grocer has no intention of ever correcting the misconception of the shoppers.

a botanical museum (a museum is a different sort of place—a different genre of place—from a grocery store) would create a problem for visitors about the curator's intentions: that is, in a botanical museum, visitors expect scientific truthfulness to be relevant.[20]

Animal Sacrifice Feeds God? (Lev 1:9)

Animal sacrifice was one of the chief topics to which both Jews and Christians applied the notion of accommodation.[21] Their concern was to explain how God employed different practices throughout history to teach his people truth according to their capacity.[22] My interest here is to use animal sacrifice to illustrate how interpretive conclusions might be warranted or unwarranted depending on which premises the interpreter draws from among several accessible contextual assumptions.

From Mesopotamia to Egypt, food was offered to the gods in order to supply their needs.[23] This function was associated with animal sacrifice in Mesopotamia and the Levant. For example, when the flood hero of Mesopotamian lore sacrificed an animal at the end of the deluge, the gods hovered around the sacrifice like flies because they had been effectively starved from lack of sacrifices during the deluge.[24] Associating sacrifice with providing for divine needs was a contextual assumption necessary for the audience to draw upon in order to understand the behavior of the gods in the story and the threat that the deluge had been for the well-being of the gods. The Mesopotamian flood account portrays the deluge as a catastrophic mistake.

---

20. I thank Todd Patterson, a collegial fellow at the Henry Center during fall 2016, for suggesting the botanical museum counterpart as an illustration of the effect of genre on cognitive assumptions and expectations of truthfulness.

21. See chapter 3.

22. Benin, *The Footprints of God*, 43

23. Hundley, *Gods in Dwellings*, 282, 331, 360–61.

24. Epic of Gilgamesh xi 161–163 (in George, trans., *The Epic of Gilgamesh*, 94) and Atrahasis III iv, lines 34–36 (in Foster, *Before the Muses*, 251). In similar manner, the goddess Ishtar complains to the Assyrian king Esarhaddon that her physical beauty is diminishing due to lack of adequate offerings (Parpola, ed., *Assyrian Prophecies*, 3.5 lines iii 25–37, as well as Parpola, ed., *Assyrian Prophecies*, 2.3 lines ii 24–27; Parpola, ed., *Assyrian Prophecies*, 16, 26). Egyptian deities could fall back on other manifestations for survival if their cult statues became malnourished (Hundley, *Gods in Dwellings*, 204–5).

This common assumption—associating animal sacrifice with provisions for the gods—was deeply embedded in ancient Israel's cognitive environment and led to misunderstanding in many Israelites' interpretation of Levitical sacrifice:

> And the priest shall burn the whole of it on the altar, as a whole burnt offering, an offering by fire, a pleasing aroma to the Lord. (Lev 1:9)

Let's consider some possible premises and conclusions that an Israelite might infer from their contextual assumptions accessible in their cognitive environment about animal sacrifice:

> Contextual Assumption 1: humans need acceptance by deities.
> Contextual Assumption 2: deities need food.
>
> Conclusion 1: humans' animal sacrifices contribute to humans' acceptability before the Lord.
> Conclusion 2: sacrifice provides for the Lord's needs.

Contextual Assumption 1 is made manifest by the language of "atonement" in Lev 1 as well as the word "pleasing" in Lev 1:9, which explicates it. Contextual Assumption 2 is also accessible to an Israelite living in the ancient cognitive environment. Furthermore, some aspects of the ritual of sacrifice might even encourage the supply of Contextual Assumption 2 as a premise for interpreting the meaning of the instruction (e.g., the symbolism of an altar as God's table, the fact that one type of sacrifice, the peace offering, is shared as a meal, including by worshipers with the Lord [Lev 3:5; 7:15]). The translation of the Hebrew word *'iššeh* as "food offering" (e.g., ESV) illustrates how close the association was between sacrifice and food for God. Thus, Contextual Assumption 2 was implicit in the minds of some Israelites. But it did not need to be implicated in the informative intention of Lev 1:9. (Indeed, this accessible assumption is denied explicitly in Ps 50:12–13. The fact that it received denial is evidence that some Israelites actually supplied Contextual Assumption 2 as a premise and inferred Conclusion 2.) All of the assumptions associated with eating (e.g., it supplies needed nutrition) are not necessarily implicated in the meaning. The language of Lev 1 was optimized to teach the basic procedures of a ritual and its effect (i.e., atonement), not the reasons that underlie its efficacy.

Deaf Vipers? (Ps 58:4–5)

The difficulties in Ps 58:4–5 were mentioned in chapter 3. Calvin wrestled with this verse because it suggests that David believed in the efficacy of magical incantations. Calvin explained this passage as David's accommodation to an erroneous assumption of his time in order to portray the stubborn wickedness of his enemies. There is another difficulty in this verse of which Calvin seems unaware—that snakes do not have ears to hear. Ps 58:4b and 5a form lines that are logically parallel: the stubborn refusal of a viper to use its hearing faculty results in an ineffective incantation. This provides the source for a metaphor targeting David's enemies. Let's examine more closely the assumptions at play in the context of this verse.

[A/author decries that David's enemies are]
like a deaf viper that stops its ear, (4b)
it does not hear the voice of charmers (5a)

Contextual Assumption 1a: vipers have ears that they can plug
Contextual Assumption 1b: [therefore] vipers can refuse to respond to incantations
    (a viper resisting incantations is analogous to David's enemies)
Conclusion: David's enemies ignore the pleas of their victim

Before dismissing Contextual Assumption 1 as absurd, we should note that this premise was actually suggested by Augustine.[25] By pressing one ear in the dirt and plugging the other ear with its tail, a viper can render itself impervious to incantations. But the difficulty is not how, in the real world, a viper can plug its own ears; rather, the image presupposes that vipers actually have ears when in fact they do not. As Calvin recognized, this metaphor is constructed on the premise of an erroneous belief that David conceded for the sake of literary effect. For Calvin it was the effectiveness of magic; for our interest it is the physiology of snakes.

It is helpful at this point to recall Poythress's argument mentioned above that a statement of truth cannot be built on "the false assumptions of the audience."[26] The truth statement of this verse is the characterization of David's enemies, not any state of affairs in the real world of

---

25. Wesselschmidt, *Psalms 51–150*, 35.
26. Poythress, "Adequacy of Language and Accommodation," 368.

zoology. This characterization of the wicked remains true whether the word picture used to describe it is fact or fiction. Drawing conclusions about snake physiology is not part of this passage's intended implications; rather, the imagery here accommodates a false assumption in order to guide readers to a conclusion that is not dependent on the truthfulness of the assumption.[27]

Accommodation in Cosmological Language

A difficult aspect of accommodation is the expression by biblical authors of geographical or physiological perceptions that are by some measure not true in the real world. The cosmology (world picture) of ancient Near Eastern peoples was discussed at length in chapter 2, where I attempted to demonstrate that the language of the Old Testament is not merely an assertion of ordinary observation; embedded in such language are aspects of a model of the world that held truth for ancient peoples. They seem not to have been interested in describing how this model worked in terms of natural causality; rather, their model was primarily theological. Nevertheless, physical-spatial relationships between features of the cosmos "show through" the language that was used, both in ancient Near Eastern texts and the Old Testament. I begin with an example that is cosmological in nature. The second example, an astronomical one, is perhaps the most commonly used one—that of the sun "rising." Those that follow these two examples are samples from Gen 1.

The Underground Realm of the Dead (1 Samuel 28:11–15)

The episode in 1 Sam 28, concerning King Saul, the necromancer, and the spirit of Samuel, offers an important case study in accommodation. It incorporates an erroneous assumption regarding the spacial location of the realm of the dead. As noted in chapter 2, the narrative constitutes accommodation on two levels. There is accommodation to the audience in the text's narrative report, but there is also an accommodation in Saul's and the necromancer's encounter with Samuel when they experienced his return from the dead, ascending from out of the ground:

---

27. In a relevance-theoretic account of metaphor, the "literal meaning" plays no role in any event.

[A/author reports that the necromancer said]
"I see a divine being coming up from the earth" (1 Sam 28:13)

Contextual Assumption: the realm of the deceased is located under the earth's surface

Conclusion: the being who is ascending from under ground is a deceased person

Saul sought an encounter with the dead prophet Samuel through the skills of a necromancer. God facilitated an experience for the necromancer and Saul that accommodated their erroneous assumption, creating a significant cognitive effect—terror on the part of the necromancer (evidently the encounter was more tangible than her customary experience), and resignation on the part of Saul regarding his doom (the deceased prophet had returned to deliver God's word). Both interpreted the encounter as authentic, in part because it met their expectations about what a return from the dead entails. The veracity of the prophetic speech-act did not depend on whether Sheol is underground—only upon the fact that the genuine prophet, Samuel, had returned to speak. But accommodation to Saul's assumptions optimized the communicative act without compromising the truthfulness of the informative intention: the prophet Samuel indeed returned from the dead to deliver a message of doom to Saul.

The Sun Rising (Gen 19:23)

Perhaps the most familiar example discussed regarding cosmological accommodation is that of the sun "rising" (e.g., Gen 19:23; 32:31 [Eng.]; Jonah 4:8).[28] The ancient author and audience both shared the same incorrect, contextual assumption that the sun was an object moving daily across the heavens to the west and then back to its appointed place of entry in the east. As noted in chapter 2, while such language can be explained by modern interpreters as merely phenomenological, for the ancients it was not, since it involved a schema of associations with solar movement. Of the many possible assumptions associated with the sun rising reported in Gen 19:23, let's presume several to sort through.

---

28. One could add New Testament references as well (Matt 5:45; 13:6; Mark 16:2; Jas 1:11).

A/author reports that "the sun rose" (Gen 19:23).

Contextual Assumption 1: The sun rising is the beginning of morning.

Contextual Assumption 2: Exposure to the sun has harmful effects.

Contextual Assumption 3a: The sun revolves around the earth.

Contextual Assumption 3b: The earth rotates on its axis.[29]

Conclusion 1: It was early morning.

Conclusion 2: The person in the narrative will get burned.

Conclusion 3a: The sun traveled (in its revolution around the earth).

Conclusion 3b: The sun's position changed (as the earth rotated).

All of these contextual assumptions are embedded in different encyclopedic entries about the word "sun." The question is, what is explicated in the text? Conclusion 1 is a correct inference intended by both the divine and human authors for Gen 19:23. Contextual Assumption 1, upon which it is based, is strongly explicated; first, because the association between the sun rising and early morning is a very accessible cognition that is likely to be triggered by the phrase "the sun rose"; and second, in terms of relevance, this expression satisfies the audience's expectation for temporal orientation in the narrative prompted by the previous verse. Conclusion 2 is also a possible inference, but Contextual Assumption 2, upon which it is based, is not as accessible: a very special context must make it manifest (e.g., Jonah is soon to be exposed [Jonah 4:8], or perhaps a princess gets a tan from spending time out in the field [see Song 1:6]). Contextual Assumption 2 is true but not explicated in the text of Gen 19:23. How strong or weak are Assumptions 3a and 3b with respect to informative intention? Does Gen 19:23 explicate these?

Assumption 3a is a fairly accessible cognition to an ancient person, and it may be close to conscious awareness for the author or the audience. But it is only weakly related to the informative intention ("it is morning" [Gen 19:23]), and even activating this cognition with the word "rose" does not disrupt the author's intended meaning. One might say that the potential activation of erroneous Assumption 3a was allowed by the divine author and conceded for the sake of optimal relevance in communication. Correcting the ancients' Assumption 3a, would have necessitated considerably more words and demanded excessive

---

29. Or perhaps the length of arc between the sun's position and the earth's horizon increases through the day as the earth revolves on its axis.

processing effort unnecessary to convey the informative intention of the utterance, which is Conclusion 1. Similarly, Assumption 3b was not even accessible to the original audience and not intended to be activated by the divine author. It would be a correct inference by modern interpreters but was not explicated as part of intended meaning.

The "Great Lights" (Gen 1:16)

Similar to the question of the operational relationship between the sun and earth is the comparison of the source and intensity of the "great lights" (the sun and moon) in relation to the stars (Gen 1:16). In what sense are sun and moon "great"? In the cognition of the ancients, these two objects are larger and more intense than stars, but we know this is not true absolutely. This recognition led to the application of the idea of accommodation on this example as early as Augustine (see chapter 3). Probably, the ancients conceived of the moon as a source of light rather than merely a reflection of solar light, and they could hardly have imagined that in absolute terms the size differences are quite contrary to observation. Let's consider some possible assumptions and their conclusions:

> A/author reports that "God made the two 'great lights' . . . and the stars" (Gen 1:16)
>
> Contextual Assumption 1: The sun and moon are more conspicuous than the stars.
> Contextual Assumption 2: The sun gives heat and the moon has spots but not stars.
> Contextual Assumption 3a: The sun and moon are absolutely larger and brighter than stars.
> Contextual Assumption 3b: The sun and moon are larger and brighter by relative distance.
>
> Conclusion 1: The sun and the moon are appropriate objects to mark the calendar.
> Conclusion 2: The sun and moon have unique properties compared to stars.
> Conclusion 3a: The sun and moon dominate stars by virtue of their absolute scale.
> Conclusion 3b: The sun and moon dominate stars by virtue of their relative scale.

All the listed contextual assumptions are potential cognitions associated with the actual linguistic code "great lights." However, Contextual Assumption 1 is strongly explicated since the word "great" makes the relative brightness of the sun and moon to the stars highly accessible in a way that is important to the informative intention of the passage. But Contextual Assumptions 2 and 3a/b are only weakly related. Let's explain this further. In terms of relevance, the utterance of Gen 1:14–18 directs the audience to consider how God's creative work regulates days and seasons. That calendrical matters are of foremost concern is validated by texts such as Gen 8:22 and Ps 74:16–17, besides the "code" in Gen 1:14 explicating seasons and years. So the most accessible cognitive assumption that satisfies relevance is the fact that the sun and moon are more conspicuous than stars, both in terms of visibility and cyclical nature, making them the primary calendar markers. The audience can quit processing at this point, satisfied that the assumption of relative conspicuity makes sense of the utterance. Further speculation about *why* these objects are more unique or conspicuous probes beyond the language of Gen 1:14–18, which was optimally chosen to affect cognitions about cycles of days and seasons. God can allow erroneous Contextual Assumptions 2 and 3a to remain unaddressed without disrupting this cognitive effect.[30] Contextual Assumption 1 is explicated, and Conclusion 1 is the intended meaning, but the audience must bear sole responsibility for assuming and concluding 2 or 3a/3b.

The Waters Above (Gen 1:6–8)

A more difficult example of accommodation is the utterance in Gen 1:6–8 that God separated water above the heavens. It is possible that this refers merely to the source of water from the sky; the ancient Israelite's way of speaking of clouds and rain. This possibility was discussed in chapter 2. However, several lines of thought suggest that people in the ancient Near East conceived of a cosmic sea in the upper reaches of the sky.[31] Assuming the more difficult position, that the human author conceived

---

30. Assumption 2 is false because stars have spots (as the sun does) and project heat in their domains; many are more intense than the sun in absolute scale.

31. The difficulty here is the nature of the heavenly water source (whether heavenly ocean or merely clouds), not the more contested nature of the firmament (whether a solid barrier or merely a loose term for the "sky"). For discussion, see chapter 2 (above, pages 69–72, 77–82).

of the waters above as a reservoir, how might one analyze the nature of accommodation in Gen 1:6–8?

> And God made the expanse . . . and divided the waters which were under the expanse and *the waters which were above the expanse* (Gen 1:7)
>
> A/author reports that God positioned "the waters which are above the expanse"
>
> Contextual Assumption 1a: Rain comes from water in the sky.
> Contextual Assumption 1b: Rain is a crucial provision for life.
> Contextual Assumption 2: The water in the sky is a cosmic sea.
> Contextual Assumption 3: Cosmogony involves theogony (the origin of the gods).
>
> Conclusion 1a/b: God structured the cosmos in such a way as to provide rain to sustain life.
> Conclusion 2: God placed a cosmic sea in the sky.
> Conclusion 3: God created a nondeified cosmos (Assumption 3 corrected).

Contextual Assumptions 1a and 2 are linked to language in the text that makes them highly *accessible* for the task of inferring the author's informative intention. Contextual Assumption 1b is only implicit in the set of assumptions about rain; it is not embedded in the meaning of the word "waters" itself, so it is an implicated assumption. Contextual Assumption 3 is implicit, contained in the encyclopedic entries of ancient Near Eastern people regarding stories of origins, the contextual topic of Gen 1. It may be strongly implicit if one considers that many ancients identified the primeval waters with divine entities. Even if this was not part of *Israel's* orthodox faith, such a concept is strongly manifest in the cognitive environment.

Contextual Assumption 1a is observably true to anyone ancient or modern. Assumption 1b is also true and strongly implicated in the text, since provision of water for drinking and agriculture is highly relevant across the ancient Near East, creation stories frequently address this particular expectation of relevance, and God's provision for the flourishing of life is a major theme in Gen 1 as a whole.[32] Implicit Assumption 3 is

---

32. See Walton, *Genesis 1 as Ancient Cosmology*, 40–41, 57–58, 164, 170, 194; and

also readily accessible as a common feature to all ancient Near Eastern creation traditions; but it is implicated only to be *challenged* by Gen 1.

But what do we make of Contextual Assumption 2, which is explicated (encouraged by the wording of Gen 1:7) but erroneous regarding *some* of the properties of these waters? The important question is *how* its explication guides readers toward relevant conclusions. In short, Assumption 2 is explicated in order to make manifest Assumption 1a and at the same time *efficiently* implicate Assumption 3 for refutation. The exact nature of these waters (i.e., their physical properties) are weakly communicated, since the informative intention lies with Assumptions 1a and 3. For the sake of optimal relevance, the divine author accommodated the assumption that these waters had the properties of a cosmic sea. But even the human author does not rely on assumptions about the physical properties of the waters above in order to communicate his informative intention. Two considerations highlight how explicating the "waters above" efficiently guides the relevance expectations of the audience toward the author's informative intention.

First, the use of the phrase "waters above the expanse" explicates Assumption 1a and thereby implicates Assumption 1b. The message about God's goodness in the supply of life-giving water does not *rely* on the false Assumption 2 for its warrant. That there is water in the sky remains true even if the manner in which its properties are conceived is mistaken by those sharing Assumption 2.[33] The utterance "waters above the expanse" is sufficient to facilitate a valid Conclusion 1 (it merely utilizes the common name for the source of water). At the same time the divine author accommodates Assumption 2 without demanding from the audience the extensive processing effort that would be necessary to correct it. This method of accommodation is similar to those found in Ps 58:4–5 and 1 Sam 28:11–15. In those two cases, erroneous assumptions in the audience's encyclopedic entries about snakes and the underworld are allowed to remain in order to *efficiently* communicate the relevant point. The erroneous assumption is weakly communicated relative to more manifest contextual interests.

Second, in the case of Gen 1:7, the description of God dividing waters also *efficiently* guides ancient readers to draw comparisons with

---

Averbeck, "The Three 'Daughters' of Ba'al," 237–56.

33. See above the comments by Poythress (page 138 and note 16) that truth affirmations cannot rely on a false assumption. Poythress would not share my interpretation of heavenly waters (see chapter 2), but his assertion is helpful here.

other ancient Near Eastern creation traditions, the *theological* aspects of which are refuted by the alternative version offered in Gen 1.³⁴ This makes manifest *implications* related to Assumption 2—specifically, assumptions about the origin of the gods and their relation to the natural world (Contextual Assumption 3). Implicating Contextual Assumption 3 is important for the intended meaning. It is a literary way of saying, "For the sake of argument, consider the placement of the cosmic sea"—creation traditions in Israel's ancient world that are theogonic and pan(en)theistic whereby the waters above are divine.³⁵ Enuma Elish, to which Gen 1:7 possibly alludes, additionally associates cosmic battle with the separation of waters. By alluding to the alternative creation accounts, Gen 1 also replaces those accounts with a demythologized alternative. The author *implicates* that those accounts are false (gods did not emerge from the waters, and there was no cosmic battle). All of this complies with the way effective communication operates:

> The aim is to find an interpretation of the speaker's meaning that satisfies the presumption of optimal relevance. To achieve this aim, the hearer must enrich the decoded sentence meaning at the explicit level, and complement it at the implicit level by supplying contextual assumptions which will combine with it to yield enough conclusions (or other cognitive effects) to make the utterance relevant *in the expected way*. What route should he follow in disambiguating, assigning reference, constructing a context, deriving conclusions, etc.? According to the relevance-theoretic comprehension heuristic, he should follow a path of least effort. This is the key to relevance-theoretic pragmatics.³⁶

The *expectations* of ancient Israelites were conditioned by the types of answers their ancient Near Eastern cognitive environment gave to questions of origins and the place of humanity in the cosmos. Foremost in ancient Near Eastern accounts is concern for the relationships of the various deities to one another and to humanity. Gen 1:6–8 addresses these expectations of relevance by attributing to Israel's God the provision of a

---

34. In terms of the *efficiency* of language from ancient Near Eastern stories, Averbeck argues that biblical use of mythic imagery "provided a set of motifs that could be used to speak powerfully about Yahweh" (Averbeck, "Ancient Near Eastern Mythography," 345).

35. I think this is close to what Collins means by the rhetorical use of language as *arguendo* (C. J. Collins, *Reading Genesis Well*, 100).

36. Sperber and Wilson, "Pragmatics," 474–75 (italics added).

cosmos in which human life could flourish. At the same time, the account is told in such a way as to simultaneously address another highly relevant question: how is the cosmos related to the divine? In this regard, Israel's God is unique. This uniqueness is conveyed in part by way of contrast to the beliefs of Israel's neighbors regarding the nature of cosmos and its origins relative to the divine realm.

Conclusions

Explicated and Implicated Meanings

Not every possible assumption in a cognitive environment is part of the context needed to infer meaning. Only assumptions that are relevant to the informative intention are explicated or implicated for inferential processing. At the same time, some assumptions are stronger, and some are weaker, depending on the degree to which an author's discourse makes them manifest to the audience. Some assumptions are not part of the context from which an audience should infer meaning, or are only weakly related. If an audience draws upon such an assumption as a premise to infer a conclusion about the author's meaning, they take full responsibility for doing so, and any errors concluded in this process are the reader's responsibility. What is important in this is that false assumptions can exist in the knowledge of an author or readers—assumptions that are not explicated or implicated in the informative intention.

Dual Authorship of Scripture and False Assumptions

If one presupposes that God verbally inspires the words of Scripture, then there exists a dual authorship of the text. Yet the divine author and human author inhabit different cognitive environments: the former has perfect knowledge while the latter does not; and there are many false assumptions in the cognitive environment of the human author and audience that are implicit in the background of biblical discourse. The critical consideration for those concerned with the veracity of Scripture is whether false assumptions are explicated or implicated by the discourse *in such a way as to be part of the informative intent*. The focus of interpretation is only on those assumptions that are necessary for the author's informative intention. Accommodation allows unity between the human and divine authors relating some explicated and implicated assumptions but excludes erroneous assumptions held by the human author that do not contribute to this meaning.

Accommodation in Cosmology

In terms of Old Testament creation texts, the language of Scripture addresses the nature of God, the relationship between God and creation, and the place of humanity in it. In doing so, God accommodates the language of Scripture to the ancient context, which is characterized by many competing creation traditions attempting to answer these same questions. In some instances, there exist erroneous cosmological assumptions on the part of the ancient author and audience that they *might* supply to enrich scriptural utterances; however, such assumptions do not contribute to the informative intention. The audience remains responsible for entertaining any erroneous thoughts. Another way of stating this is, in God's accommodative language, he allowed the potential that certain erroneous assumptions are supplied by the audience; but even if the audience mistakenly infers conclusions from these, they do not interfere with the informative intention of the utterance.[37] Accommodation allows for the adaptation of language for the purpose of explicating and implicating the informative intention without affirming the full encyclopedic range of ideas about cosmology associated with the utterance used. This concession is based on good communication practice; that is, optimal relevance in the use of language.

---

37. Green notes that communication in general is not "risk free" (Green, "Relevance Theory and Biblical Interpretation" [2009], 224).

5

Validation of Relevance and Theological Implications

Introduction

Secondary communication situations are inherently more difficult for interpretation because the audience does not share the same set of encyclopedic assumptions as the original audience, nor does it have the same reflexes regarding priority of accessibility for those assumptions.[1] Therefore, attending to how interpreters within the original communication context understood a text is helpful for testing the assumptions of modern interpreters. The first part of this chapter examines the expectations of relevance in the ancient Israelite cognitive environment. In keeping with previous chapters, I will restrict my discussion to intertextual links between Gen 1 and other Old Testament texts. As a clue to contextual relevance, we might ask to what use did later Old Testament interpreters put Gen 1?

In addition, the categories of relevance theory are helpful in evaluating specific, theological issues in Gen 1. In the last chapter, we explored how the existence of contextual assumptions does not necessarily mean that a given assumption is explicated or implicated in a discourse. In other words, an author might hold an assumption to be true but not necessarily explicate it or implicate it in the meaning of the text. In cases of divine accommodation, this explains how propositional content (what the author asks readers to believe) does not include every assumption in

---

1. See discussion in chapter 1 (pages 10–13, 18–19).

the background of the text that could potentially be activated. The second part of this chapter applies the same distinction (between what is implicit and what is explicated or implicated) to several important theological questions.

Validating the Expectation of Relevance in Genesis 1

Methodological Considerations

Establishing an intentional allusion between two texts necessitates three things: (1) demonstrating a set of verbal links between the two texts that render it likely that an audience would recognize a unique relationship between these texts; (2) determining directionality, or chronological order, between the texts; and (3) demonstrating a plausible rhetorical use of the source text by the later text.[2] At times, similarity between two texts may not be due to intertextual allusion; rather, both texts may have drawn from a third, common textual tradition.[3]

The intertextuality between Gen 1 and other Old Testament texts is a narrower question than the use of creation motifs shared between them. The latter question involves utilization of creation theology in general, but the former necessitates establishing a dependent textual relationship between the two. When directionality can be established, the interpretation of Gen 1 in later texts offers the best window into the meaning of Genesis in its original communication situation. But when directionality or even intertextuality cannot be established, the sharing of similar creation motifs still reveals something about the cognitive assumptions that were relevant in the ancient context. This helps modern readers judge the availability and perhaps the hierarchy of accessibility of

---

2. See the discussion of "echoes" of ancient Near Eastern traditions in chapter 1. Hoffman's ("The First Creation Story," 37–38) criterion that there must be "a literal repetition of at least one syntactical unit" for a "citation" is too restrictive, since repetition of an array of unique or statistically rare elements in the source text points to literary dependence and therefore to the likelihood that keywords are directly borrowed. For example, his denial that Jer 4:23-26 depends upon Gen 1 sets aside what even he calls an "impressive" array (Hoffman, "The First Creation Story," 45–47). This leads him to call links between several other prophetic texts and Gen 1 "utterly unfounded" (Hoffman, "The First Creation Story," 49 n. 47; see below for Hosea and Zephaniah).

3. Bauks, "Intertextuality in Ancient Literature," 29.

assumptions. With these challenges in mind, the following examples are important in the discussion.

Pentateuch

Exod 20:11 is the most significant text in the Old Testament regarding the meaning of "day" in Gen 1 and its chronological implications; yet the interpretive relationship between the two texts is more complicated than is often realized. It is crucial to recall that Gen 1 was not written before the initiation of a new calendar pattern immediately following the exodus (Exod 16:4-5, 22-26).[4] Israel's seven-day workweek was established before the Sabbath command at Sinai, and it reoriented the nation away from the organization of work and life in the rest of the ancient Near East, particularly of Egypt, which observed a ten-day work cycle and would have been ancient Israel's starting framework.[5] In addition, the traditions of Israel's ancestors show no evidence of Sabbath observance (in spite of many other narrative episodes in Genesis that anticipate Mosaic law). So it is unlikely that a seven-day creation tradition was passed down from antiquity.[6] The sevenfold sabbatical pattern was used not only for the workweek but also for the larger liturgical calendar.[7] It was the central sign of the covenant and the primary distinctive that set Israel apart from

---

4. It is conceivable that the motive clause in Exod 20:11 is secondary to the original wording of the fourth commandment (cf. the different motive clause in Deut 5:15), and therefore it constitutes a later addition, perhaps subsequent to the composition of Gen 1. This still does not preclude the interpretation preferred in my discussion, namely, the analogical use of the human workweek for structuring the account of God's creation.

5. R. A. Parker, "Ancient Egyptian Astronomy," 53; Spalinger, "Calendars," 1:226. The Egyptian workweek was a ten-day cycle rather than a seven-day, thus breaking the pattern set by Israel's former suzerain. According to Hallo, Mesopotamia shows no evidence of a seven-day work cycle either (Hallo, *Origins*, 127-28). However, a seven-day-week concept existed in Late Babylonian times, witnessed in astronomical cuneiform texts (Scurlock and Al-Rawi, "A Weakness for Hellenism," 357-82). It is also attested in Old Assyrian texts of the early second millennium (Veenhof, "The Old Assyrian *Hamuštum* Period," 5-26).

6. This seemingly obvious conclusion was first pointed out to me by Gordon Johnston.

7. "Sabbaths" (plural; Exod 31:13); land recovery and manumission in the seventh year (Exod 21:2; Lev 25:1-7); new moons and feasts (2 Chr 2:4; Amos 8:5); Feast of weeks following Passover (Lev 23:15) and Ingathering in the seventh month (Lev 23:24); Jubilee (Lev 25:8); eschatological expectations (Isa 66:22-23).

the other nations (Exod 31:12–17; Ezek 20:20). Gen 1, then, was written in support of an already existing sabbatical structure. As Collins argues, this passage uses the analogy of a human workweek; and Exod 20:11 functions in the same manner—not commenting on the text of Gen 1 but reflecting the same analogical motif.[8] The parallel to Exod 20:11 that is found in Exod 31:17 stresses this analogical nature through a strongly anthropomorphic assertion that God refreshed himself (*Niphal* of *npš*, cf. 2 Sam 16:14). God no more took six days to create than he "refreshed himself" on the seventh. The seven-day schema conforms to the expectation that creation moves toward completion of a dwelling for God, recognized by the wilderness generation in the construction and dedication of the tabernacle and later in Solomon's temple.[9] As I already noted in chapter 1, seven of any object or activity was a schema by which one organized a narrative, set out poetry, or planned ritual. As a literary schema, it did *not necessarily* correspond to real passage of days; rather, it was simply the way one structured thought—how else would you characterize God's work? Indeed, Gen 1 itself employs no fewer than ten other heptad literary features besides the seven-day scheme.[10] Implicit assumptions about completion and perfection in a sevenfold schema, and what constitutes a proper work pattern, are explicated in both Gen 1 and Exod 20:11. Insisting that these texts explicate assumptions about divine action in real-time earth history begs the question by defaulting to a literalism on such matters that finds no counterpart anywhere else in

---

8. C. J. Collins, *Genesis 1–4*, 77, 88–94, 122–25; C J. Collins, *Reading Genesis Well*, 163. The work of Michael LeFebvre, *The Liturgy of Creation*, came to my attention too late for developed discussion here. Similar to Collins, LeFebvre argues "that the creation week narrative contains the history of God's ordering the world, mapped to Israel's observance schedule for stewarding that order with labor and worship, without any concern to preserve the events' original occurrence timing" (117).

9. Walton, *Genesis 1 as Ancient Cosmology*, 100–119, 178–92. Cf. Lev 8:33–35; 1 Kgs 6:38; 8:65; 2 Chr 7:8–9; and the sevenfold structure of the tabernacle instructions marked by the formula, "The LORD said to Moses" culminating with Sabbath instruction (Exod 25:1; 30:11; 30:17; 30:22; 30:34; 31:1; 31:12). Thus, the relevance of the sevenfold pattern utilized in Exod 20:11 receives complement in the ensuing context of tabernacle construction. The temple significance of creation has roots in ancient rabbinic interpretation and modern Jewish commentary (see Weinfeld, "Sabbath," 505–10; Levenson, *Creation and the Persistence of Evil*, 95–99); it is not a post-Enlightenment effort to avoid a more literalistic interpretation of Gen 1. See the discussion in chapter 1 (pages 37–38 n. 143) for the breadth of the sevenfold schema in the ancient Near East.

10. See the summary in chapter 1 (page 38 n. 143) and in Levenson, *Creation and the Persistence of Evil*, 67.

Israelite textual traditions. As I discussed in chapter 1, there is no evidence that the ancients had expectations of relevance for natural history. Inferences about theology, rather than six real-time days for God's work, are more likely for ancient Israelites. The following discussion supports this assessment by examining the intertextual use of Gen 1 in the Old Testament.

The Latter Prophets

Isaiah

There are numerous intertextual links between Isaiah and Gen 1 that offer a window into how a competent, ancient reader understood the text of Genesis.[11] Thomas Mann writes, "Whatever actions in history may be attributed to Yahweh, they are grounded in a theology of Yahweh as 'creator of the ends of the earth'! In this sense, a theology of creation is prior to and foundational for a theology of history."[12] He notes that this is a particularly relevant theme for the exiles, whose captivity might be ascribed to the hand of the Babylonian creator-god, Marduk (cf. Enuma Elish). Sun, moon, and stars, appointed by Marduk and associated with deities, are merely part of the natural order (Isa 40:18; cf. Gen 1:16).[13] The effective agency of God's Spirit (*ruaḥ 'elohim*) over creation in Isa 40:13 (note contextual allusions to Gen 1 in vv. 12, 21–22) supports a similar

---

11. This assumes directionality from Gen 1 to the Isaiah texts (see Fishbane, *Biblical Interpretation*, 325–26). If this is not the case, then one could simply state that Isaiah echoes assumptions from Israel's faith that are shared with assumptions related to Gen 1, which is still useful for exploring the cognitive environment of Gen 1. But Hosea, Zephaniah, and Jeremiah's intertextual relationship with Gen 1 strongly suggests the existence of this tradition in the preexilic period from both northern and southern regions. Elsewhere I have argued on the basis of comparative studies with ancient Near Eastern prophetic and scribal culture that the oracles of Second Isaiah are ostensibly preexilic, even if redacted for an exilic community (Hilber, "Isaiah as Prophet," 151–74). Arguments that passages related to Gen 1 in these prophets must be later redactions, based upon an assumed postexilic date for P, are circular. Hoffman insists that if Gen 1 were a canonical priority (chronologically and theologically) it would find far more quantitative reuse in later Scripture (Hoffman, "The First Creation Story," 32–53). But this is an undemonstrated assumption. One might argue, for example, that the covenantal tradition is so dominant that creation theology plays a minor role relative to it.

12. Mann, "Stars, Sprouts, and Streams," 142.

13. Mann, "Stars, Sprouts, and Streams," 138–40.

interpretation in Gen 1:2, where God's effective presence presides over the precreation chaos.[14] Thus, "mighty wind" is an unlikely interpretation for Gen 1:2.[15] The capacity to create sets Israel's God apart from the gods of the nations and the impotent idols created by humans for their embodiment. In Isa 40:28, the prophet denies any assumption potentially implicit in Gen 2:1–2 that God's work might weary him, reinforcing what was noted in connection with Exod 20:11—that there is only an analogy between Gen 1 and the human workweek.

More will be said below regarding Isaiah's use of Gen 1 and the doctrine of creation ex nihilo, specifically about Isa 45:7 and other texts referring God's eternality over against creation. Here suffice it to say that Isaiah utilizes the imagery of light and darkness (specifically darkness and calamity in Isa 13:10) to affirm that even judgment is within God's firm control. If uncreation is the measure of severe judgment, Gen 1 also serves as the model for final redemption. Isa 65:25 couples this hope with the future Davidic King of Isa 11, whose just rule restores order. In Isa 66, this includes the proper cultic function of God's servants from all nations within God's temple of creation.[16] Chaos is neutralized, and order restored through proper worship.[17] But ultimate victory comes only through the intervention of the Creator, whose glory will fill the earth, which is his temple, and will render the natural luminaries of Gen 1 unnecessary by comparison (Isa 60:19–20).

Jeremiah

Jeremiah announces the undoing of creation in terms that echo the beginning state of affairs in Gen 1 (*tohu wabohu*, "formless and void," Jer. 4:23).[18] The absence of light, birds, fruitful land, and humans as well as

---

14. Mann ("Stars, Sprouts, and Streams," 142–47) suggests that Isaiah also proclaims a new defeat of the Sea (Isa 27:1; 51:9–11). The idea of *Chaoskampf* will be treated below in connection with Jeremiah's use of creation imagery. For note here, there is no *battle* with chaos in Gen 1:2.

15. See Hildebrandt, *An Old Testament Theology*, 39–41 (cf. Ps 33:6).

16. For the created world as God's temple, see Walton, *The Lost World of Genesis 1*.

17. For this general notion, albeit nuanced differently in some details, see Levinson, *Creation and the Persistence of Evil*, 121–27.

18. Some consider this collocation to be missing from the Old Greek witness because only the word *outhen* appears; however, the Greek term ("nothing") is a possible interpretive gloss for the whole Hebrew phrase (see Rutten, "Back to Chaos," 22 n. 2).

the motif of "saw" add to the allusion, as does reference to the instability of land (Jer 4:23–29).[19] The hyperbolic nature of this imagery is indicated by the description that birds only "fled" (Jer 4:25); and this is further clarified in verses 26 and 27 by Jeremiah's announcement that fertility is destroyed and warfare has decimated the population (Jer 4:7; 50:39; 51:37, 42–43). Similar use of creation imagery appears in Jer 9:10–11 [Heb., 9–10] (beasts and birds flee; cf. 33:10, 12).[20] The New Covenant promise utilizes Gen 1 imagery for reversal of this judgment (Jer 31:35; cf. Jer 33:20, 25, and 5:24, which may allude to Gen 8:22). The theme "maker of heaven and earth" (Jer 10:11; 27:5; 32:17; [cf. 32:27; 33:2]) may also allude to Gen 1.[21]

It is relevant at this point to address whether *tohu wabohu* (Jer 4:23) explicates any notion of chaos. As I noted briefly in chapter 1, David Tsumura challenges this interpretation, arguing instead that the phrase simply means "emptiness" (more specifically, "aridness and unproductiveness" in Jer 4:23, and "unproductive and uninhabited" in the context of Gen 1).[22] Before considering the connotations of this expression, it is necessary to examine the proposed relationship between *tohu* and the glosses "desert" or "desert-like," which are central to Tsumura's discussion.[23] The word *tohu* appears once in parallelism with desert (*midbar*; Deut 32:10), and in three references, the word is used metonymically for the desert place (Job 6:18; 12:24=Ps 107:40). But proposing that "desert" is a primary meaning of *tohu* confuses the subject (desert) for the adjunct (*tohu*). In other words, *tohu* can be used figuratively for the desert, not because a primary meaning is "desert" but because deserts are inherently *tohu*. So even in Deut 32:10, *tohu* is an appropriate echo for *midbar*

---

19. See Rutten, "Back to Chaos," 27–29. The verbal links are impressive, Tsumura's arguments notwithstanding (Tsumura, *Creation and Destruction*, 29–30). On the other hand, Fishbane ("Jeremiah iv 23–26 and Job iii 3–13," 151–67) perhaps forces details of the parallel regarding the "days" of creation.

20. One might note, however, that the simple taxonomy of "beasts" and "birds" appears to be rather generic, without specific allusion, in Jer 16:4; 19:17.

21. The phrase "all flesh" also points to awareness of the flood narrative (Gen 6:13, 17). Brueggemann ("Jeremiah," 159–60) and others argue for a sapiential source for these "doxological" sayings (Jer 51:15–19; cf. Prov 3:19–20; 8:22–31), but a Genesis allusion is supported by the plethora of allusions.

22. Tsumura, *The Earth and the Waters*, 41 (with slight revision in Tsumura, *Creation and Destruction*, 31, 35; Tsumura, "The Doctrine of Creation *Ex Nihilo*," 13–15); followed by R. S. Watson, *Chaos Uncreated*, 16, 269–70.

23. Tsumura, *Creation and Destruction*, 22–23, 32.

because it further describes the conditions of the wilderness. It is not just another word for "desert." The disjunct between *tohu* and "desert" is underscored by Gen 1:2, where the earth is *tohu* beneath the watery abyss! Similarly, in Job 26:7, *tohu* stands in parallelism with the word "nothing" (*beli*). Tsumura translates it "empty space," yet he offers as an alternative: "a desert-like place." Nothing about Job 26:7 should suggest a desert. As Bauks notes, the description is not sociocultural (pertaining to human habitat) in such contexts, as Tsumura asserts, but cosmological.[24]

With regard to the phrase *tohu wabohu* in Jer 4:23, Tsumura's interpretation that it means "desert-like" is insufficient.[25] He correctly notes the inclusio between Jer 4:23 and 28, where the word 'bl in v. 28 parallels *tohu wabohu* in v. 23 as descriptions of the earth.[26] Some translations assign the meaning in v. 28 to 'bl (I), which means "to mourn" (e.g., NRSV; ESV; NIV). This does not appear to provide a good semantic match with *tohu*; consequently, Tsumura prefers the root 'bl (II), which means "to dry up." But assuming that "dry up" is the correct meaning for 'bl in this context, this does not exhaust considerations for the meaning of *tohu wabohu*. First, the image of something drying up carries with it a mental picture of something withered and misshapen. More than just desert-like conditions (Jer 4:26 [*midbar*]), the earth as *tohu wabohu* is in a state of cosmic disruption (Jer 4:24). While the earth's normal state is one of stability (Ps 24:2; 75:3; 104:5), the undoing of cosmic stability occurs through war (Ps 46:1–3) and judgment (Amos 8:8; Hab 3:6). Furthermore, in Jer 4:26, the cities are not merely empty but are reduced to rubble. As observed above, *tohu wabohu* appropriately describes "desert-like" conditions, but that does not exhaust the image. Wider connotations come into play than just dictionary meanings, which are the basis of Tsumura's appeal.[27]

Examining why deserts are *tohu wabohu*, there are implicit assumptions in the broader cognitive environment of ancient Israel that are potentially explicated by this phrase. Elsewhere in the Old Testament, the desert waste is the habitation of not only untamed creatures but also

---

24. See Bauks, *Die Welt am Anfang*, 117–18.

25. Tsumura, *Creation and Destruction*, 32. However, more recently, he has translated Jer 4:23 "waste and void" (Tsumura, "The Doctrine of Creation *Ex Nihilo*," 14).

26. Tsumura, *Creation and Destruction*, 30.

27. A new dictionary under development, the *Semantic Dictionary of Biblical Hebrew*, expressly takes into account connotations of words, and it supplies "chaos" as a secondary gloss for *tohu* (www.sdbh.org).

demons (Lev 17:7 with Deut 32:17 and Ps 106:37; 2 Chr 11:15; Isa 13:20–22; 34:14; Zeph 2:14).²⁸ In the ancient Near East, these places stood in contrast to the created order that emanated from the temple presence of benevolent gods.²⁹ This idea is well illustrated in Mesopotamian and Egyptian texts. For example, an Assyrian prophet uses the phrase "evil wilderness of chaos" (*ṣeri lemni balli*) to describe the unfortunate abode of gods who are exiled away from the Babylonian temple to the desert.³⁰ The Egyptian *Prophecies of Neferti* describes the undoing of creation: "what was made has been unmade." Details of this include the emptying land, encroaching darkness, the drying water sources, strange wildlife appearing, desert flocks moving into the heartland, and disappearing center points of creation—temples—that gave birth to gods. In this "prophecy," a king emerges who restores "order" (*m ' t*) to what was "chaos" (*isft*).³¹ Isaiah's use of *tohu* in Isa 24:10 cannot be divorced from his adaptation of *Chaoskampf* in the broader context of Isa 24–27 (Isa 25:8 [Mot]; 27:1 [Leviathan]).³² William Barker carefully nuances the links between the serpentine traditions across the ancient Near East (Mesopotamia–Ugarit–Egypt–the Bible) and concludes that the image symbolizes the evil, antagonistic cosmic forces that the chief deity must defeat in order for a cosmic temple to be built.³³ Thus, the conditions from which Yahweh rescues his people in Isa 24–27 are cosmic in scope. The conditions that are concurrent with *tohu* include such descriptions as "twisted" (*'wh*; Isa 24:1), "cursed" (*'lh*; Isa 24:6), "horrifying desolation" (*šmmh*; Isa 24:12; cf. verb uses in 1 Sam 5:6; 1 Kgs 9:8; Jer 4:9). As I noted above, Jeremiah's use of the phrase *tohu wabohu* as a description of judgment can hardly be regarded as a neutral state of affairs. This tone is reinforced

---

28. The necessity of ancient Near Eastern monarchs to conquer wild animals is based upon their duty to uphold creation over against the evil state of disorder. Also, the desert is where the ghosts of the unsettled dead dwell.

29. Hundley, *Gods in Dwellings*, 41–48, 80–82, 134–36. The architecture of Solomon's temple reflected the notion of the temple as microcosm, where "wild" things resided in the court (wild bulls undergirding the "Sea") under Yahweh's watchful eye, but as one moved into the building itself, the imagery changed to garden, then heavenly symbols. In reverse, the spheres of holiness radiated from the sanctuary, to the camp/city/people, to the desert where things unclean resided and to which the scapegoat carried Israel's sins on the Day of Atonement.

30. SAA 9.2 ii 24; cf. SAA 9 9:8–15 (Parpola, ed., *Assyrian Prophecies*, 16, 41).

31. Lichtheim, *Ancient Egyptian Literature*, 1:141–44. Cf. *COS* 1.45: 110 n. 39.

32. Cf. J. J. Collins, "The Beginning of the End," 145–49.

33. Barker, *Isaiah's Kingship Polemic*, 169.

in Gen 1 by virtue of its contrast with "good." So while the lexical glosses for *tohu* denote an empty place, the connotation is inferentially linked to a broader range of assumptions in the mind of an ancient Israelite. These associations can have cosmic relevance when the context suggests it, such as in Jer 4:23–24 and Gen 1:2. The presence of the watery abyss in Gen 1:2 indicates that "nothing" or "empty" are inadequate glosses in this context, and the notions of "unproductive and uninhabited" are too benign. Without necessarily involving personified cosmic forces or combat, the phrase *tohu wabohu* explicates assumptions in Gen 1:2 that are conceptually parallel to our notion of chaos.

Ezekiel

The prophet's taxonomy in Ezek 38:20 ("the fish of the sea, the birds of the heavens, the beasts of the field, all the creeping things that creep on the earth, and all the men who are on the face of the earth") is unique to Gen 1 and the flood narrative (Gen 9:2), strong evidence for intertextuality. Ezekiel also uses the phrase "according to [its] kind" (*lemin*) with respect to fish in Ezek 47:10, which is restricted to Gen 1, the related flood narrative, and categories of clean or unclean foods in Lev 11 and Deut 14.[34] These two texts illustrate Ezekiel's use of Gen 1 for both judgment (Ezek 38:20) and restoration (Ezek 47:10). Another image of judgment associated with Gen 1, perhaps directly alluding to it, is the collocation of sun, moon, and stars in Ezek 32:7–8 (cf. Ezek 30:18).

While Gen 2 is outside the purview of this study, the prophet's many references to God's garden and Eden (Ezek 28:13; 31:1–18; 36:35) show his awareness of traditions related to Gen 2 in combination with Gen 1. The allusion to Gen 1 in Ezek 47:10 is set in the context of river imagery, alluding to Gen 2:10–14 and the "living creatures" that "swarm"

---

34. Gen 1 (five times); Gen 6:20; 7:14; Lev 11 (six times); Deut 14 (four times). See also Ezek 29:5 (fish, beasts, birds). Other references to beasts and birds (e.g., Ezek 31:6; 32:4; 38:29) appear to be common taxonomy not unique to the Genesis creation tradition (1 Sam 17:46; 21:10; Ps 79:2). Petersen ("Creation and Hierarchy in Ezekiel," 169–78) argues that Ezekiel did not use "creation traditions" from Gen 1 or 2 "in consequential ways." Rather, the only substantial use, the garden motif, is from a paradise/expulsion tradition that differs from any creation tradition. He does not take the examples of this paragraph into account, nor does he discuss Ezekiel's unification of motifs from both Gen 1 and 2 discussed in the next paragraph. The verbal correspondence between Ezekiel and Genesis texts is too significant to disregard.

(Ezek 47:9, *nepeš ḥayyah, šrṣ*; cf. Gen 1:20–21),[35] suggesting that for Ezekiel these two traditions were undivided. This is important in that it reinforces the understanding of creation as temple building and includes Gen 1, particularly when these references are knit together with Ezekiel's dominant concern for the sanctuary of God (Ezek 37:26–28; 48:35).

Daniel

There is possibly an allusion to Gen 1 in Dan 7. Robert Wilson observes that the waters of the sea in Dan 7:2–3 are not contained within boundaries, such as in Gen 1:9 (cf. Prov 8:29; Job 38:1–11), and therefore it is as though they have returned to their original chaotic state (Gen 1:2).[36] Furthermore, mutant animals prevail in contrast to the orderly reproduction of animals "after their kind"; hence they are "violations of the natural order that God set up in creation."[37] Human rulers have failed to function properly as image bearers (Dan 2:38; 3:1; 4:31; cf. Gen 1:29).[38] Therefore, re-creating the world necessitates placing a "son of man" back in control who properly regulates the cult and its calendar. If the thesis is correct that Gen 1 refers to temple building, then Dan 7 is a negative counterpart, depicting anticreation, and the son of man is the key to the restoration of temple/creation.

Hosea 2:13 [Heb. 12], 20 [Heb. 18]; 4:3

Deroche observes that Hosea's use of the collocation "beasts," "birds," and "creeping things" (Hos 2:18 [Heb. v. 20]) is shared only with Gen 1:30.[39] Contextually, Hosea announces a reversal of covenant sanctions in terms of a restoration of a harmony in creation that blesses rather than destroys (Hos 2:21–23 [Heb. vv. 23–25]; cf. Lev 26:6, 22).[40] There is slight variation of this taxonomy in Gen 8:17, 19, and 9:2, but it could be argued that these represent the same textual tradition as Gen 1. Similarly, Hos

---

35. For parallels between Ezek 47:1–12 and the primordial creation accounts, including Gen 2:10–14, see Tuell, "The Rivers of Paradise," 172.
36. R. R. Wilson, "Creation and New Creation," 201.
37. R. R. Wilson, "Creation and New Creation," 202.
38. Cf. Klingbeil, "Creation in the Prophetic Literature of the Old Testament," 284.
39. DeRoche, "The Reversal of Creation," 400–409.
40. Cf. Tucker, "The Peaceable Kingdom," 222–23.

4:3 announces the annihilation of living creatures, birds, creeping things, and fish. This is a more drastic destruction of life than the flood, which spared the fish.

Amos 5:8; 9:6

The reference in Amos 5:8 to constellations, separation of light and darkness, separation of water and earth, coupled with the possible mention of the heavenly sea in Amos 9:6 (cf. Ps 104:3), echo the creation in Gen 1. Amos appeals to this tradition to highlight Yahweh's sovereign power to judge. Other, more general uses of creation and cosmological imagery occur in Amos 4:13; 5:20, 26; and 8:9.

Zephaniah 1:2–3

The reversal of Gen 1 creation appears in Zeph 1:2–3 with allusion to the removal of "man," "beast," "birds," and "fish" (in reverse order of Gen 1).[41] Due to the mention of "face of the earth," some commentators maintain that the allusion is to Gen 6:7; 7:4; and 8:8. However, as DeRoche observes, the inclusion of fish points rather to Gen 1. As noted with regard to Hos 2, it is difficult to separate the text of Gen 1 from the flood narrative. On the surface level, Zephaniah's announcement of judgment contradicts the Noahic covenant; but if one interprets Zephaniah's use of Gen 1 imagery as hyperbolic, then he merely expresses Yahweh's punishment of Judah and the nations in the most severe terms—in the undoing of creation.[42]

Summary

The prophets alluded to Gen 1 and related creation motifs to assert Yahweh's sovereign mastery over the universe, thereby substantiating their claims that he is able to execute both judgment and salvation (theological use), particularly over against non-Yahwistic religious claims (polemical use or countertext). The prophets also utilized creation motifs related to Gen 1 for rhetorical images (literary use).

---

41. DeRoche, "Zephaniah i 2–3," 104–9.
42. DeRoche, "Zephaniah i 2–3," 106–7.

After surveying the prophetic theology of creation, Martin Klingbeil asserts:

> [The prophets] saw creation as a literal and historical given ... Any discussion of whether the prophets considered creation anything other than a historical event or even that they only used it for literary or theological purposes cannot be sustained from the textual data and would be projecting a nineteenth-century AD rationalist debate into a first-millennium BC context.[43]

No doubt the prophets viewed creation as a "historical event." For God to be Creator necessitates divine action in space and time. This creative and providential power undergirds their theology, as noted above. The more nuanced question is to what extent they would have considered Gen 1 to have implications for our understanding of earth history—which is what I think Klingbeil means by "literal." In this regard, nothing in the prophets contributes to the question. Denial of chronological concord between Gen 1 and earth history does not entail denial of divine action in whatever processes actually transpired. The imposition of such chronological expectations is itself a projection of modern expectations of relevance on an ancient Near Eastern text. What Julie Galambush asserts for Ezekiel is true for all the prophets: "[The prophet] is not concerned with how the world came into existence, but with re-forming a world gone awry."[44] What the prophets reveal is the expectation of relevance in the original communication situation. Their instinct in terms of accessible assumptions pertains to theological implications of the text. If any questions could have entered their minds regarding the process of natural history, they offer no encouragement to postulate that this was the case.

The Psalms

While creation theology in the book of Psalms is pervasive, there are only a few references that can be linked to Gen 1 with any confidence. Most of these passages are addressed in chapter 2 for their contribution to questions of cosmography: Ps 19:1 (Heb. 2) uses *raqia'* ("firmament/expanse") in a cosmographic sense, as in Gen 1:6–8; Pss 24:2 and 136:6 allude to the foundation of earth relative to the waters (Gen 1:9–10); and

---

43. Klingbeil, "Creation in the Prophetic Literature of the Old Testament," 289.
44. Galambush, "God's Land and Mine," 91.

Ps 148:4 contributes to our understanding of waters above the heavens. But several other psalms remain for comment:

Psalm 8

The taxonomy of creatures and objects of creation arrayed in this short psalm render a direct allusion to Gen 1 highly probably. Primarily the psalm constitutes a commentary on the function of humans as God's image, even though the words "image" (*ṣelem*) and "likeness" (*demut*) do not appear. The explanation of these terms in Ps 8 confirms the importance of cultural enrichment in Gen 1, since the honorific connotations of image-bearing are only implicit there. For example, one can have authority without honor—e.g., a slave may be given management responsibility over household children yet not be elevated above them in honor. While authority is explicated in the very wording of Gen 1:26–28, the degree of honor conferred is explicated only through enrichment of the concept of a divine image from contextual assumptions, which have primarily royal connotations. Ps 8 confirms this.

Psalm 33

The striking feature of Ps 33 is the emphasis on creation by spoken word (Ps 33:6, coupled with allusion to Gen 1:9–10 in the parallel verse 7). The implication that God created with sovereign ease is generally inferred from Gen 1, but Ps 33:8–9 confirms this inference and applies its consequences for the earth's inhabitants. They are to fear him, recognizing that his word overwhelmed the powerful elements of creation. His ability to command the creation assures his people of his ability to save (Ps 33:10–19).

Based on the explication of creation by "word" in Ps 33, Alexej Muráň concludes that the psalmist "believed in a literal creation."[45] But "literal" is not straightforward. It could be argued on the basis of "literal" that God has organs for vocalization, or at least that he emitted sound waves. This illustrates the problem with the word "literal." The meaning of an utterance must be enriched by the contextual assumptions that are either explicated or implicated. The choice is not between "it happened 'literally' or nothing happened at all." The question is one of referential

---

45. Muráň, "The Creation Theme in Selected Psalms," 222.

intent on the part of the author—that is, what events does the language explicate? See the discussion below for the poetics of Ps 104 in relation to Gen 1.

Psalm 74

There has been debate as to whether Ps 74:13–14 alludes to creation (Gen 1 specifically), alludes instead to the parting of the Sea at the exodus, or is only a metaphorical reference to conflict with Israel's physical enemies (the nations).[46] It is difficult to ignore the concentration of references in Ps 74:16–17 ("day," "night," "lights and sun," the earth/sea boundary, and the appointed seasons) that points to Gen 1; but this does not force the imagery of vv. 13–14 into the same allusion. The language of v. 15, *nahar* ("rivers"; NIV) could allude to the "rivers" of Egypt (*nahar*; cf. Isa 19:5–7), hence to the exodus. So the psalm could utilize an amalgam of both creation theology from Genesis and divine-warfare imagery from the exodus. Since vv. 13–14 more closely follow the exodus imagery, its point of reference is more likely the exodus. The creation theology in vv. 16–17, then, would support the same message of divine sovereignty, only from the Gen 1 creation tradition rather than from the exodus.

Tsumura argues that *Chaoskampf* is an inappropriate label for Ps 74:13–14 altogether. He reserves *Chaoskampf* for traditions such as Enuma Elish, which actually portray battle between deities in a creation context, and he prefers "theomachy" for the Baal traditions from Ugarit, which do not involve creation.[47] However, while it is true that creation plays no role in the Baal traditions, Baal's conflict with both the Sea and Death affect the cosmic order in its ongoing function. The Ugaritic story involves the would-be king of the gods in battle with anticreation forces for maintenance of world order. In this regard, it is not so far removed after all from *Chaoskampf* in the Mesopotamian tradition (Enuma Elish), in which Marduk's victory over the Sea is a necessary prerequisite to creation of a world in which the gods can rest. Similarly, even if Ps 74:16–17 does not draw creation theology into the context of Yahweh's victory over the Sea, it remains possible that Israelites inferred cosmic significance regarding the battle with Israel's enemies. This is particularly relevant when the context of Ps 74 is the destruction of God's temple, the center of

---

46. See Tsumura, "The Creation Motif in Psalm 74:12–14?," 548.
47. Tsumura, "The Creation Motif in Psalm 74:12–14?," 554.

cosmic order. As I discussed above with regard to the question of chaos in Jer 4:23, contextual schemas provide a wider range for explicated or implicated assumptions than simple lexicography.

The options become more complicated, still, in the light of our distinction between implicit assumptions and implication of assumptions in a text. Even if Gen 1:2 and 1:7 do not implicate a cosmic battle with the Sea, since the emphasis of Gen 1 is on the tranquility of God's creative work, a cosmic battle could still be implicit in the broader Israelite tradition about ordering the cosmic waters. In this case, the author of Ps 74:13–15 utilizes *Chaoskampf* from this broader stock of tradition, even though it is not implicated in the context of Gen 1. So, as Averbeck argues, it is Gen 1 that transforms the tradition of *Chaoskampf* into more tranquil imagery in order to stress the sovereign ease of creation, only to draw upon the more martial aspect for the narrative of Gen 3: the conflict is not at initial creation; rather, it is in an ongoing battle over the allegiance of humans to the rule of God.[48] In any event, the *message* of Gen 1 does not involve *Chaoskampf*; at most *Chaoskampf* constitutes an implicit assumption linked with creation, which is not implicated in Gen 1.

Psalm 104

Ps 104 parallels the sequence of days in Gen 1 in general structure, yet draws out the implications of the creation account in terms of God's providential care. The result is that the thematic content in each of the days of Genesis is not carefully separated in Ps 104 due to the psalm's own theological interest.[49] For example, as Averbeck observes, humans cultivate the plants of day 3 (Ps 104:14–15); and while animals hunt in the night of day 4 (Ps 104:20–22), humans do their labor during the daylight (Ps 104:23).[50] The author of Ps 104, then, has taken less poetic liberty with the sequence of days in Gen 1 than is sometimes suggested. The psalm merely associates animal and human *activity* with the applicable day of creation. As noted in chapter 2, the contribution of Ps 104:2 to our understanding of the nature of heavenly water is inconclusive. However, Ps 104:20–22 explicates the surprising assumption that predation is a natural part of God's design.

48. Averbeck, "Ancient Near Eastern Mythography," 352–54.
49. Averbeck, "The Three 'Daughters' of Ba'al," 245–46.
50. Averbeck, "Psalms 103 and 104," 143.

Summary

The intertextual use to which the psalmists put Gen 1 is poetic, and an author's theological and literary foundation in Gen 1 does not limit poetic creativity in adapting the content. Such poetic license does, however, reinforce what has already been said about expectations of relevance from the prophets: The interests of readers in the original communication situation are exclusively theological and literary.

The Wisdom Literature

Just as it does in the Psalms, creation theology and creation texts abound in wisdom literature. Focusing on the more clearly recognized echoes of Gen 1, however, narrows the list considerably. Prov 3:19–20 received brief comment in chapter 2 due to its potential contribution to the cosmological assumptions of ancient Israelites, but it is doubtful that it echoes Gen 1 directly. On the other hand, Prov 8:22–29 contains a greater concentration of words and concepts that link to Gen 1. Lady Wisdom's preexistence to creation substantiates her credibility. The theological implications are discussed below regarding creation ex nihilo. As Clifford has noted, the interest of these two texts do "not differ from many ancient Near Eastern cosmologies: to ground or explain an element of 'culture.' In this instance the reality is not a temple or a king, but a way of life—the pursuit of wisdom."[51]

As in Prov 8:27–29, there is a likely echo of Gen 1:6–10 in Job 38:8–11. This text is situated conceptually between Gen 1 and *Chaoskampf* texts (Ps 74:12–17; Isa 27:1; 51:9–10). On the one hand, Genesis presents creation as completely tranquil, and similarly, Job 38:8–11 describes no struggle between Yahweh and the Sea. On the other hand, Job 38:8–11 should be read in context with other *Chaoskampf* passages within the book (Job 3:8; 7:12; 9:8; 26:12). There is no hint of battle in Job 38, but the author of Job likely conceived of the Sea as potentially hostile. It needs restraint in its destructive potential, like the Accuser in Job 1:12; 2:6.[52] This is another example in support of the above discussion on Jer 4:23 (see pages 158–62). Chaos, and even its destructive potential, is implicit in Israel's cognitive association with the Sea, but battle with it need not

---

51. R. J. Clifford, *Creation Accounts*, 181.
52. Mettinger, *In Search of God*, 191–98.

be *implicated* in Gen 1. It is to some degree implicated in Job 38:8–11, as potentially hostile but not in conflict with Yahweh.

Summary

This survey highlights the interest of competent readers who were close to the original communication situation of Gen 1. While Exod 20:11 is not a commentary on Gen 1, it reflects the same seven-day creation tradition. But the corollary regulation in Exod 31:17 shows that the seven-day schema in this tradition follows the analogy of the human workweek, which was established just prior to Sinai. Every echo of Gen 1 in later texts highlights the theological and literary interests of ancient Israelites. While *national* history looms large in the Old Testament, interest in *natural* history is limited to the proposition that Israel's God is the sovereign, active agent of creation. The expectation of relevance for ancient Israelites suggests that accessible assumptions pertain to religious values, not processes of nature.

Polemics

Defining Polemics

The status of Gen 1 as a polemic against ancient Near Eastern beliefs about creation is not as straightforward as is often assumed. It is common to read that elements of Gen 1 are direct criticisms of Mesopotamian, Canaanite, and Egyptian texts or traditions.[53] But more recently, the definition of what constitutes a polemic has been reconsidered.[54] Walton expresses concern that texts are too quickly labeled polemical.[55] First, such efforts must establish a direct link between the biblical text and specific foreign texts or traditions. Second, one must demonstrate that the purpose of the Old Testament text was to refute that foreign tradition. Those two requirements set polemics at one end of a continuum with other

---

53. E.g., Hasel and Hasel, "The Unique Cosmology of Genesis 1," 25.

54. For example, because the language of Gen 1 is tranquil, Collins prefers the phrase "alternative story" to "polemic" (C. J. Collins, *Genesis 1–4*, 242).

55. Walton, "Interactions in the Ancient Cognitive Environment," 333–39. Hasel claims that Walton "ignores the active polemic of the Genesis account" (Hasel and Hasel, "The Unique Cosmology of Genesis 1," 13 n. 16). But this accusation disregards the careful methodological criteria that Walton insists on.

ways Old Testament literature interacts with foreign texts and traditions. Walton offers a typology of five possible relationships between Old Testament texts and their cognitive environment: (1) borrowing—direct adaptation from foreign literary sources in the positive construction of an Old Testament passage;[56] (2) polemic—direct refutation of another text or tradition, using language that either names the target of the attack or at least assumes the target is demonstrably well-known; (3) countertext—similar to polemic, but whereas a polemic is a direct refutation of the claims of a foreign tradition, a countertext offers only an alternative perspective;[57] (4) echo—an allusion in theme or content to another text with no critical intent;[58] (5) diffusion—a sharing of a motif or a theme without a specific text or tradition in view (no polemics in any sense).

Walton's typology is a helpful advance, but the boundary between polemic and countertext remains fuzzy.[59] Consider the following reframe of Walton's definitions, taking into account the continuum between strong and weak communication utilized in relevance theory.

Polemic: The source text/tradition must be *mutually* manifest to the author and audience in order for the refutation to have its cognitive effect. The disposition of the author toward the source is negative; and the criticism is at least strongly implicated, since the target of attack is mutually manifest and the style of argumentation against it is clear.

Countertext: The source text/tradition need not be mutually manifest with the audience to impact their assumptions with the desired perspective. In the case of a countertext, any contrast with the source tradition or any negative disposition on the part of the author is only

---

56. While Walton does not use this example, I argue for direct borrowing in the case of the Instruction of Amenemope in Prov 22–24 (see chapter 1, page 21, esp. n. 66).

57. Walton adopts this category from Eckart Frahm, who notes that a countertext can completely reverse the plot of another text (Frahm, *Babylonian and Assyrian Text Commentaries*, 345). For Frahm's treatment of Gen 1 as countertext to Enuma Elish, see his discussion in Frahm, 364–66.

58. Walton uses the term "echo" in a more restrictive manner than Richard Hays and Christopher Hays. The correspondence of relevance theory to their use of "echo" is discussed in chapter 1 (pages 23–25).

59. Even in Eckart Frahm's discussion, the distinctions are blurred. So, the Erra Epic is a countertext to Enuma Elish (Frahm, *Babylonian and Assyrian Text Commentaries*, 348) but is a "farcical sequel," hence quite disparaging. Similarly, the Marduk Ordeal is a countertext that "rereads" Marduk's Akitu Festival at which Enuma Elish was liturgically read, yet Frahm characterizes them as having a "polemical tone" (Frahm, *Babylonian and Assyrian Text Commentaries*, 352, 367).

implicit but not *strongly implicated*. In the cases of both polemic and countertext, the author's attitude toward the source is negative. If this is explicated or strongly implicated, the passage is polemical; if the author's attitude remains only implicit, then countertext is perhaps a preferable category.

Walton argues that for polemic to be intended, the link to the source tradition must at least be "demonstrably so well known that general recognition by the audience could be assumed."[60] But implicature functions on a continuum between strong and weak; and if the litmus test for polemic is an authorially intended refutation, then any critical implicature could qualify an utterance for polemic. A countertext might be merely a less strongly implicated polemic. The line is crossed from merely implicit to implicated when there is sufficient encouragement from the code of a text to make the source tradition manifest and thereby available for inferential processing. It seems reasonable to argue that countertext can implicate refutation of another tradition if the *contrast* between two traditions is mutually manifest. Perhaps the only difference that can be stated between polemic and countertext is the degree to which the code directly targets the source tradition. For example, Isa 46:1 is polemical because it names the god Bel in the code. But Ps 19:1–6 is countertext because it teaches that Yahweh's glory spreads throughout the earth through the instrumentality of the sun, concerning whose deity (or lack thereof) the psalm does not explicate or strongly implicate.

Examples

Utilizing Walton's categories, but granting more weight to the dynamic of implicature, the following illustrations revisit examples from Gen 1 discussed in previous chapters:

Gen 1:1 on its own is perhaps an echo. It incorporates specific language ("in the beginning"/"heaven and earth") commonly used to introduce creation accounts. It guides the audience's expectation of relevance using a topic sentence to introduce the literary unit. This is probably not simply the result of diffusion, because language makes comparative traditions manifest, supporting countertextual implicatures that follow. If Gen 1:1 were explicating or implicating creation ex nihilo,

---

60. Walton, "Interactions in the Ancient Cognitive Environment," 334.

then it could be considered a countertext; but as will be argued below, this is probably not the case.

Gen 1:2 is countertext. The language in this verse and the motif of watery preexistence are close enough to Egyptian creation traditions as to make the latter mutually manifest. The resulting cognitive effect is a comparison, with contrast, between the Genesis account and Egyptian ideas. A comparison to Mesopotamian cosmology might also be implicated due to the shared motif of a watery beginning in some Mesopotamian accounts, particularly the cognate use of the word *tehom* (the "deep"). But the comparison also invites contrast, implicating the dismissal of foreign traditions on some important points. Specifically, the primeval elements are not the source for God, as in the theogonies of Egypt or Mesopotamia. Rather, Israel's God exists independent of them and superintends them. In addition, there is no *Chaoskampf* in which God *battles* against the waters of chaos. So this verse presents an alternate narrative about the origin of god(s) and cosmos. The contrast is manifest enough to implicate a corrective intention on the part of the author, even though this correction does not take the form of more direct refutation. If the contrast implicates a refutation strongly enough, then one might judge this to be polemical.

Gen 1:6–8 is countertext. There is ample similarity with the separation motif in both Mesopotamian and Egyptian traditions to make a comparison manifest. Particularly striking is the separation of waters in order to construct heaven. As I argued in the last chapter, the optimal use of language in these verses precluded the addition of corrective teaching concerning Israel's assumptions about the properties of heavenly water. But by *implicating* the alternative creation accounts, Gen 1 dismisses those accounts by presenting a demythologized alternative. The possible allusion to Enuma Elish (due to the specific motif shared only with Genesis) might draw this particular tradition to the foreground for contrastive purposes. Recall that relevance works by providing new information, reinforcing an assumption, or challenging it. In the case of Gen 1:6–8, the most relevant implications involve challenging *religious* assumptions, not assumptions about cosmic geography. Still, the challenge to *religious* assumptions behind competing cosmological traditions would satisfy readers' expectations of relevance.

Gen 1:16 is probably countertext. Many commentators have noted the switch in code from the common names for "sun/moon" (also proper names of deities) to "greater/lesser light." In relevance terms, this avoidance of the expected words might be ostensive, that is, it makes manifest a peculiarity in the text, bringing accessible assumptions to the foreground for inferential processing. Since these objects were known throughout the ancient Near East as divine beings, the avoidance of their names was insulting inasmuch as the passage reassigned them to the same category the rest of creation. This reading would constitute a polemic. However, it is also possible that this text might not implicate any assumption about foreign religious traditions. Walton points out that in terms of calendrical function, "lights" is an appropriate label.[61] Smith notes that Ugaritic literature uses the equivalent cognate expression, "great light," for the sun without any special connotation.[62] In relevance theory terms, no religious assumptions regarding the divine nature of the sun, moon, and stars would be activated for processing. In short, it is a matter of opinion as to how strongly the language of the text implicates religious assumptions, thereby advocating (or not) an alternative belief. The intertextual allusions to Gen 1 in Pss 104:19 and 148:3 (cf. Ps 136:7–9) refer to these astral objects with their usual (and potentially divine) names, and Ps 104:19 explicates the relevance of these objects as seasonal markers. But even if the de-deification of these elements of the cosmos is not implicated in the text, the assumption about the divine nature of the astrological bodies was commonly held and available for processing at the inferential discretion of readers (similar to creation ex nihilo discussed below). So, a valid theological inference could be the de-deification of heavenly bodies even if this conception were not implicated in Gen 1 itself.

Summary

This section examined the question of polemics. Walton is correct to insist on a more rigorous methodology for such labels, and his typology is useful: borrowing, polemic, countertext, echo, and diffusion. Relevance theory offers complementary categories of thought. The boundary between polemic and countertext is fuzzy. Perhaps the best distinction is found in how strongly the code targets the object of criticism. Such judgments are often difficult to assess because the code of the text still needs reference assignment, disambiguation, and enrichment from implicit, contextual

---

61. Walton, *Genesis 1 as Ancient Cosmology*, 171–72.

62. Smith, *The Priestly Vision of Genesis 1*, 94 (*KTU* 1.3 v 17; 1.4 viii 21; 1.6 i 8–9 and ii 24; 1:16 i 36–38).

assumptions. The strength of explicature and implicature relies on judgment calls as to how manifest these assumptions are in the primary communication situation, something we as modern interpreters find difficult to judge.

Creation ex Nihilo

Does Gen 1:1 Explicate Creation ex Nihilo?

One of the best-known interpretive issues in Gen 1 concerns the function of Gen 1:1 relative to Gen 1:2-3. At the risk of oversimplifying, there are three primary interpretive options in contemporary debate: (1) The traditional view that Gen 1:1 states God's first act of creation—an absolute beginning—in which v. 2 describes the result of this first stage; (2) Gen 1:1 introduces the creation account as a relative beginning, with the preexistent conditions of the earth described in v. 2 as the starting point;[63] or (3) Gen 1:1 introduces the creation account with a summary title.[64] In this third view, the account might still present a relative beginning, since the first creative act begins in v. 3, utilizing the preexisting conditions described in v. 2. Only the traditional view necessarily *explicates* creation

---

63. E.g., "When God began to create..." (NJPS); or "In the beginning when God created..." (NRSV). A more recent permutation, often neglected in discussion, is that of Holmstead ("Restrictive Syntax of Gen i, 1," 56-67). A substantial argument against interpreting Gen 1:1 as a relative clause is based on functional grammar. Placing elements in first position in a sentence ("fronting") introduces new topics with spatiotemporal framing. So, as Winther-Nielsen argues, "From this point of view, the first element in the Genesis 1:1 clause may be taken as the time setting, while the rest of the clause ["God created"] expresses a highly foregrounded state of affairs: God created the universe" (Winther-Nielsen, "'In the Beginning," 77-78). The conclusion is that the entire verse is a main clause, not a subordinate relative clause that sets up the following narrative.

64. Similar is the position of Bauks, who suggests that Gen 1:1 is an incomplete sentence but that there is no grammatical link between Gen 1:1 and 1:2-3 (i.e., anacoluthon). While the verse serves as a topic heading for the narrative unit (neither absolute nor relative beginning), it is an incomplete sentence, grammatically speaking: "In the beginning when God created the world. But the earth was not yet present, rather there was darkness over the ur-sea. And a wind of God was blowing over the waters. Then God said, 'Let there be light.' And there was light." (Bauks, *Die Welt am Anfang*, 146, my translation). In her analysis, Gen 1 does not present creation ex nihilo, nor does it affirm the eternal, preexistence of matter. Her view is followed in Keel and Schroer, *Creation*, 139-40.

ex nihilo—that is, the specific wording chosen for the discourse describes creation out of nothing explicitly.

It is not my purpose to rehearse all the major arguments here regarding the syntax of Gen 1:1–3; rather, I aim to explore the consequences for the theology of creation ex nihilo of applying relevance theory to Gen 1. In my judgment, the parallel structure that Gen 1:1 shares with Gen 2:4–7 as well as the collocation "heavens and earth" for the ordered cosmos in Gen 1:1 are both pieces of strong evidence that Gen 1:1 is a topic sentence for the creation account (rather than a relative clause or the first creative act). Perhaps the best presentation of this position remains that of Waltke.[65] Critiques of his arguments have only chipped away at the margins of his view and have not fundamentally undermined his understanding of the structure of these verses.[66] More recent arguments from discourse grammar to support the traditional interpretation that Gen 1:1 is the first act of creation ex nihilo are inconclusive.[67] Summary openings in other

---

65. Waltke, "The Creation Account in Genesis," 216–28.

66. This is true of Poythress's extensive critique of the summary interpretation of Gen 1:1 (Poythress, "Genesis 1:1," 97–121). At most, he shows that alternative interpretations of various details in the summary view are viable. But are they preferable? A brief comment on two major issues is warranted: (1) "heavens and earth" as the ordered universe. Poythress contends that this cannot be a merism and does not always designate the ordered universe. In my view, the collocation "heavens and earth" most often makes a structural assertion about the cosmos; it is organized as they knew it (a bipartate whole—see the extensive parallel examples in chapter 2). The technical nature of merisms is irrelevant. Separation is organization (cf. Isa 45:18; 48:13). In Prov 3:19 and 8:27–29 the heavens are the finished product of creative processes; and in Isa 66:17, 22 the new reordered cosmos is cast in terms that echo Gen 1:1. So, contrary to Poythress, organization is part of the sense of the collocation, which is not just a referent to "everything." This meaning is contextually preferred in Gen 1:1 by the fact that the heavens are not created until the second day (organized structure through separation), by the fact that the earth (as Israelites knew it) is not created until the third day, and by the *inclusio* with Gen 2:1. (2) the structural parallel with Gen 2:4–7, i.e., a topic sentence, followed by a disjunctive clause listing three conditions in verses 5–6, and then the first creative act in verse 7. Poythress stresses differences between Gen 1:1 and 2:4 (e.g., finite verb versus nonverb for the main clause). But the parallel structure (with three disjunctive conditions each) remains striking, a clue to how the author conceives the discourse flow of these two units. Interpreting Gen 1:1 as a summary introduction to the first unit of Genesis (Gen 1:1—2:3) is consistent with the organizing technique for the rest of the book, which utilizes *toledot* as summary introduction, a term that would not have been appropriate to introduce Gen 1.

67. Using discourse grammar, Collins argues that it is grammatically possible but unlikely that Gen 1:1 is a summary statement; since, in his view, a perfect tense in the opening of a pericope describes "an event that precedes the main storyline" (C. J. Collins, *Genesis 1–4*, 51–52; cf. Poythress, "Genesis 1:1," 100–101). Many occasions of

creation accounts in Mesopotamia (see chapter 1) as well as the watery preconditions of the universe in both Mesopotamian and Egyptian traditions (see chapter 2) reinforce this interpretive path for Gen 1:1 (i.e., as a summary heading), based on the original audience's expectations. It is of course possible that the author offers *new* information that was contrary to any existing assumption about creation. But if this had been the case, one would expect *more explicit code* (language) in the discourse that is necessary to override existing assumptions. The text as is offers no guidance away from this expectation but rather accommodates to it. If Gen 1:1 is a topic sentence, then creation ex nihilo is not *explicated* in Gen 1:1 unless the rest of the chapter informs readers of ex nihilo creation, which v. 1 summarizes. Of course, it is important to note that the *eternality* of preexisting matter is *also* not explicated.[68] There remains the possibility, however, that creation ex nihilo is *implicit* in Gen 1:1–2 or

---

the disjunctive construction do function as he describes, wherein the action begins with a perfect-tense verb in a disjunctive clause followed in temporal sequence by a *wayyiqtol* verb form (e.g., Gen 3:1; 4:1; 15:1; Exod 24:1). But when opening a new pericope with a disjunctive clause (signaled by use of a nonverb as in Gen 1:1), it is the opening of a new literary unit that is stressed; the temporal relationship between the perfect tense and following verbs is incidental to the construction. In some cases of a new pericope, the action is *antecedent* to the opening of the new pericope, not the first action (e.g., Gen 16:1; 39:1). Some of these provide background information expressed by a stative perfect (Gen 24:1; 43:1). But two examples open the pericope with summary action, both of which Collins discusses, since they are problematic to his argument. It is true that in Exod 19:1 the perfect-tense verb, *ba'u*, does not summarize the entire pericope. But *ba'u* in verse 1 subsumes the action of the next verb, both of which *together* set the chronological and geographical context for everything that follows. So the important point remains, that there is no necessary sequential relationship between the perfect tense of the disjunctive clause and the *wayyiqtol* form that follows. In Gen 22:1, the new pericope opens with a fronted temporal clause followed by a perfect tense that summarizes the events of the pericope. The difference between Gen 22:1 and Gen 1:1 is that in Gen 22:1, the fronted temporal element is a clause rather than a noun. But the temporal clause sets the chronological context for the pericope and the perfect tense expresses action that summarizes what follows. Not discussed by Collins is Josh 24:1–2; a perfect tense introduces the temporal and geographical background to action that is *concurrent* with the *wayyiqtol* verb action. If the collocation "heavens and earth" is the structured whole (see above note 66), then Gen 1:1 must be a summary, which the grammar allows. Indeed, if an author wishes to front a sentence with a temporal phrase to open a pericope (as in Gen 1:1), there is no other option than to use the perfect tense. Temporal sequence between verbs is subordinate to other considerations.

68. Bauks argues that the origin of matter ontologically is simply not addressed by the text, so neither ex nihilo nor the eternality of matter is taught (Bauks, *Die Welt am Anfang*, 63–64).

Gen 1 as a whole; and if it is, does the author *implicate* this assumption in the informative intention of the passage?

Does Gen 1:2 Implicate Creation ex Nihilo?

The language of Gen 1:2 explicitly teaches the independence of God from the material universe and his superintendence of it. Independence is explicated by the preposition "over" (the waters), and superintendence is explicated by the image of "hovering" (Deut 32:11).[69] Closely related to this is God's transcendent sovereignty, since this assumption implicitly underlies independence and superintendence. The rest of the chapter confirms this contextually, not only through the image of creation by spoken word but also the shaping, organizing, and naming of the universe's fundamental parts. Thus, transcendent sovereignty is strongly implicated. This is the crucial theological point of Gen 1:2. It offers *new* information through an alternative narrative to ancient Near Eastern cosmogonies where the physical properties of the universe are manifestations of various gods and goddesses. But transcendent sovereignty does not necessarily *implicate* creation ex nihilo.

The rest of Gen 1 leaves the question of creation ex nihilo underdetermined as well. One might argue that the degree of emphasis on God's transcendent sovereignty (i.e., creation by spoken word) implicates an assumption of creation ex nihilo (cf. Ps 33:6, 9). But creation by spoken word offers no assurance that ex nihilo is implicated. The Egyptian Memphite creation features Ptah fashioning the universe by thought and word, but this is not ex nihilo.[70] Conversely, it is possible that Marduk's

---

69. The image is disputed, but Hamilton's argument remains cogent (Hamilton, *The Book of Genesis 1–17*, 114–15). Scurlock notes the Ugaritic cognate *rḥp*, used in reference to the goddess Anat, who with wings flies in heaven (Scurlock, "Searching for Meaning," 53). One might consider the "hovering" image as an example of contextual enrichment—the lexical semantics of the participle + preposition coupled with the *contrast* to other creation accounts in the ancient Near East where deities emerge from *within* the primordial deep. Given the frequency with which *ruaḥ 'elohim* denotes God's personal Spirit (e.g., Gen 41:38; Exod 31:3; 1 Sam 10:10; Ezek 11:24) as well as the intertextual understanding in Ps 33:6, it is unlikely that the "spirit" is anything other than God's presence.

70. Lichtheim, *Ancient Egyptian Literature*, 51–57. It is not often recognized that this pantheistic model of creation differs substantially from creation by word in Gen 1, in which God exists independent of the cosmic waters. Ptah subsists in the primordial waters (Ptah-Nun), and creation emerges out of his being (see cols. 50–51). Unfortunately, the excerpt provided in *COS* 1.15 begins only with col. 53, omitting this crucial information about Ptah's identity.

verbal command to destroy and re-create a constellation in Enuma Elish (iv 19–26) demonstrates ex nihilo power, although this may be only the scattering of stars and their reorganization into a fixed constellation.[71] But creation as a whole in Enuma Elish emerges from the preexisting waters of chaos as it does in Egyptian creation tradition. In my judgment, if Gen 1 implicates creation ex nihilo, it is at best a relatively weak implicature on the continuum of strong communication to weak communication. Others applying relevance theory to the interpretive possibilities might judge the relative strength or weakness of this implicature differently.

Is ex Nihilo Implicit in Genesis 1:2?

On the basis of God's separation from his creation (explicated by the preposition "over") and creation's dependency on him (implicated by his superintendence of it), one might infer that creation is not eternally coexistent with him and therefore must be ex nihilo.[72] Such a belief is consistent with Israelite faith expressed in other Old Testament passages (to be discussed below), some of which use language from Gen 1. If ex nihilo creation is an accessible assumption to the ancient readers of Gen 1, then one can argue that ex nihilo is an implicit assumption in the background of Gen 1:2 and can be inferred from it, even if it is not implicated in the informative intention of Gen 1.[73] In this case, Gen 1 would have

---

71. This observation seems to escape discussion, but see Scurlock, "Searching for Meaning," 50. The possibility that other ancient Near Eastern religions ascribed limited ex nihilo power to some deities needs revisiting. However, such power would not negate the pantheistic notions inherent in these creation accounts.

72. This is not a tight philosophical argument; rather, it involves loose inference by which normal communication operates. It is logically possible for creation to be dependent on the Creator yet still coexist eternally with him, if it eternally emanates from his being. However, the separation between God's Spirit and creation explicated in Gen 1:2 suggests that such ontological continuity is not a valid assumption, particularly in contrast with other ancient Near Eastern creation narratives that explicitly involve a pantheistic emergence of the gods from the primordial waters and the emanation of the rest of creation from them. Additionally, creation can be contingent on the Creator (a stronger proposition than mere dependence) yet still coexist eternally with him, if the existence of creation is necessitated by God's eternal attributes. These are theological problems that extend beyond the scope of this monograph. I thank Marc Cortez for stimulating my thoughts about this in a more complex way, although my reflections should not be construed as representing his conclusions on these matters.

73. Readers might wish to consult the discussion in that last chapter regarding true implicit assumptions that are not necessarily implicated in the informative intention of a speaker or author. See page 130.

theological relevance to the question of ex nihilo external to the meaning of the passage itself. Of course, if one's judgment is that creation ex nihilo is at least weakly implicated in Gen 1, then the following intertextual examples support this judgment as well. In cases of weakly communicated ideas, readers take responsibility for their inferences. But if theological inferences are validated by ancient (especially canonical) interpretation, then they are more strongly warranted. The following paragraphs discuss Old Testament passages that in my judgment do implicate creation ex nihilo.

Isaiah

Isaiah's arguments that redemption is rooted in creation do not depend on inferring creation ex nihilo from Genesis; rather only God's transcendent sovereignty is necessary to assure Israel that God is capable of accomplishing his future redemptive work.[74] But the allusion in Isa 45:7 to Gen 1:2–3 ("light and darkness"; cf. Isa 45:18) is exceptional, explicitly affirming that even the existence of darkness, with which creation begins (Gen 1:2), comes at God's initiation.[75] There is an even stronger argument for ex nihilo in Isaiah, not from his echo of Gen 1:2 but from the prophet's insistence on the eternality of God over against creation. This is strongly implicated in Isa 46:10 ("I make known the end from the beginning"). Other texts could be added (Isa 40:28; 41:4 [cf. Gen 1:1 with 2:4]; 44:6 [ṣeba'ot / 'elohim precludes even the "angels" of Job 38:7]; 48:12–13). When coupled with declarations of incomparability, the doctrine of Yahweh as eternal Creator over against the other gods is one of Isaiah's ways of affirming monotheism.[76] There were no other entities in existence when he created; hence, ex nihilo. So, while ex nihilo is underdetermined in Gen 1, Isaiah shows that it is an implicit assumption that was salient to a reader in the original communication situation. As such, it is a canonically authorized theological inference from Gen 1.

---

74. I thank John Oswalt for focusing my attention on Isaiah's doctrine of creation ex nihilo (Oswalt, "*Creatio ex Nihilo*"), although we differ on whether creation ex nihilo is explicit in Gen 1; see also Oswalt, "Creation Ex Nihilo."

75. DeRoche ("Isaiah xiv 7," 11–21) labors to demonstrate that "darkness" is part of the created cycle of the universe with light, and that "evil" is merely a necessary facet of Yahweh's creation of an ethical universe. This infers too much from the text.

76. H. Clifford, "Deutero-Isaiah and Monotheism," 267–69, 273–77.

Proverbs

As I noted above, Prov 8:22–29 echoes Gen 1. What is most important in our discussion here is the argument underlying this passage, that Lady Wisdom precedes the elements of creation temporally, including the "deeps" (v. 24, *tehomot*; cf. *tehom*, Gen 1:2). Strongly implicated in Prov 8:24 is the assumption that there was a time when the conditions described in Gen 1:2 did not exist.[77] While this does not necessitate that creation ex nihilo is implicated in Gen 1:2, it does demonstrate that the range of implicit assumptions associated with Gen 1:2 includes the understanding that creation is ex nihilo, which Gen 1:2 entails even though it is not implicated in that context.

Psalms

In Ps 104:6, the same precreation conditions described in Gen 1:2 are called God's handiwork. While this verse does not necessarily echo the language of Gen 1, other passages from the book of Psalms set the assumption about God's eternality over against the contingency of creation—both Ps 90:2 and Ps 102:25–27 contrast God's eternality with creation. This suggests that such theology was in Israel's cognitive environment and therefore likely implicit in Gen 1.

Summary

One can speculate as to why creation ex nihilo seems less important to biblical authors than transcendent sovereignty. Had it been more important, it would be explicated or implicated more strongly. Certainly, it is not expressed in the terms we might wish to find. But the doctrine is nevertheless there, assumed by orthodox Israelites, implicated in Isaiah, Proverbs, and Psalms, and likely implicit in Gen 1 even though it is neither explicated nor implicated in that particular passage.

---

77. See Waltke, *The Book of Proverbs*, 1:412 and his counter to the suggestion that this interpretation is too exceptional to be valid.

Trinitarianism in Genesis 1

The explanation of *sensus plenior* in the light of relevance theory contributes to another commonly discussed interpretive issue in Gen 1. In the same way that a canonical reading of Gen 1 can find hints of the doctrine of creation ex nihilo, so a canonical reading of Gen 1 can also find implications in the text that are consistent with a Trinitarian formulation—only in this case one needs the full New Testament testimony. With respect to creation ex nihilo, the doctrine was implicit in the assumptions of the human author but not implicated. Regarding the doctrine of the Trinity, however, it is implicit in the assumptions of the *divine* author, even though this assumption was not shared by the *human* author or audience in the original context.[78] New Testament revelation makes manifest the divine author's assumptions. So, creation by the word in Gen 1 receives a christological interpretation in John 1:1, allowing the Son to be identified in Gen 1. Following this, Father and Spirit can be explicated as the Speaker and active Agent over the precreation waters, respectively. The frequently debated plural in Gen 1:26 (cf. Gen 3:22) also lends itself to this expanded meaning. In the contextual environment of the human author and audience, the plural verbs and pronouns would access assumptions about a divine council made up of numerous supernatural (otherworldly) beings (cf. 1 Kgs 22:19; Ps 82:1, 6–7; Job 1:6). However, the language can also function to explicate plurality within the Godhead. In the expanding experience of the God's people, especially in the light of the Christ event and Pentecost, contextual assumptions not accessible to the original Old Testament community became manifest for inferential processing. As Green argues, for Christians, reading the plural "us" in Gen 1:26 as divine offers the greatest cognitive effect for the least processing effort.[79]

Conclusions

Validation of Relevance

Intertextual allusions to Gen 1 in other Old Testament texts reveal interest in theological implications of the creation account but no attention to what we might call natural processes. Only Exod 20:11 draws upon

---

78. Green, "Relevance Theory and Theological Interpretation," 89.

79. Green, "Relevance Theory and Theological Interpretation," 89–90.

the same seven-day schema as Gen 1, but it cannot be a commentary on the Genesis. Rather, both texts utilize the analogy of the human workweek, which the Bible indicates was established before the composition of either text. From Gen 1, the prophets and sages inferred that God's transcendent sovereignty, as revealed in creation, secured the basis for his divine action in judgment and salvation. One might argue, of course, that the Old Testament primarily conveys theological truth, so one would not expect information about cosmography to be explicated or implicated in later uses of Gen 1. But that reinforces the point—reading Gen 1 with the reflexes of the original audience means ignoring assumptions relevant to what we would call natural history or science.

Polemics and Countertext

Intertextuality between the Old Testament and other ancient Near Eastern creation traditions can take several forms: these are best delineated in Walton's typology: direct borrowing, polemical attack, countertext, and rhetorical echo. A fifth possibility involving no intertextuality is simple cultural diffusion. Relevance theory complements this careful nuance of intertextuality by focusing on varying strengths of explicature or implicature. Perhaps the boundary between polemic and countertext is best delineated by how strongly the code targets the object of criticism—polemics involve code that explicates or strongly implicates the target of attack whereas countertexts implicate the comparative tradition more weakly.

Creation ex Nihilo

Relevance theory's distinction between implicit assumptions and implicated assumptions is helpful for thinking about the doctrine of creation ex nihilo. Compared to theological interest in this question beginning in late antiquity, the doctrine was evidently less important to the faith of ancient Israel than transcendent sovereignty; otherwise it would be explicated more strongly. However, creation ex nihilo is implicit in Gen 1, even if not implicated by the author, since it is implicated in other Old Testament texts and therefore likely existed as an implicit assumption for Gen 1.

The Trinity

The dual authorship of Scripture adds a layer of complexity to interpretation. If one grants the existence of Scripture's divine author, then relevance theory's notion of explicature and implicature, when considered within the expanding cognitive environment of salvation history, opens the possibility of *sensus plenior*. Proposals of *sensus plenior* in theological interpretation of the Old Testament depend on canonical validation, and through such effort one can find explication of triune plurality in the Creator God of Gen 1.

Bibliography

Albertz, Rainer, and Rüdiger Schmitt. *Family and Household Religion in Ancient Israel and the Levant*. Winona Lake, IN: Eisenbrauns, 2012.

Alexander, Robert. "Šaušga and the Hittite Ivory from Megiddo." *JNES* 50 (1991) 161–82.

Allen, James P. *Genesis in Egypt: The Philosophy of Ancient Egyptian Creation Accounts*. Yale Egyptological Studies 2. New Haven: Yale University Press, 1988.

———. "The World of Ancient Egyptian Thought." In *The Adventure of the Human Intellect: Self, Society, and the Divine in Ancient World Cultures*, edited by Kurt A. Raaflaub, 73–88. The Ancient World: Comparative Histories. Chichester, UK: Wiley, 2016.

Allert, Craig D. *Early Christian Readings of Genesis One: Patristic Exegesis and Literal Interpretation*. Downers Grove, IL: InterVarsity, 2018.

Augustine. *On Genesis: Two Books on Genesis against the Manichees; and, On the Literal Interpretation of Genesis, an Unfinished Book*. Fathers of the Church 84. Washington, DC: Catholic University of America Press, 1991.

———. *The Literal Meaning of Genesis*. 2 vols. Translated by John Hammond Taylor. Ancient Christian Writers 41–42. New York: Newman, 1982.

Austin, J. L. *How to Do Things with Words*. William James Lectures 1955. Cambridge: Harvard University Press, 1975.

Averbeck, Richard E. "Ancient Near Eastern Mythography as It Relates to Historiography in the Hebrew Bible: Genesis 3 and the Cosmic Battle." In *The Future of Biblical Archaeology: Reassessing Methodologies and Assumptions*, edited by James K. Hoffmeier and Alan Millard, 328–56. Grand Rapids: Eerdmans, 2004.

———. "Psalms 103 and 104: Hymns of Redemption and Creation." In *Interpreting the Psalms for Teaching and Preaching*, edited by Herbert W. Bateman IV and D. Brent Sandy, 132–48. St. Louis: Chalice, 2010.

———. "The Three 'Daughters' of Ba῾al and Transformations of Chaoskampf in the Early Chapters of Genesis." In *Creation and Chaos: A Reconsideration of Hermann Gunkel's Chaoskampf Hypothesis*, edited by JoAnn Scurlock and Richard H. Beal, 237–56. Winona Lake, IN: Eisenbrauns, 2013.

Balserak, Jon. *Divinity Compromised: A Study of Divine Accommodation in the Thought of John Calvin*. Studies in Early Modern Religious Reforms 5. Dordrecht: Springer, 2006.

Barker, William D. *Isaiah's Kingship Polemic: An Exegetical Study in Isaiah 24–27*. FAT 70. Tübingen: Mohr/Siebeck, 2014.

Baroway, Israel. "The Bible as Poetry in the English Renaissance: An Introduction." *Journal of English and Germanic Philology* 32 (1933) 447–80.

Bartholomew, Craig G. *Introducing Biblical Hermeneutics: A Comprehensive Framework for Hearing God in Scripture*. Grand Rapids: Baker, 2015.

Batto, Bernard F. *In the Beginning: Essays on Creation Motifs in the Bible and the Ancient Near East*. Siphrut: Literature and Theology of the Hebrew Scriptures 9. Winona Lake, IN: Eisenbrauns, 2013.

———. "The Combat Myth in Israelite Tradition Revisited." In *Creation and Chaos: A Reconsideration of Hermann Gunkel's Chaoskampf Hypothesis*, edited by JoAnn Scurlock and Richard H. Beal, 217–36. Winona Lake, IN: Eisenbrauns, 2013.

Bauks, Michaela. *Die Welt am Anfang: Zum Verhältnis von Vorwelt und Weltentstehung in Gen 1 und in der altorientalischen Literatur*. WMANT 74. Neukirchen-Vluyn: Neukirchener, 1997.

———. "Intertextuality in Ancient Literature in Light of Textlinguistics and Cultural Studies." In *Between Text and Text: The Hermeneutics of Intertextuality in Ancient Cultures and Their Afterlife in Medieval and Modern Times*, edited by Michaela Bauks et al., 27–46. Journal of Ancient Judaism Supplements 6. Göttingen: Vandenhoeck & Ruprecht, 2013.

Bavinck, Herman. *In the Beginning: Foundations of Creation Theology*. Edited by John Bolt. Translated by John Vriend. Grand Rapids: Baker, 1999.

———. *Reformed Dogmatics*. 4 vols. Edited by John Bolt. Translated by John Vriend. Grand Rapids: Baker, 2003.

Beall, Todd. "Reading Genesis 1–2: A Literal Approach." In *Reading Genesis 1–2: An Evangelical Conversation*, edited by J. Daryl Charles, 45–59. Peabody, MA: Hendrickson, 2013.

Beck, Pirhiya. "The Art of Palestine During the Iron Age II: Local Traditions and External Influences (10th–8th Centuries BCE)." In *Imagery and Representation—Studies in the Art and Iconography of Ancient Palestine: Collected Articles*, 203–22. Journal of the Institute of Archaeology of Tel Aviv University, Occasional Publications 3. Tel Aviv: Emery and Claire Yass Publications in Archaeology, 2002.

Benin, Stephen D. *The Footprints of God: Divine Accommodation in Jewish and Christian Thought*. SUNY Series in Judaica. Albany: State University of New York Press, 1993.

Block, Daniel I. *The Book of Ezekiel*. Vol. 2, *Chapters 25–48*. 2 vols. NICOT. Grand Rapids: Eerdmans, 1998.

Boman, Thorleif. *Hebrew Thought Compared with Greek*. Translated by Jules L. Moreau. Norton Library. New York: Norton, 1960.

Breasted, James Henry. "The Philosophy of a Memphite Priest." *ZÄS* 39 (1901) 39–54.

———. *Ancient Records of Egypt*. Vol. 4, *The Twentieth to the Twenty-Sixth Dynasties*. Chicago: University of Chicago Press, 1906.

Breucker, Geert de. "Berossos between Tradition and Innovation." In *The Oxford Handbook of Cuneiform Culture*, edited by Karen Radner and Eleanor Robson, 637–57. Oxford Handbooks. Oxford: Oxford University Press, 2011.

Brown, A. J. *The Days of Creation: A History of Christian Interpretation of Genesis 1:1—2:3*. History of Biblical Interpretation Series. Blandford Forum, UK: Deo, 2014.

Brown, Jeannine K. *Scripture as Communication: Introducing Biblical Hermeneutics*. Grand Rapids: Baker Academic, 2007.

Brueggemann, Walter. "Jeremiah: *Creation in Extremis*." In *God Who Creates: Essays in Honor of W. Sibley Towner*, edited by William P. Brown and S. Dean McBride,

152–70. Grand Rapids: Eerdmans, 2000. Reprinted in Brueggemann, *The God of All Flesh*, 25–43. Eugene, OR: Cascade Books, 2015.

Buck, Adriann de. *The Egyptian Coffin Texts: II (Spells 76–163)*. Chicago: University of Chicago Press, 1938.

———. *The Egyptian Coffin Texts: VI (Spells 472–787)*. Oriental Institute Publications 81. Chicago: University of Chicago Press, 1956.

Budge, E. A. Wallis. *The Gods of the Egyptians: or, Studies in Egyptian Mythology*. 2 vols. London: Methuen, 1904.

Byrne, Ryan. "Self, Substance, and Social Metaphysics: The Intellectual Adventures of Israel and Judah." In *The Adventure of the Human Intellect: Self, Society, and the Divine in Ancient World Cultures*, edited by Kurt A. Raaflaub, 105–26. The Ancient World: Comparative Histories. Chichester, UK: Wiley, 2016.

Calvin, John. *Commentaries on the First Book of Moses Called Genesis*. Translated by John King. Grand Rapids: Eerdmans, 1948.

———. *Commentary on the Book of Psalms*. Translated by James Anderson. Grand Rapids: Eerdmans, 1949.

———. *Institutes of the Christian Religion*. Translated by Ford Lewis Battles. Philadelphia: Westminster, 1960.

———. *Ioannis Calvini Opera Quae Supersunt Omnia*. Edited by G. Baum et al. Corpus Reformatorum 31. Bad Feilnbach, Germany: Schmidt, 1990.

Cameron, Nigel M. de S. *Biblical Higher Criticism and the Defense of Infallibilism in 19th Century Britain*. Texts and Studies in Religion 33. Lewiston, NY: Mellen, 1987.

Campos, Marcio D'Olne. "Búzios Island: Knowledge and Belief among a Fishing and Agricultural Community at the Coast of the State of São Paulo." In *Songs from the Sky: Indigenous Astronomical and Cosmological Traditions of the World*, edited by John Von Del Chamberlain et al., 236–43. Bognor Regis, UK: Ocarina, 2005.

Carey, Susan, and Elizabeth Spelke. "Science and Core Knowledge." *Philosophy of Science* 63 (1996) 515–33.

Carston, Robyn. *Thoughts and Utterances: The Pragmatics of Explicit Communication*. Oxford: Blackwell, 2002.

———. "Relevance Theory and the Saying/Implicating Distinction." In *The Handbook of Pragmatics*, edited by Laurence R. Horn and Gregory L. Ward, 633–56. Blackwell Handbooks in Linguistics 16. Oxford: Blackwell, 2004.

———. "Word Meaning, What is Said and Explicature." In *What Is Said and What Is Not*, edited by Carlo Penco and Filippo Domaneschi, 175–203. CSLI Lecture Notes 207. Stanford: CSLI Publications, 2013.

Clifford, Hywel. "Deutero-Isaiah and Monotheism." In *Prophecy and the Prophets in Ancient Israel*, edited by John Day, 267–89. Library of Hebrew Bible/Old Testament Studies 531. T. & T. Clark Library of Biblical Studies. New York: T. & T. Clark, 2010.

Clifford, Richard J. *Creation Accounts in the Ancient Near East and in the Bible*. Catholic Biblical Quarterly Monograph Series 26. Washington, DC: Catholic Biblical Association, 1994.

Clines, David J. A. "The Image of God in Man." *Tyndale Bulletin* 19 (1968) 53–103.

Cohen, Yoram. *Wisdom from the Late Bronze Age*. WAW 34. Atlanta: SBL, 2013.

Colet, John. *Letters to Radulphus on the Mosaic Account of the Creation Together with Other Treatises*. Translated by J. H. Lupton. London: Bell, 1876.

Collins, Billie Jean. *The Hittites and Their World*. ABS 7. Atlanta: SBL, 2007.

Collins, C. John. *Genesis 1-4: A Linguistic, Literary, and Theological Commentary*. Phillipsburg, NJ: P & R, 2006.

———. "Noah, Deucalion, and the New Testament." *Biblica* 93 (2012) 403-26.

———. *Reading Genesis Well: Navigating History, Poetry, Science, and Truth in Genesis 1-11*. Grand Rapids: Zondervan, 2018.

Collins, John J. "The Beginning of the End of the World in the Hebrew Bible." In *Thus Says the Lord: Essays on the Former and Latter Prophets in Honor of Robert R. Wilson*, edited by John J. Ahn and Stephen L. Cook, 137-55. Library of Hebrew Bible/Old Testament Studies 502. T. & T. Clark Library of Biblical Studies. New York: T. & T. Clark, 2009.

Cornelius, Izak. "The Visual Representation of the World in the Ancient Near East and the Hebrew Bible." *JNSL* 20 (1994) 193-218.

Csapo, Eric. *Theories of Mythology*. Ancient Cultures. Oxford: Blackwell, 2005.

Cummings, Louise. *Pragmatics: A Multidisciplinary Perspective*. Edinburgh: Edinburgh University Press, 2005.

Currid, John D. *Ancient Egypt and the Old Testament*. Grand Rapids: Baker, 1997.

Davies, Graham I. "Was There an Exodus?" In *In Search of Pre-Exilic Israel: Proceedings of the Oxford Old Testament Seminar*, edited by John Day, 23-40. JSOTSup 406. London: T. & T. Clark, 2004.

Day, John. "The Flood and the Ten Antediluvian Figures in Berossus and in the Priestly Source in Genesis." In *On Stone and Scroll: Essays in Honour of Graham Ivor Davies*, edited by James K. Aitken et al., 211-23. BZAW 420. Berlin: de Gruyter, 2011.

DeRoche, Michael. "Zephaniah i 2-3: The 'Sweeping' of Creation." *VT* 30 (1980) 104-9.

———. "The Reversal of Creation in Hosea." *VT* 31 (1981) 400-409.

———. "Isaiah xlv 7 and the Creation of Chaos?" *VT* 42 (1992) 11-21.

Dietrich, M., et al. *Die Keilalphabetischen Texte aus Ugarit*. AOAT 24. Neukirchen-Vluyn: Neukirchener, 1976.

Dijk, Jacobus van. "Paradise." In *The Ancient Gods Speak: A Guide to Egyptian Religion*, edited by Donald B. Redford, 309-11. Oxford: Oxford University Press, 2002.

Dillery, John. *Clio's Other Sons: Berossus and Manetho*. Ann Arbor: University of Michigan Press, 2015.

Doty, William G. *Mythography: The Study of Myths and Rituals*. Tuscaloosa: University of Alabama Press, 2000.

Enns, Peter. *Inspiration and Incarnation: Evangelicals and the Problem of the Old Testament*. Grand Rapids: Baker Academic, 2005.

———. *Inspiration and Incarnation: Evangelicals and the Problem of the Old Testament*. 2nd ed. Grand Rapids: Baker Academic, 2015.

Erichsen, W. *Papyrus Harris I: Hieroglyphische Transkription*. Brussels: Fondation égyptologique reine Élisabeth, 1933.

Evans-Pritchard, E. E. *Theories of Primitive Religion*. Sir D. Owen Evans Lectures 1962. Oxford: Clarendon, 1965.

Fantin, Joseph D. *The Greek Imperative Mood in the New Testament: A Cognitive and Communicative Approach*. Studies in Biblical Greek 12. New York: Lang, 2010.

Faulkner, Raymond O. *A Concise Dictionary of Middle Egyptian*. Oxford: Griffith Institute, 1962.

Finnestad, Ragnhild Bjerre. "Ptah, Creator of the Gods: Reconsideration of the Ptah Section of the Denkmal." *Numen* 23 (1976) 81-113.

Fishbane, Michael. *Biblical Interpretation in Ancient Israel.* Oxford: Clarendon, 1985.

———. "Jeremiah iv 23–26 and Job iii 3–13: A Recovered Use of the Creation Pattern." *VT* 21 (1971) 151–67.

Foster, Benjamin R. *Before the Muses: An Anthology of Akkadian Literature.* 3rd ed. Bethesda, MD: CDL, 2005.

———. "On Speculative Thought in Ancient Mesopotamia." In *The Adventure of the Human Intellect: Self, Society, and the Divine in Ancient World Cultures,* edited by Kurt A. Raaflaub, 89–104. The Ancient World: Comparative Histories. Chichester, UK: Wiley, 2016.

Frahm, Eckart. *Babylonian and Assyrian Text Commentaries: Origins of Interpretation.* GMTR 5. Münster: Ugarit-, 2011.

Frame, John M. *The Doctrine of the Word of God.* A Theology of Lordship 4. Philipsburg, NJ: P & R, 2010.

Frankfort, H., et al. *The Intellectual Adventure of Ancient Man.* Chicago: University of Chicago Press, 1946.

Funkenstein, Amos. *Theology and the Scientific Imagination from the Middle Ages to the Seventeenth Century.* Princeton: Princeton University Press, 1986.

Furlong, Anne. "A Modest Proposal: Linguistics and Literary Studies." *Canadian Journal of Applied Linguistics/Revue canadienne de linguistique appliquée* 10 (2007) 325–47.

Galambush, Julie. "God's Land and Mine: Creation as Property in the Book of Ezekiel." In *Ezekiel's Hierarchical World: Wrestling with a Tiered Reality,* edited by Stephen L. Cook and Corrine L. Patton, 91–108. SymS 31. Atlanta: SBL, 2004.

Galileo. *Discoveries and Opinions of Galileo.* Translated and introduced by Stillman Drake. Anchor Books. New York: Doubleday, 1957.

Garr, W. R. *In His Own Image and Likeness.* CHANE 15. Leiden: Brill, 2003.

Gelb, Ignace J., et al., eds. *The Assyrian Dictionary of the Oriental Institute of the University of Chicago.* 21 vols. Chicago: Oriental Institute, 1964–2010.

George, A. R. *The Babylonian Gilgamesh Epic: Introduction, Critical Edition and Cuneiform Texts.* Oxford: Oxford University Press, 2003.

George, Andrew, trans. *The Epic of Gilgamesh: A New Translation.* London: Penguin, 1999.

Glassner, Jean-Jacques. *Mesopotamian Chronicles.* Edited by Benjamin R. Foster. WAW 19. Atlanta: SBL, 2004.

Glucksberg, Sam. *Understanding Figurative Language: From Metaphor to Idioms.* Oxford Psychology Series 36. Oxford: Oxford University Press, 2001.

Goren, Y., H. Mommsen, et al. "A Provenance Study of the Gilgamesh Fragment from Megiddo." *Archaeometry* 51 (2009) 763–73.

Görg, Manfred. *Gott-König-eden in Israel und Ägypten.* BWA(N)T 105. Stuttgart: Kohlhammer, 1975.

Gray, Louis Herbert, ed. *The Mythology of All Races.* Vol. 5, *Semitic,* by Stephen Herbert Langdon. 13 vols. New York: Cooper Square, 1964.

Green, Gene L. "Lexical Pragmatics and Biblical Interpretation." *JETS* 50 (2007) 799–812.

———. "Lexical Pragmatics and the Lexicon." *BBR* 23 (2012) 315–33.

———. "Relevance Theory and Biblical Interpretation." In *The Linguist as Pedagogue: Trends in the Teaching and Linguistic Analysis of the Greek New Testament,* edited by Stanley E. Porter and Matthew Brook O'Donnell, 217–40. New Testament Monographs 11. Sheffield: Sheffield Phoenix, 2009.

———. "Relevance Theory and Biblical Interpretation." In *The Oxford Encyclopedia of Biblical Interpretation*, edited by Steven L. McKenzie, 266–73. Oxford: Oxford University Press, 2013.

———. "Relevance Theory and Theological Interpretation: Thoughts on Metarepresentation." *Journal of Theological Interpretation* 4 (2010) 75–90.

Greene-McCreight, K. E. *Ad Litteram: How Augustine, Calvin, and Barth Read the "Plain Sense" of Genesis 1–3*. Issues in Systematic Theology 5. New York: Lang, 1999.

Greenfield, Jonas C. "Apkallu." In *Dictionary of Deities and Demons in the Bible*, edited by Karel van der Toorn et al., 72–74. 2nd ed. Leiden: Brill, 1999.

Greenwood, Kyle. *Scripture and Cosmology: Reading the Bible between the Ancient World and Modern Science*. Downers Grove, IL: IVP Academic, 2015.

Grice, Paul. "Logic and Conversation." In *Studies in the Way of Words*, 22–40. Cambridge: Harvard University Press, 1967.

Gundlach, Bradley J. *Process and Providence: The Evolution Question at Princeton, 1845–1929*. Grand Rapids: Eerdmans, 2013.

Gutt, Ernst-August. "Aspects of 'Cultural Literacy' Relevant to Bible Translation." *Journal of Translation* 2 (2006) 1–16.

———. *Relevance Theory: A Guide to Successful Communication in Translation*. New York: Summer Institute of Linguistics, 1992.

———. *Translation and Relevance: Cognition and Context*. Manchester: St. Jerome, 2000.

Hallo, William W. *Origins: The Ancient Near Eastern Background of Some Modern Western Institutions*. SHANE 6. Leiden: Brill, 1996.

Hallo, William W., and K. Lawson Younger Jr., eds. *The Context of Scripture: Canonical Inscriptions, Monumental Inscriptions, and Archival Documents from the Biblical World*. 4 vols. Leiden: Brill, 1997–2017.

Hamilton, Victor P. *The Book of Genesis: Chapters 1–17*. NICOT. Grand Rapids: Eerdmans, 1990.

Harris, Robert A. "Medieval Jewish Biblical Exegesis." In *A History of Biblical Interpretation*. Vol. 2, *The Medieval through the Reformation Periods*, edited by Alan J. Hauser and Duane F. Watson, 141–71. 2 vols. Grand Rapids: Eerdmans, 2003.

Harrison, Peter. *The Bible, Protestantism, and the Rise of Natural Science*. Cambridge: Cambridge University Press, 1998.

Hasel, Gerhard F., and Michael G. Hasel. "The Unique Cosmology of Genesis 1 against Ancient Near Eastern and Egyptian Parallels." In *The Genesis Creation Account and Its Reverberations in the Old Testament*, edited by Gerald A. Klingbeil, 9–29. Berrien Springs, MI: Andrews University Press, 2015.

Hauser, Alan J., and Duane F. Watson, eds. *A History of Biblical Interpretation*. 2 vols. Grand Rapids: Eerdmans, 2003.

Hays, Christopher B. *A Covenant with Death: Death in the Iron Age II and Its Rhetorical Uses in Proto-Isaiah*. Grand Rapids: Eerdmans, 2015.

———. "Echoes of the Ancient Near East? Intertextuality and the Comparative Study of the Old Testament." In *The Word Leaps the Gap: Essays on Scripture and Theology*

in Honor of Richard B. Hays, edited by J. Ross Wagner et al., 20-43. Grand Rapids: Eerdmans, 2008.
Hays, Richard B. *Echoes of Scripture in the Letters of Paul*. New Haven: Yale University Press, 1989.
Henst, Jean-Baptiste van der, and Alexander Sperber. "Testing the Cognitive and Communicative Principles of Relevance." In *Meaning and Relevance*, by Deirdre Wilson and Dan Sperber, 279-306. Cambridge: Cambridge University Press, 2012.
Hilber, John W. "Isaiah as Prophet and Isaiah as Book in Their Ancient Near Eastern Context." In *Bind Up the Testimony: Explorations in the Genesis of the Book of Isaiah*, edited by Daniel I. Block and Richard L. Schultz, 151-74. Peabody, MA: Hendrickson, 2015.
Hildebrandt, Wilf. *An Old Testament Theology of the Spirit of God*. Peabody, MA: Hendrickson, 1995.
Hodge, Archibald Alexander. *Outlines of Theology*. New York: Armstrong, 1891.
Hodge, Charles. *Systematic Theology*. 3 vols. Grand Rapids: Eerdmans, 1952.
Hoffman, Yair. "The First Creation Story: Canonical and Diachronical Aspects." In *Creation in Jewish and Christian Tradition*, edited by Henning Graf Reventlow and Yair Hoffman, 32-53. JSOTSup 319. London: Sheffield Academic, 2002.
Hoffmeier, James K. "Egyptian Religious Influences on the Early Hebrews." In *Did I not Bring Israel Out of Egypt? Biblical, Archaeological, and Egyptological Perspectives on the Exodus Narratives*, edited by James K. Hoffmeier et al., 3-35. BBRSup 13. Winona Lake, IN: Eisenbrauns, 2016.
———. "Some Thoughts on Genesis 1 & 2 and Egyptian Cosmology." *JANES* 15 (1983) 39-49.
Hoffner, Harry A., Jr. *Hittite Myths*. Edited by Gary M. Beckman. WAW 2. Atlanta: Scholars, 1998.
Hofmann, Rudolf. "Accommodation." In *The New Schaff-Harzog Encyclopedia of Religious Knowledge*, edited by Samuel Macauley Jackson, 22-24. Grand Rapids: Baker, 1960.
Holmstead, Robert D. "Restrictive Syntax of Gen i, 1." *VT* 58 (2008) 56-67.
Hooykaas, Reijer. "Calvin and Copernicus." *Organon* 10 (1974) 139-48.
Hornung, Erik. *The Ancient Egyptian Books of the Afterlife*. Translated by David Lorton. Ithaca, NY: Cornell University Press, 1999.
Horowitz, Wayne. *Mesopotamian Cosmic Geography*. Mesopotamian Civilizations 8. Winona Lake, IN: Eisenbrauns, 2011.
Horowitz, Wayne, et al. *Cuneiform in Canaan: Cuneiform Sources from the Land of Israel in Ancient Times*. Jerusalem: Israel Exploration Society, 2006.
Houtman, Cornelis. *Der Himmel im Alten Testament: Israels Weltbild und Weltschauung*. OtSt 30. Leiden: Brill, 1993.
Howell, Kenneth J. "Natural Knowledge and Textual Meaning in Augustine's Interpretation of Genesis: The Three Functions of Natural Philosophy." In *Nature and Scripture in the Abrahamic Religions*, edited by Jitse M. van der Meer and Scott Mandelbrote, 1:117-45. 2 vols. Brill's Series in Church History 36-37. Leiden: Brill, 2008.
Huijgen, Arnold. *Divine Accommodation in John Calvin's Theology: Analysis and Assessment*. Reformed Historical Theology 16. Göttingen: Vandenhoeck & Ruprecht, 2011.

Hundley, Michael B. *Gods in Dwellings: Temples and Divine Presence in the Ancient Near East.* WAWSup 3. Atlanta: Society of Biblical Literature, 2013.
Hunger, Hermann, ed. *Astrological Reports to Assyrian Kings.* SAA 8. Helsinki: University of Helsinki Press, 1992.
Izre'el, Shlomo. *The Amarna Scholarly Tablets.* CM 9. Gröningen: Styx, 1997.
Janowski, Bernd. "Das Biblische Weltbild: Eine Methodologische Skizze." In *Das Biblische Weltbild und seine altorientalischen Kontexte,* edited by Bernd Janowski and Beate Ego, 3–36. FAT 32. Tübingen: Mohr/Siebeck, 2001.
Johnson, Elliott E. *Expository Hermeneutics: An Introduction.* Grand Rapids: Zondervan, 1990.
Johnston, Gordon H. "Genesis 1 and Ancient Egyptian Creation Myths." *BSac* 165 (2008) 178–94.
Johnston, Philip S. *Shades of Sheol: Death and Afterlife in the Old Testament.* Leicester, UK: Apollos, 2002.
Kaiser, Walter C., and Moisés Silva. *An Introduction to Biblical Hermeneutics.* Grand Rapids: Zondervan, 1994.
Kämmerer, Thomas. "Das Sintflutfragment aus Ugarit (RS 22.241)." *UF* 25 (1993) 189–200.
Kannengiesser, Charles. "Augustine of Hippo (354–430)." In *The Handbook of Patristic Exegesis,* 2:1149–218. 2 vols. The Bible in Ancient Christianity 1. Leiden: Brill, 2004.
———. "The Literal Meaning of Scripture." In *Handbook of Patristic Exegesis,* 1:167–205. 2 vols. The Bible in Ancient Christianity 1. Leiden: Brill, 2004.
Keel, Othmar. "Das Sogenannte Altorientalische Weltbild." *BK* 40 (1985) 157–61.
———. *The Symbolism of the Biblical World: Ancient Near Eastern Iconography and the Book of Psalms.* Translated by Timothy J. Hallett. New York: Seabury, 1978.
Keel, Othmar, and Silvia Schroer. *Creation: Biblical Theologies in the Context of the Ancient Near East.* Translated by Peter T. Daniels. Winona Lake, IN: Eisenbrauns, 2015.
Keel, Othmar, and Christoph Uehlinger. *Gods, Goddesses, and Images of God in Ancient Israel.* Translated by Thomas H. Trapp. Minneapolis: Fortress, 1998.
King, L. W. *Babylonian Boundary Stones and Memorial Tablets.* London: British Museum, 1912.
Kitchen, Kenneth A. "Egypt and East Africa." In *The Age of Solomon: Scholarship at the Turn of the Millennium,* edited by Lowell K. Handy, 106–26. Studies in the History and Culture of the Ancient Near East 11. Leiden: Brill, 1997.
Klauber, Martin I., and Glenn S. Sunshine. "Jean-Alphones Turrettini on Biblical Accommodation: Calvinist or Socinian?" *CTJ* 25 (1990) 7–27.
Klein, William W., et al. *Introduction to Biblical Interpretation.* 2nd ed. Nashville: Nelson, 2004.
Klingbeil, Martin G. "Creation in the Prophetic Literature of the Old Testament: An Intertextual Approach." In *The Genesis Creation Account and Its Reverberations in the Old Testament,* edited by Gerald A. Klingbeil, 257–89. Berrien Springs, MI: Andrews University Press, 2015.
Lamb, Weldon. "Tzotzil Maya Cosmology." In *Songs from the Sky: Indigenous Astronomical and Cosmological Traditions of the World,* edited by Von Del Chamberlain et al., 163–72. Bognor Regis, UK: Ocarina, 2005.

Lambert, W. G. *Babylonian Creation Myths*. Mesopotamian Civilizations 16. Winona Lake, IN: Eisenbrauns, 2013.
———. *Babylonian Wisdom Literature*. Oxford: Clarendon, 1960.
Lamoureux, Denis O. *Evolutionary Creation: A Christian Approach to Evolution*. Eugene, OR: Wipf & Stock, 2008.
Lee, Hoon J. "Accommodation—Orthodox, Socinian, and Contemporary." *WTJ* 75 (2013) 335–48.
———. "Biblical Accommodation and Authority in Eighteenth- and Nineteenth-Century Germany: The Accommodation Debate of 1761–1835." PhD diss., Trinity Evangelical Divinity School, 2014.
LeFebvre, Michael. *The Liturgy of Creation: Understanding Calendars in Old Testament Context*. Downers Grove, IL: InterVarsity, 2019.
Lemaire, André. "The United Monarchy: Saul, David and Solomon." In *Ancient Israel: From Abraham to the Roman Destruction of the Temple*, edited by Hershel Shanks, 85–128. Washington, DC: Biblical Archaeology Society, 2010.
Lesko, Leonard H. "Ancient Egyptian Cosmogonies and Cosmology." In *Religion in Ancient Egypt: Gods, Myths, and Personal Practice*, edited by Byron E. Shafer, 88–122. Ithaca, NY: Cornell University Press, 1991.
Levenson, Jon D. *Creation and the Persistence of Evil: The Jewish Drama of Divine Omnipotence*. San Francisco: Harper & Row, 1988.
Lévy-Bruhl, Lucien. *Primitive Mentality*. Translated by Lilian A. Clare. Boston: Beacon, 1966.
Lewis, D. "Voyaging Stars: Aspects of Polynesian and Micronesian Astronomy." In *The Place of Astronomy in the Ancient World*, edited by F. R. Hodson, 133–48. London: Oxford University Press for the British Academy, 1974.
Lichtheim, Miriam. *Ancient Egyptian Literature: A Book of Readings*. 3 vols. Berkeley: University of California Press, 1973–1980.
Lindberg, David C. *The Beginnings of Western Science: The European Scientific Tradition in Philosophical, Religious, and Institutional Context, Prehistory to A.D. 1450*. 2nd ed. Chicago: University of Chicago Press, 2008.
Livingstone, Alasdair, ed. *Court Poetry and Literary Miscellanea*. SAA 3. Helsinki: University of Helsinki Press, 1989.
Lloyd, G. E. R. *Ancient Worlds, Modern Reflections: Philosophical Perspectives on Greek and Chinese Science and Culture*. Oxford: Clarendon, 2004.
Longman, Tremper, III. "What Genesis 1–2 Teaches (and What It Doesn't)." In *Reading Genesis 1–2: An Evangelical Conversation*, edited by J. Daryl Charles, 103–28. Peabody, MA: Hendrickson, 2013.
Loud, Gordon. *The Megiddo Ivories*. The University of Chicago Oriental Institute Publications 52. Chicago: University of Chicago, 1939.
Lowery, Daniel DeWitt. *Toward a Poetics of Genesis 1–11: Reading Genesis 4:17–22 in Its Ancient Near Eastern Background*. BBRSup 7. Winona Lake, IN: Eisenbrauns, 2013.
Luther, Martin. *Lectures on Genesis (Chapters 1–5)*. Luther's Works 1. St. Louis: Concordia, 1958.
———. *Lectures on Genesis (Chapters 6–14)*. Luther's Works 2. St. Louis: Concordia, 1960.
———. *Word and Sacrament III*. Luther's Works 37. Philadelphia: Muhlenberg, 1961.

Mann, Thomas W. "Stars, Sprouts, and Streams: The Creative Redeemer of Second Isaiah." In *God Who Creates: Essays in Honor of W. Sibley Towner*, edited by William P. Brown and S. Dean McBride, 135–51. Grand Rapids: Eerdmans, 2000.

Mattox, Mickey L. "Cosmology." In *The Oxford Encyclopedia of Martin Luther*, edited by Derek Nelson and Paul Hinlicky, 1:296–313. 3 vols. Oxford: Oxford University Press, 2017.

McCabe, Robert V. "A Critique of the Framework Interpretation of the Creation Week." In *Coming to Grips with Genesis: Biblical Authority and the Age of the Earth*, edited by Terry Mortenson and Thane H. Ury, 211–49. Green Forest, AR: Master, 2008.

McCalla, Arthur. *The Creationist Debate: The Encounter between the Bible and the Historical Mind*. London: T. & T. Clark, 2006.

Merrick, James R. A., and Stephen M. Garrett, eds. *Five Views on Biblical Inerrancy*. Counterpoints: Bible and Theology. Grand Rapids: Zondervan, 2013.

Mettinger, Tryggve N. D. *In Search of God: The Meaning and Message of the Everlasting Names*. Translated by Frederick H. Cryer. Philadelphia: Fortress, 1988.

Mickelsen, A. Berkeley. *Interpreting the Bible*. Grand Rapids: Eerdmans, 1963.

Millard, Alan R. "Cartography in the Ancient Near East." In *The History of Cartography*. Vol. 1, *Cartography in Prehistoric, Ancient, and Medieval Europe and the Mediterranean*, edited by J. B. Harley and David Woodward, 107–16. 6 vols. in 5. Chicago: University of Chicago Press, 1987.

Miller, Johnny V., and John M. Soden. *In the Beginning . . . We Misunderstood: Interpreting Genesis 1 in Its Original Context*. Grand Rapids: Kregal, 2012.

Molen, Rami van der. *A Hieroglyphic Dictionary of Egyptian Coffin Texts*. PAe 15. Leiden: Brill, 2000.

Muller, Richard A. *Post-Reformation Reformed Dogmatics: The Rise and Development of Reformed Orthodoxy, ca. 1520 to ca. 1725*. Grand Rapids: Baker Academic, 2003.

Muráň, Alexej. "The Creation Theme in Selected Psalms." In *The Genesis Creation Account and Its Reverberations in the Old Testament*, edited by Gerald A. Klingbeil, 189–223. Berrien Springs, MI: Andrews University Press, 2015.

Needham, Joseph. "Astronomy in Ancient and Medieval China." In *The Place of Astronomy in the Ancient World*, edited by F. R. Hodson, 67–82. Oxford: Oxford University Press for the British Academy, 1974.

———. "The Cosmology of Early China." In *Ancient Cosmologies*, edited by Carmen Blacker and Michael Loewe, with contributions by J. M. Plumley et al., 87–109. London: Allen & Unwin, 1975.

Neugebauer, Otto. *The Exact Sciences in Antiquity*. 2nd ed. 1957. Reprint, New York: Dover, 1969.

Nobes, Gavin, and Georgia Panagiotaki. "Mental Models or Methodological Artefacts? Adults' 'Naïve' Responses to a Test of Children's Conceptions of the Earth." *British Journal of Psychology* 100 (2009) 347–63.

Noll, Mark. *The Princeton Theology (1812–1921)*. Grand Rapids: Baker Academic, 2001.

Norris, Richard A., Jr. "Augustine and the Close of the Ancient Period." In *A History of Biblical Interpretation*. Vol. 1, *The Ancient Period*, edited by Alan J. Houser and Duane F. Watson, 380–408. 2 vols. Grand Rapids: Eerdmans, 2003.

O'Connor, David. "From Topography to Cosmos: Ancient Egypt's Multiple Maps." In *Ancient Perspectives: Maps and Their Place in Mesopotamia, Egypt, Greece, and Rome*, edited by Richard J. A. Talbert, 47–79. The Kenneth Nebenzahl, Jr., Lectures in the History of Cartography. Chicago: University of Chicago, 2012.

Ocker, Christopher. "Scholastic Interpretation of the Bible." In *A History of Biblical Interpretation*. Vol. 2, *The Medieval through the Reformation Periods*, edited by Alan J. Houser and Duane F. Watson, 254–79. 2 vols. Grand Rapids: Eerdmans, 2003.

Ogonowski, Zbigniew. "Faustus Socinus." In *Shapers of Religious Traditions in Germany, Switzerland, and Poland, 1560–1600*, edited by Jill Raitt, 195–209. New Haven: Yale University Press, 1981.

Olmo Lete, Gregorio del. *Canaanite Religion according to the Liturgical Texts of Ugarit*. Translated by Wilfred G. E. Watson. Bethesda, MD: CDL, 1999.

Oswalt, John N. "*Creatio ex Nihilo*: An Exploration of the Biblical Message." Unpublished paper delivered at the Dabar Conference, Henry Center–Trinity Evangelical Divinity School, Deerfield, IL, June 2017.

———. "Creation Ex Nihilo: Is It Biblical, and Does It Matter?" *Trinity Journal* 39 (2018) 165–80.

Otten, Heinrich, and Jana Siegelova. "Die Hethitischen Gulš-Gottheiten und die Erschaffung der Menschen." *AfO* 23 (1970) 32–38.

Overland, Paul. "Paleographic Dating of the Egyptian Museum Ostracon of *the Wisdom of Amenemope* (EM 1840–4)." Paper presented at the Wisdom in Israelite and Cognate Traditions Section of the SBL, Chicago, IL, November 2012.

———. "Structure in the Wisdom of Amenemope and Proverbs." In *"Go to the Land I Will Show You": Studies in Honor of Dwight W. Young*, edited by Joseph E. Coleson and Victor H. Matthews, 275–91. Winona Lake, IN: Eisenbrauns, 1996.

Parker, R. A. "Ancient Egyptian Astronomy." In *The Place of Astronomy in the Ancient World*, edited by F. R. Hodson, 51–65. Oxford: Oxford University Press for the British Academy, 1974.

Parker, Simon B., ed. *Ugaritic Narrative Poetry*. Translated by Mark S. Smith et al. WAW 9. Atlanta: Scholars, 1997.

Parpola, Simo, ed. *Assyrian Prophecies*. SAA 9. Helsinki: University of Helsinki Press, 1997.

———. *Letters from Assyrian and Babylonian Scholars*. SAA 10. Helsinki: University of Helsinki Press, 1993.

Pattemore, Stephen. *The People of God in the Apocalypse: Discourse, Structure and Exegesis*. SNTSMS 128. Cambridge: Cambridge University Press, 2004.

Petersen, David L. "Creation and Hierarchy in Ezekiel: Methodological Perspectives and Theological Prospects." In *Ezekiel's Hierarchical World: Wrestling with a Tiered Reality*, edited by Stephen L. Cook and Corrine L. Patton, 169–78. SymS 31. Atlanta: SBL, 2004.

Pitard, Wayne T. "The 'Libation Installations' of the Tombs at Ugarit." *BA* 57 (1994) 20–37.

Plantinga, Alvin. *Where the Conflict Really Lies: Science, Religion, and Naturalism*. Oxford: Oxford University Press, 2011.

Pongratz-Leisten, Beate. "*Mental Map* und Weltbild in Mesopotamien." In *Das Biblische Weltbild und seine altorientalischen Kontexte*, edited by Bernd Janowski and Beate Ego, 261–79. FAT 32. Tübingen: Mohr/Siebeck, 2001.

Poythress, Vern S. "Adequacy of Language and Accommodation." In *Hermeneutics, Inerrancy, and the Bible: Papers From ICBI Summit II*, edited by Earl D. Radmacher and Robert D. Preus, 351–76. Grand Rapids: Zondervan, 1984.

———. "Genesis 1:1 Is the First Event, Not a Summary." *WTJ* 79 (2017) 97–121.

———. *Interpreting Eden: A Guide to Faithfully Reading and Understanding Genesis 1–3*. Wheaton, IL: Crossway, 2019.

———. "Rain Water versus a Heavenly Sea in Genesis 1:6–8." *WTJ* 77 (2015) 181–91.

———. "Three Modern Myths in Interpreting Genesis 1." *WTJ* 76 (2014) 321–50.

Pritchard, James B., ed. *Ancient Near Eastern Texts Relating to the Old Testament*. 3rd ed. Princeton: Princeton University Press, 1969.

Reventlow, Henning Graf. *History of Biblical Interpretation*. Vol. 2, *From Late Antiquity to the End of the Middle Ages*. Translated by James O. Duke. RBS 61. Atlanta: SBL, 2009.

Richardson, Peter, and Paul W. Gooch. "Accommodation Ethics." *TynBul* 29 (1978) 89–142.

Robins, Gay. "Mathematics, Astronomy, and Calendars in Pharaonic Egypt." In *Civilizations of the Ancient Near East*, edited by Jack M. Sasson et al., 3:1799–1813. 4 vols. 1996. Reprint, 4 vols. in 2. Peabody, MA: Hendrickson, 2000.

Rochberg, Francesca. *Before Nature: Cuneiform Knowledge and the History of Science*. Chicago: University of Chicago Press, 2016.

———. "A Critique of the Cognitive-Historical Thesis of *the Intellectual Adventure*." In *The Adventure of the Human Intellect: Self, Society, and the Divine in Ancient World Cultures*, edited by Kurt A. Raaflaub, 16–28. The Ancient World: Comparative Histories. Chichester, UK: Wiley, 2016.

———. "The Expression of Terrestrial and Celestial Order in Ancient Mesopotamia." In *Ancient Perspectives: Maps and Their Place in Mesopotamia, Egypt, Greece & Rome*, edited by Richard J. A. Talbert, 9–46. The Kenneth Nebenzahl, Jr., Lectures in the History of Cartography. Chicago: University of Chicago Press, 2012.

———. *The Heavenly Writing: Divination, Horoscopy, and Astronomy in Mesopotamian Culture*. Cambridge: Cambridge University Press, 2004.

———. "Mesopotamian Cosmology." In *A Companion to the Ancient Near East*, edited by Daniel C. Snell, 316–29. Blackwell Companions to the Ancient World. Ancient History. Malden, MA: Blackwell, 2005.

Roe, Peter G. "Mythic Substitution and the Stars: Aspects of Shipibo and Quechua Ethnoastronomy Compared." In *Songs from the Sky: Indigenous Astronomical and Cosmological Traditions of the World*, edited by Von Del Chamberlain et al., 193–228. Bognor Regis, UK: Ocarina, 2005.

Rogers, Jack B., and Donald K. McKim. *The Authority and Interpretation of the Bible: An Historical Approach*. San Francisco: Harper & Row, 1979.

Rollston, Christopher A. "Inscriptional Evidence for the Writing of the Earliest Texts of the Bible: Intellectual Infrastructure in Tenth- and Ninth-Century Israel, Judah, and the Southern Levant." In *The Formation of the Pentateuch: Bridging the Academic Cultures of Europe, Israel, and North America*, edited by Jan C. Gertz et al., 15–45. FAT 111. Tübingen: Mohr/Siebeck, 2016.

———. "Scribal Curriculum during the First Temple Period: Epigraphic Hebrew and Biblical Evidence." In *Contextualizing Israel's Sacred Writings: Ancient Literacy, Orality, and Literary Production*, edited by Brian B. Schmidt, 71–101. Society of Biblical Literature: Ancient Israel and Its Literature 22. Atlanta: SBL Press, 2015.

Rumelhart, David E. "Some Problems with the Notion of Literal Meanings." In *Metaphor and Thought*, edited by Andrew Ortony, 71–82. Cambridge: Cambridge University Press, 1993.

Rutten, Jacques T. A. G. M. van. "Back to Chaos: The Relationship Between Jeremiah 4:23–26 and Genesis 1." In *The Creation of Heaven and Earth: Re-Interpretation of Genesis 1 in the Context of Judaism, Ancient Philosophy, Christianity, and Modern Physics*, edited by George H. van Kooten, 21–30. TBN 8. Leiden: Brill, 2005.

Schroer, Silvia, and Othmar Keel. *Die Ikonographie Palästinas/Israels und der Alte Orient: Eine Religionsgeschichte in Bildern*. Vol. 2, *Die Mittelbronzezeit*. 4 vols. Fribourg: Academic Press, 2008.

———. *Die Ikonographie Palästinas/Israels und der Alte Orient: Eine Religionsgeschichte in Bildern*. Vol. 3, *Die Spätbronzezeit*. Fribourg: Academic Press, 2011.

Schroer, Silvia, and Othmar Keel. *Die Ikonographie Palästinas/Israels und der Alte Orient: Eine Religionsgeschichte in Bildern*. Vol. 1, *Vom Ausgehenden Mesolithikum bis zur Frühbronzezeit*. Fribourg: Academic Press, 2005.

Scurlock, JoAnn. "Death and the Afterlife in Ancient Mesopotamian Thought." In *Civilizations of the Ancient Near East*, edited by Jack M. Sasson, 3:1883–93. 4 vols. 1996. Reprint, Peabody, MA: Hendrickson, 2000.

———. "Divination between Religion and Science." In *Divination as Science: A Workshop Conducted during the 60th Rencontre Assyriologique Internationale, Warsaw, 2014*, edited by Jeanette C. Fincke, 1–10. Winona Lake, IN: Eisenbrauns, 2016.

———. "Searching for Meaning in Genesis 1:2: Purposeful Creation out of Chaos without Kampf." In *Creation and Chaos: A Reconsideration of Hermann Gunkel's Chaoskampf Hypothesis*, edited by JoAnn Scurlock and Richard H. Beal, 48–61. Winona Lake, IN: Eisenbrauns, 2013.

Scurlock, JoAnn, and F. Al-Rawi. "A Weakness for Hellenism." In *If a Man Builds a Joyful House: Assyriological Studies in Honor of Erle Verdun Leichty*, edited by Ann K. Guinan et al., 357–82. CM 31. Leiden: Brill, 2006.

Searle, John R. *Speech Acts: An Essay in the Philosophy of Language*. Cambridge: Cambridge University Press, 1969.

Seely, Paul H. "The Firmament and the Water Above. Part I: The Meaning of *raqia'* in Genesis 1." *WTJ* 53 (1991) 227–40.

———. "The Firmament and the Water Above. Part II: The Meaning of 'the Water above the Firmament' in Gen 1:6–8." *WTJ* 54 (1992) 31–46.

———. "The Geographical Meaning of 'Earth' and 'Seas' in Genesis 1:10." *WTJ* 59 (1997) 231–55.

Segal, Robert A. "The Modern Study of Myth and Its Relation to Science." *Zygon* 50 (2015) 757–71.

———. *Theorizing about Myth*. Amherst: University of Massachusetts Press, 1999.

Shedd, William G. T. *Dogmatic Theology*. 3 vols. Limited Classical Reprint Library. Minneapolis: Klock & Klock, 1979.

Shupak, Nili. "The Contribution of Egyptian Wisdom to the Study of Biblical Wisdom Books." In *Was There a Wisdom Tradition? New Prospects in Israelite Wisdom Studies*, edited by Mark R. Sneed, 265–304. SBL Ancient Israel and Its Literature 23. Atlanta: SBL Press, 2015.

———. "The Instruction of Amenemope and Proverbs 22:17–24:22 from the Perspective of Contemporary Research." In *Seeking Out the Wisdom of the Ancients: Essays Offered to Honor Michael V. Fox on the Occasion of His Sixty-Fifth Birthday*, edited by Ronald L. Troxel et al., 203–20. Winona Lake, IN: Eisenbrauns, 2005.

Silva, Moisés. "Old Princeton, Westminster, and Inerrancy." *WTJ* 50 (1988) 65–80.

Sim, Margaret G. *A Relevant Way to Read: A New Approach to Exegesis and Communication.* Eugene, OR: Pickwick Publications, 2016.
Smith, Mark S. *The Priestly Vision of Genesis 1.* Minneapolis: Fortress, 2010.
Snobelen, Stephen D. "'In the Language of Men': The Hermeneutics of Accommodation in the Scientific Revolution." In *Nature and Scripture in the Abrahamic Religions.* Vol. 1, *Up to 1700*, edited by Jitse M. van der Meer and Scott Mandelbrote, 691–732. 2 vols. Brill's Series in Church History 36–37. Leiden: Brill, 2008.
Socinus, Faustus. *An Argument for the Authority of Holy Scripture; From the Latin of Socinus, After the Steinfurt Copy.* Translated by Edward Combe. London: Meadows, 1731.
———. "Epitome of a Colloquium Held in Raków in the Year 1601." In *The Polish Brethren: Documentation of the History and Thought of Unitarianism in the Polish-Lithuanian Commonwealth and in the Diaspora, 1601–1685*, edited by George H. Williams, 1:83–126. 2 vols. HTS 30. Missoula, MT: Scholars, 1980.
Spalinger, Anthony J. "Calendars." In *The Oxford Encyclopedia of Ancient Egypt*, edited by Donald B. Redford, 1:224–27. 3 vols. Oxford: Oxford University Press, 2001.
Sparks, Kenton L. *God's Word in Human Words: An Evangelical Appropriation of Critical Biblical Scholarship.* Grand Rapids: Baker Academic, 2008.
Sperber, Dan. "Intuitive and Reflective Beliefs." *Mind and Language* 12 (1997) 67–83.
Sperber, Dan, and Deirdre Wilson. "Pragmatics." In *The Oxford Handbook of Contemporary Philosophy*, edited by Frank Jackson and Michael Smith, 468–501. Oxford: Oxford University Press, 2005.
———. "Précis of Relevance: Communication and Cognition." In *The Semantics-Pragmatics Boundary in Philosophy*, edited by Maite Ezcurdia and Robert J. Stainton, 220–46. Peterborough, ON: Broadview, 2013.
———. *Relevance: Communication and Cognition.* The Language and Thought Series. Cambridge: Harvard University Press, 1986.
———. *Relevance: Communication and Cognition.* 2nd ed. Oxford: Blackwell, 1995.
Spinoza, Baruch. *Theological-Political Treatise.* 2nd ed Translated by Samuel Shirley. Indianapolis: Hackett, 2001.
Sproul, Barbara C. *Primal Myths: Creating the World.* San Francisco: Harper & Row, 1979.
Stadelmann, Luis I. J. *The Hebrew Conception of the World: A Philological and Literary Study.* AnBib 39. Rome: Pontifical Biblical Institute Press, 1970.
Stemmer, Brigitte. "Neuropragmatics." In *The Oxford Handbook of Pragmatics*, edited by Yan Huang, 1–30. Oxford: Oxford University Press, 2013.
Sternberg, Robert J., and Karin Sternberg. *Cognitive Psychology.* 7th ed. Boston: Cengage Learning, 2017.
Strong, Augustus Hopkins. *Systematic Theology.* 3 vols. Philadelphia: Judson, 1907.
Sunshine, Glenn S. "Accommodation in Calvin and Socinus: A Study in Contrast." MA thesis, Trinity Evangelical Divinity School, 1985.
———. "Accommodation Historically Considered." In *The Enduring Authority of the Christian Scriptures*, edited by D. A. Carson, 238–65. Grand Rapids: Eerdmans, 2016.
Talon, Philippe. *The Standard Babylonian Creation Myth: Enūma Eliš.* State Archives of Assyria Cuneiform Texts 4. Helsinki: University of Helsinki Neo-Assyrian Text Corpus Project, 2005.

Toorn, Karel van der. *Sin and Sanction in Israel and Mesopotamia: A Comparative Study.* SSN 22. Assen: Van Gorcum, 1985.
Trotter, David. "Analysing Literary Prose: The Relevance of Relevance Theory." *Lingua* 87 (1992) 11–27.
Tsumura, David Tashio. *Creation and Destruction: A Reappraisal of the "Chaoskampf" Theory in the Old Testament.* Winona Lake, IN: Eisenbrauns, 2005.
———. "The Creation Motif in Psalm 74:12–14? A Reappraisal of the Theory of the Dragon Myth." *JBL* 134 (2015) 547–55.
———. "The Doctrine of Creation *Ex Nihilo* and the Translation of *tōhû wābōhû*." In *Pentateuchal Traditions in the Late Second Temple Period: Proceedings of the International Workshop in Tokyo, August 28-31, 2007,* edited by Akio Moriya and Gohei Hata, 1–21. JSJSup 158. Leiden: Brill, 2012.
———. *The Earth and the Waters in Genesis 1 and 2: A Linguistic Investigation.* JSOTSup 83. Sheffield: Sheffield Academic, 1989.
Tucker, Gene M. "The Peaceable Kingdom and a Covenant with the Wild Animals." In *God Who Creates: Essays in Honor of W. Sibley Towner,* edited by William P. Brown and S. Dean McBride, 215–25. Grand Rapids: Eerdmans, 2000.
Tuell, Steven. "The Rivers of Paradise: Ezekiel 47:1–12 and Genesis 2:10–14." In *God Who Creates: Essays in Honor of W. Sibley Towner,* edited by William P. Brown and S. Dean McBride, 171–89. Grand Rapids: Eerdmans, 2000.
Unger, Christoph. *Genre, Relevance and Global Coherence: The Pragmatics of Discourse Type.* Palgrave Studies in Pragmatics, Language and Cognition. Basingstoke, UK: Palgrave Macmillan, 2006.
Van de Mieroop, Marc. *Philosophy before the Greeks: The Pursuit of Truth in Ancient Babylonia.* Princeton: Princeton University Press, 2016.
Vanhoozer, Kevin J. "Augustinian Inerrancy: Literary Meaning, Literal Truth, and Literate Interpretation in the Economy of Biblical Discourse." In *Five Views on Biblical Inerrancy,* edited by James R. A. Merrick and Stephen M. Garrett, 199–235. Counterpoints: Bible and Theology. Grand Rapids: Zondervan, 2013.
———. "From Speech Acts to Scripture Acts." In *After Pentecost: Language and Biblical Interpretation,* edited by Craig Bartholomew et al., 1–49. Scripture and Hermeneutics 2. Grand Rapids: Zondervan, 2001.
———. *Is There a Meaning in This Text? The Bible, the Reader, and the Morality of Literary Knowledge.* Grand Rapids: Zondervan, 1998.
Veenhof, K. R. "The Old Assyrian *Hamuštum* Period." *Jaarbericht van het vooraziatisch-egyptisch Genootschap Ex Orient Lux* 34 (1995) 5–26.
Vogt, Hermann J. "Origen of Alexandria (185–253)." In *Handbook of Patristic Exegesis: The Bible in Ancient Christianity,* edited by Charles Kannengiesser, 1:536–74. 2 vols. Leiden: Brill, 2004.
Waltke, Bruce K. *The Book of Proverbs.* Vol. 1, *Chapters 1–15.* 2 vols. NICOT. Grand Rapids: Eerdmans, 2004.
———. "The Creation Account in Genesis 1:1–3, Part III: The Initial Chaos Theory and the Precreation Chaos Theory." *BSac* 132 (1975) 216–28.
Walton, John H. *Genesis 1 as Ancient Cosmology.* Winona Lake, IN: Eisenbrauns, 2011.
———. "Interactions in the Ancient Cognitive Environment." In *Behind the Scenes of the Old Testament: Cultural, Social, and Historical Contexts,* edited by Jonathan S. Greer et al., 333–39. Grand Rapids: Baker Academic, 2018.

———. *The Lost World of Genesis One: Ancient Cosmology and the Origins Debate*. Downers Grove, IL: IVP Academic, 2009.

———. "Reading Genesis 1 as Ancient Cosmology." In *Reading Genesis 1–2: An Evangelical Conversation*, edited by J. Daryl Charles, 141–69. Peabody, MA: Hendrickson, 2013.

Walton, John H., and D. Brent Sandy. *The Lost World of Scripture: Ancient Literary Culture and Biblical Authority*. Downers Grove, IL: IVP Academic, 2013.

Warfield, Benjamin Breckinridge. "The Biblical Idea of Inspiration." In *The Inspiration and Authority of the Bible*, 131–66. Philadelphia: P & R, 1948. Reprint, 1970.

———. "On the Antiquity and the Unity of the Human Race." In *Biblical and Theological Studies by Benjamin Breckinridge Warfield*, edited by Samuel G. Craig, 238–61. Philadelphia: P & R, 1968.

———. "The Real Problem of Inspiration." In *The Inspiration and Authority of the Bible*, 169–226. Philadelphia: P & R, 1948. Reprint, 1970.

Watson, Rebecca S. *Chaos Uncreated: A Reassessment of the Theme of "Chaos" in the Hebrew Bible*. BZAW 341. Berlin: de Gruyter, 2005.

Watson, Rita, and Wayne Horowitz. *Writing Science before the Greeks: A Naturalistic Analysis of the Babylonian Astronomical Treatise MUL.APIN*. CHANE 48. Leiden: Brill, 2011.

Weeks, Kent R. "Medicine, Surgery, and Public Health in Ancient Egypt." In *Civilizations of the Ancient Near East*, edited by Jack M. Sasson, 3:1787–98. 4 vols. 1996. Reprint, Peabody, MA: Hendrickson, 2000.

Weeks, Noel K. "Cosmology in Historical Context." *WTJ* 68 (2006) 283–93.

Weinfeld, Moshe. "Sabbath, Temple and the Enthronement of the Lord—the Problem of the *Sitz im Leben* of Genesis 1:1–2:3." In *Mélanges bibliques et orientaux en l'honneur de M. Henri Cazelles*, edited by A. Caquot and M. Delcor, 501–12. AOAT 212. Kevelaer: Butzon & Bercker, 1981.

Wellman, Henry M., and Susan A. Gelman. "Cognitive Development: Foundational Theories of Core Domains." *Annual Review of Psychology* 43 (1992) 337–75.

Wesselschmidt, Quentin F., ed. *Psalms 51–150*. ACCS: Old Testament 8. Downers Grove, IL: InterVarsity, 2007.

Wilson, Deirdre. "Relevance Theory and Literary Interpretation." In *Reading beyond the Code: Literature and Relevance Theory*, edited by Terrence Cave and Deirdre Wilson, 185–204. Oxford: Oxford University Press, 2018.

Wilson, Deirdre, and Dan Sperber. "Inference and Implicature." In *Pragmatics: A Reader*, edited by Steven Davis, 377–93. New York: Oxford University Press, 1991.

———. "Relevance and the Interpretation of Literary Works." *UCL Working Papers in Linguistics* 23 (2011) 69–80.

———. "Relevance Theory." In *The Handbook of Pragmatics*, edited by Laurence R. Horn and Gregory L. Ward, 607–32. Blackwell Handbooks in Linguistics 16. Oxford: Blackwell, 2004.

———. "Truthfulness and Relevance." In *Meaning and Relevance*, edited by Deirdre Wilson and Dan Sperber, 47–83. Cambridge: Cambridge University Press, 2012.

Wilson, Robert R. "Creation and New Creation: The Role of Creation Imagery in the Book of Daniel." In *God Who Creates: Essays in Honor of W. Sibley Towner*, edited by William P. Brown and S. Dean McBride, 190–203. Grand Rapids: Eerdmans, 2000.

Winther-Nielsen, Nicolai. "'In the Beginning' of Biblical Hebrew Discourse: Genesis 1:1 and the Fronted Time Expression." In *Language in Context: Essays for Robert E. Longacre*, edited by Shin Ja J. Hwang and William R. Merrifield, 67–80. Summer Institute of Linguistics; the University of Texas at Arlington Publications in Linguistics 107. Dallas: Summer Institute of Linguistics and the University of Texas at Arlington, 1992.

Woodbridge, John D. *Biblical Authority: A Critique of the Rogers/McKim Proposal*. Grand Rapids: Zondervan, 1982.

Woods, Christopher E. "The Sun-God Tablet of Nabû-apla-iddina Revisited." *JCS* 56 (2004) 23–103.

Wright, J. Edward. *The Early History of Heaven*. Oxford: Oxford University Press, 2000.

Young, Davis A. *The Biblical Flood: A Case Study of the Church's Response to Extrabiblical Evidence*. Grand Rapids: Eerdmans, 1995.

Young, Frances. "Alexandrian and Antiochene Exegesis." In *A History of Biblical Interpretation*. Vol. 1, *The Ancient Period*, edited by Alan J. Hauser and Duane F. Watson, 334–54. 2 vols. Grand Rapids: Eerdmans, 2003.

Young, M. Jane. "Astronomy in Pueblo and Navajo World Views." In *Songs from the Sky: Indigenous Astronomical and Cosmological Traditions of the World*, edited by Von Del Chamberlain et al., 49–64. Bognor Regis–W. Sussex, UK: Ocarina, 2005.

Younker, Randall W., and Richard M. Davidson. "The Myth of the Solid Heavenly Dome: Another Look at the Hebrew רקיע (*rāqîaʿ*)." In *The Genesis Creation Account and Its Reverberations in the Old Testament*, edited by Gerald A. Klingbeil, 31–56. Berrien Springs, MI: Andrews University Press, 2015.

Ancient Texts Index

OLD TESTAMENT

Genesis

Reference	Pages
1:1–2:3	16, 176n66
1	2, 3, 4, 8, 15, 16, 18, 19, 25, 26, 27, 29, 30, 30n106, 33, 33n126, 35, 36, 36n141, 36n139, 37n141, 38, 38n143, 39, 41, 42, 46n7, 46n9, 78, 79, 80, 81, 85, 87, 88, 89, 91, 92, 93, 94, 95, 98, 99, 111, 112, 114, 125, 143, 148, 149, 150, 153, 154, 154n2, 155, 155n4, 156, 156n9, 157, 157n11, 158, 159, 162, 162n34, 163, 164, 165, 166, 167, 168, 169, 170, 170n54, 171n57, 174, 175, 175n64, 176, 178, 178n70, 179, 180, 180n74, 181, 182, 183, 184
1:1–3	26n81, 176
1:1–2	177
1:1	26, 26n81, 27, 28, 90, 92, 93, 113, 172, 175, 175n63, 175n64, 176, 176n66, 176n67, 177, 177n67, 180
1:2–3	175, 175n64, 180
1:2	29, 30, 113, 158, 158n14, 160, 162, 163, 168, 173, 178, 179, 180, 181
1:4	31n114
1:6–10	169
1:6–8	31n112, 78, 138, 147, 148, 150, 165, 173
1:6	96n66, 100, 102n85
1:7	31n114, 78, 79, 80, 148, 149, 150, 168
1:8	81
1:9–10	31, 165, 166
1:9	163
1:12	157
1:14–18	147
1:14–15	80
1:14	147
1:16	91, 101, 146, 157, 173
1:20–21	163
1:20	80
1:21–22	157
1:26–28	166
1:26	182
1:29	163
1:30	163
1:31	35
2	36, 87, 99, 162, 162n34
2:1	28, 176n66

2:1–2	158
2:2–3	34
2:3	34
2:4–7	176, 176n66
2:4	176n66, 180
2:7	33
2:10–14	162, 163
3	168
3:1	177n67
3:22	182
4:1	177n67
6:6	96
6:7	164
6:13	159n21
6:20	162n34
7:4	164
7:11	77, 111
7:14	162n34
8:2	77
8:8	164
8:17	163
8:19	163
8:22	147, 159
9:2	163
15:1	177n67
16:1	177n67
16:7	76
19:23	74, 144, 145
22:1	177n67
24:1	177n67
24:64	80n148
32:31	144
39:1	177n67
41:38	178n69
43:1	177n67

Exodus

2:10	21
4:15	136
14:2	76n133
16:4–5	155
16:22-26	155
19:1	177n67
20:4	72n121, 76
20:11	38n144, 72, 155, 156, 156n9, 158, 170, 182
21:2	155n7
23:12	34n131
24:1	177n67
24:10	73, 81
24:11	73, 155n4
24:16	37n143
25:1	37n143, 156n9
30:11	37n143, 156n9
30:17	37n143, 156n9
30:22	37n143, 156n9
30:34	37n143, 156n9
31:1	156n9
31:3	178n69
31:12–17	37n143, 156
31:12	156n9
31:13	155n7
31:17	156, 170
34:1	37n143, 156n9
34:12	37n143, 156n9

Leviticus

1	141
1:9	140, 141
3:5	141
7:15	141
8:33–35	37, 156n9
11	162, 162n34
17:7	161
23:3	38n143
23:7	38n143
23:15	155n7
23:24	155n7
23:36	38n143
25:1–7	155n7
25:8	155n7
26:6	163
26:22	163

Numbers

16:31-34	73
24:6	76
29:17–32	38n143

Deuteronomy

4:17	81

4:18	76	6:32	77
5:8	72n121, 76	6:38	37n143, 156n9
5:15	155	8:2	37n143
13:7	75	8:31–53	37n143
14	162, 162n34	8:65	37n143, 156n9
16:6	74	9:8	161
28:49	75	9:16	21
28:64	75	10:28–29	21
32:10	159	18:43–45	77
32:11	178	22:19	182
32:17	161		
33:2	74		
33:28	78		

Joshua

6:15–16	38n143
10:12–13	74n126
24:1–2	177n67

2 Kings

2:11	73
3:22	74n125
16:10–11	22

2 Chronicles

2:4	155n7
7:8–9	156n9
7:8–10	37n143
11:15	161

Judges

3:16	79
4:16	8n10
5	8n10
14:12	37n143

Nehemiah

9:6	72n118

1 Samuel

2:8	76
4:18	80n148
5:6	161
10:10	178
17:46	162n34
21:10	162n34
28	123, 143
28:11-15	143, 149
28:13	73, 144

Job

1:6	182
1:12	169
2:6	169
2:13	37n143
3:8	169
5:19	37n143
6:18	159
9:6	76
9:7	74
11:8–9	72n121
12:24	159
26:5–6	72n121
26:7	160
26:11	76
37:18	78n141
38	169
38:1–11	163
38:7	180
38:8–11	169, 170

2 Samuel

3:24	74
16:14	34n131, 156

1 Kings

3:1	21
5	22

38:13	75n129
38:16–17	77
38:34	77n138
38:37	78n141

Psalms

1:3	76n133
8	166
11:4	81
12:6	38n143
19:1–6	172
19:1	81, 165
19:4–5	74
19:4	75
24:2	76, 76n133, 111, 160, 165
33	166–67
33:6	158n15, 166, 178, 178n69
33:8–9	166
33:9	178
33:10–19	166
36:5	80n148
46:1–3	160
50:12–13	141
57:10	80n148
58:4–5	142–43, 149
58:4	103, 107, 123, 137n12
69:34	72n118
74	167–8
74:12–17	169
74:13–15	168
74:13–14	167
74:16–17	147, 167
75:3	76
77:17	78n141
79:2	162n34
82:1	182
82:6–7	182
89:6	78n141
89:37	78n141
90:2	181
96:11	72n118
102:25–27	181
104	167–68
104:2	168
104:3	164
104:5	76n133
104:6	181
104:14–15	168
104:19	174
104:20–22	168
104:23	168
106:37	161
107:40	159
108:4	80n148
108:5	80n148
135:6	72
135:7	77n138
136:6	76, 111, 165
136:7	101n82
136:7–9	174
139:8–9	72n121
146:6	72n118
148	80
148:1–4	80
148:1–2	81
148:1	72
148:3	174
148:4	80, 100
148:7	72
150:1	81

Proverbs

3:19–20	72, 159n21, 169
3:19	176n66
3:20	78n141
6:16–19	37n143
8:22–31	159n21
8:22–29	169
8:24	77, 181
8:27–29	169, 176n66, 181
8:27	111
8:28	78n141
8:29	163
22–24	21, 171
25:14	77n138
26:25	38n143
30:15	37n143
30:18	37n143
30:21	37n143
30:29	37n143

Ecclesiastes

1:5	74, 75n127
11:2	37n143

Song of Solomon

1:6	145

Isaiah

11	158
11:12	75
13:10	158
13:20–22	161
19:5–7	167
24–27	161
24:1	161
24:6	161
24:10	161
24:12	161
25:8	161
27:1	158n14, 169
34:14	161
40:1	136
40:13	157
40:18	157
40:28	158
41:4	180
44:6	180
45:7	158, 180
45:18	176n66, 180
46:1	172
46:10	180
48:12–13	180
48:13	176n66
48:28	180
51:9–11	158n14
58:10	74n125
60:19–20	158
65:25	158
66	158
66:17	176n66
66:22–23	155n7
66:22	176n66

Jeremiah

4:7	159
4:9	161
4:23–29	159
4:23–26	154n2
4:23–24	162
4:23	29, 158, 159, 160, 160n25, 168, 169
4:24	160
4:25	159
4:26	160
4:28	160
5:24	159
9:10–11	159
10:11	159
16:4	159n20
19:17	159n20
27:5	159
31:35	159
32:17	159
33:20	159
32:27	159
33:2	159
33:10	159
33:12	159
33:25	159
50:39	159
51:15–19	159n21
51:37	159
51:42–43	159

Ezekiel

1:22	81, 81n149
1:25	79
11:24	178n69
20:20	156
25:1–32:32	38n143
28:13	162
29:5	162n34
30:18	162
31:1–18	162
31:3–5	77
31:6	162n34
32:7–8	162
36:35	162
37:26–28	163
38:20	162
45:21–25	37n143
47:1–12	163n35
47:9	163

47:10	162
48:35	163

Daniel
2:38	163
3:1	163
4:11	75
4:31	163
7	163
7:2–3	163

Hosea
2	163
2:13	163
2:18	163
2:21–23	163
4:3	163–4

Amos
4:13	164
5:8	164
5:20	164
5:26	164
8:5	155n7
8:8	160
8:9	164
9:2–3	72
9:6	164

Jonah
1:9	72n118
2:2–6	77
4:8	144, 145

Habakkuk
3:6	160
3:11	74n126

Zephaniah
1:2–3	164
1:3	72
2:14	161

Malachi
3:10	77

NEW TESTAMENT

Matthew
5:45	144n28
13:6	144n28

Mark
16:2	144n28

Luke
16	107
16:20–21	106, 107

John
1:1	89, 182
1:14–18	84
1:14	89
6	107
6:38–39	107
6:40	107
6:54	107

1 Corinthians
5:9–11	15, 135
5:9	135
9:22	116
10:19–22	103n88

2 Timothy
3:16	136

Hebrews
1:1	136

James
1:11	144n28

2 Peter

1:21   136

~

ANCIENT NEAR EASTERN

Adapa and the South Wind   20
Aqhat   38n143
Atrahasis   19, 19n52, 19n53, 33n122, 140n24
Baal Epic   37n143, 60, 60n66, 77–79, 161, 167
Babylonian Map of the World   65–66, 67n95, 67n97
Book of Caverns   61
Book of the Dead 175   28n98
Book of Nut   62n81, 70–71, 70n110
Coffin Text 76   27, 28–29, 28n98
Coffin Text 160   62
Coffin Text 714   28n98
Enki and Ninmah   27, 30
Enuma Elish   26, 26n81, 28, 31, 32, 33n122, 34, 40n151, 58–59, 59n61, 68, 68n102, 69–71, 70n105, 78–79, 79n143, 150, 157, 167, 171n59, 173, 170

Enuma Anu Enlil   27, 31, 32
Eridu Genesis   28, 34, 68
Erra Epic   171n59
Etana   67n97
Gilgamesh and the Netherworld   60–61

Gilgamesh Epic   19, 19n52, 19n53, 37n143, 38n143, 47–48, 60, 63, 140n24
Gilgamesh, Enkidu, and the Nether World   26, 30
Gudea Cylinder B   37n143
Kirta   37n143
Instruction of Merikare   33
Megiddo Ivories   19–20
Memphite Theology   27–28, 34–35, 34n133, 37n143, 178, 178n70
Papyrus Bremner-Rhind   33
Prophecies of Neferti   161
Pyramid Text 600   32, 67
Proverbs of Amenemope   21, 21n66
SAA 8 1   49
SAA 9 2   140n24, 161n30
SAA 9 3   140n24
SAA 9 9   161n30
SAA 10 236   49n17
SAA 10 241   49
Shamash Hymn   63, 65, 68n102
Song of Illikummi   26, 59
Sumerian King List   39n145
Sun God Tablet   63–65, 65n90
The Valorous Sun   63
Theogony of Dunnu   26
Twelve Caves   61
Unilingual/Bilingual Account of Creation   27, 31

Author Index

Albertz, Rainer, 73
Alexander, Robert, 20
Allen, James P., 27, 28, 29, 31, 32, 34, 51, 61, 67, 70, 71
Allert, Craig D., 87, 88
Augustine, 86, 87, 88–91, 92, 93, 101, 142, 146
Austin, J. L., 7
Averbeck, Richard E., xiii, 32, 35, 37, 48, 77, 78, 149, 150, 168
Balserak, Jon, 103, 120
Barker, William D., 161
Baroway, Israel, 94
Bartholomew, Craig G., 16
Batto, Bernard F., 30, 64
Bauks, Michaela, 40, 154, 160, 175, 177
Bavinck, Herman, 114
Beall, Todd, 8
Beck, Pirhiya, 21, 22
Benin, Stephen D., 84, 84, 86, 87, 89, 92, 94, 96, 98, 101, 103, 121, 140
Block, Daniel I., 38
Boman, Thorleif, 46
Breasted, James Henry, 28, 35
Breucker, Geert de, 40
Brown, A. J., 36, 87, 88, 89, 90, 92, 93, 94, 95, 108, 111, 112, 113
Brown, Jeannine K., 9
Brueggemann, Walter, 159
Buck, Adriann de. 27, 28
Budge, E. A. Wallis. 62
Byrne, Ryan, 20

Calvin, John, 88, 96, 98–104, 110, 114, 123, 126, 137, 142, 143
Cameron, Nigel M. de S., 113
Campos, Marcio D'Olne, 57
Carey, Susan, 52
Carston, Robyn, 13, 17, 128, 129, 131
Clifford, Hywed, 180
Clifford, Richard J., 169
Clines, David J. A., 33
Cohen, Yoram, 20
Colet, John, 94, 99
Collins, Billie Jean, 20, 59, 60, 61
Collins, C. John, xiii, 23, 40, 53, 75, 76, 94, 137, 138, 150, 156, 170, 176, 177
Collins, John J., 161
Cornelius, Izak, 44, 46, 47, 62, 64, 76, 77
Csapo, Eric, 48
Cummings, Louise, 7, 9, 37, 142
Currid, John D., 21
Davidson, Richard M., 57, 78, 81
Davies, Graham I., 21
Day, John, 40
DeRoche, Michael, 163, 164, 180
Dietrich, M., xvi
Dijk, Jacobus van, 61
Dillery, John, 40
Doty, William G., 48, 52
Enns, Peter, 44
Erichsen, W., 35
Evans-Pritchard, E. E., 54, 55
Fantin, Joseph D., xiv, 7, 9, 18

AUTHOR INDEX

Faulkner, Raymond O., 27, 33, 34, 70
Finnestad, Ragnhild Bjerre, 28, 34, 35, 37
Fishbane, Michael, 157, 159
Foster, Benjamin R., 33, 34, 49, 63, 65, 67, 68, 140
Frahm, Eckart, 171
Frame, John M., 136
Frankfort, H., 49
Funkenstein, Amos, 92, 97
Furlong, Anne, 14, 130
Galambush, Julie, 165
Galileo, 101, 102, 108
Garr, W. R., 33
Garrett, Stephen M., 121
Gelman, Susan A., 52
George, A. R., 19, 38, 60, 140
Glassner, Jean-Jacques, 39
Glucksberg, Sam, 16, 17, 139
Goren, Y. H. Mommsen, 19
Görg, Manfred, 35
Gray, Louis Herbert, 54, 55, 56
Green, Gene L., xiv, 9, 10, 11, 12, 18, 132, 152, 182
Greene-McCreight, K. E., 89, 90, 91, 99, 103
Greenfield, Jonas, 76
Greenwood, Kyle, 44, 64, 72, 75, 77
Glice, Paul, 9, 128, 129
Gooch, Paul W., 121
Gundlach, Bradley J., xiii, 115, 116, 117
Gutt, Ernst-August, 11, 12, 18
Hallo, William W., xvi, 155
Hamilton, Victor P., 178
Harris, Robert A., 92, 111
Harrison, Peter, 95, 101, 110, 111, 119
Hasel, Gerhard F., 170
Hasel, Michael, 170
Hays, Christopher B. A., 23–25, 73, 171
Hays, Richard B., 23, 171
Henst, Jean Baptiste van der, 13
Hilber, John W., 157
Hildebrandt, Wilf, 158

Hodge, Archibald Alexander, 115–16
Hodge, Charles, 114–15, 116, 119, 120
Hoffman, Yair, 154, 157
Hoffmeier, James K., xiii, 21, 27, 29, 30, 32, 33, 34, 67, 71
Hoffner, Harry A., 59
Hofmann, Rudolf, 121, 122
Holmstead, Robert D., 175
Hooykaas, Jeijer, 103
Hornung, Erik, 32, 61, 62, 70
Horowitz, Wayne, 19, 20, 28, 31, 32, 47, 48, 50, 52, 59, 60, 61, 65, 66, 67, 68, 69, 70, 71, 75
Houtmann, Cornelius, 46, 76, 80
Howell, Kenneth J., 89, 90, 91
Huijgen, Arnold, 84, 86, 87, 89, 93, 94, 98, 103, 108, 110, 122
Hundley, Michael, 140, 161
Hunger, Hermann, 49
Isre'el, Shlomo, 20
Janowski, Bernd, 44, 46, 65
Johnson, Elliott E., 16
Johnston, Gordon H., 27, 29, 155
Johnston, Philip S., 73
Kaiser, Walter C., 16
Kämmerer, Thomas, 19
Kannengiesser, Charles, 88, 89
Keel, Othmar, 22, 45, 46, 47, 62, 76, 175
King, L. W., 64
Kitchen, Kenneth A., 21
Klauber, Martin I., 102, 104, 105, 106
Klein, William W., 16
Klingbeil, Martin G., 163, 165
Lamb, Weldon, 56
Lambert, W. G., 26, 27, 30, 31, 32, 33, 34, 59, 63, 68, 69, 70, 71, 79
Lamoureux, Denis O., 44
Lee, Hoon J., 104, 106, 107, 108
LeFebvre, Michael, 156
Lemaire, André, 21
Lesko, Leonard H., 61, 62, 67, 71
Levenson, Jon D., 38, 156
Lévy-Bruhl, Lucien, 54, 55

AUTHOR INDEX

Lewis, D., 55
Lichtheim, Miriam, 34, 161, 178
Lindberg, David C., 40, 63
Livingstone, Alasdair, 49
Lloyd, G. E. R., 44, 48, 49, 50
Longman, Tremper, III, 8
Loud, Gordon, 20
Lowery, Daniel DeWitt, 17, 18, 36, 48
Luther, Martin, 18, 19, 80, 96–98, 102, 110, 123
Mann, Thomas W., 157, 158
Mattox, Mickey L., xiii, 96
McCabe, Robert V., 36, 37
McCalla, Arthur, 112, 113
McKim, Donald K., 114, 119–121
Merrick, James R. A., 121
Mettinger, Tryggve N. D., 169
Mickelsen, A. Berkeley, 16
Millard, Alan R., 66
Miller, Johnny V., 29, 44
Molen, Rami van der, 28, 29
Muller, Richard A., 108, 121
Muráň, Alexej, 166
Needham, Joseph, 55
Neugebauer, Otto, 51
Nobes, Gavin, 52, 53
Noll, Mark, 115
O'Connor, David, 51, 67
Ocker, Christopher, 92
Ogonowski, Zbigniew, 107
Olmo Lete, Gregorio del, 60
Oswalt, John N., 80
Otten, Heinrich, 60
Overland, Paul, 21
Panagiotaki, Georgia, 52, 53
Parker, R. A., 51, 155
Parker, Simon B., 60, 78
Parpola, Simo, 49, 140, 161
Pattemore, Stephen, 9, 14, 18, 22, 23, 39–40
Petersen, David L., 162
Pitard, Wayne T., 61
Plantinga, Alvin, 39
Pontratz-Leisten, Beate, 67
Poythress, Vern S., xiii, 57, 74, 75, 77, 78, 138, 142, 149, 176
Reventlow, Henning Graf, 82
Richardson, Peter, 121
Robins, Gay, 51
Rochberg, Francesca, 49, 50, 51, 59, 67
Roe, Peter G., 56
Rogers, Jack B., 114, 119–121
Rollston, Christopher A., 20
Rumelhart, David E., 17
Rutten, Jacques T. A. G. M. van, 158, 159
Sandy, Brent, 9, 131
Schmitt, Rüdiger, 73
Schroer, Silvia, 22, 45, 46, 47, 62, 76, 175
Scurlock, JoAnn, 49, 61, 155, 178, 179
Searle, John R., 7
Seely, Paul H., 46, 53, 54, 55, 57, 67, 75, 76, 77, 79
Segal, Robert A., 56
Shedd, William G. T., 117–118
Shupak, Nili, 21
Siegelova, Jana, 60
Silva, Moisés, 16, 116
Sim, Margaret G. A., 9
Smith, Mark S., 37, 38, 174
Snobelen, Stephen D., 86, 90, 91, 101, 102
Socinus, Faustus, 104–108
Soden, John M., 29, 44
Spalinger, Anthony J., 155
Sparks, Kenton L. 135, 138
Spelke, Elizabeth, 52
Sperber, Alexander, 13
Sperber, Dan, 5, 9–14, 16–18, 26, 36, 39, 53, 128, 131–33, 136, 150
Spinoza, Baruch, 108–110
Sproul, Barbara C., 56
Stadelmann, Luis I. J., 46, 81
Stemmer, Brigitte, 17
Sternberg, Karin, 42
Sternberg, Robert J., 42
Strong, Augustus Hopkins, 118–119, 126
Sunshine, Glenn, 102, 104, 105, 106
Talon, Philippe, 70
Toorn, Karel van der, 49
Trotter, David, 14

Tsumura, David Tashio, 47, 59, 72, 159–60, 167
Tucker, Gene M., 163
Tuell, Steven, 163
Uehlinger, Christoph, 21
Unger, Christoph, xiv, 8, 14, 53
Van de Mieroop, Marc, 50
Vanhoozer, Kevin J., xiii, 9, 14, 16, 125
Veenhof, K. R. 155
Vogt, Hermann J., 87, 88
Waltke, Bruce K., 176, 181
Walton, John H., 8, 9, 22, 25, 29, 33, 35, 46, 47, 66, 131, 148, 156, 158, 170–72, 174
Walton, Kim, 64
Warfield, Benjamin Breckinridge, 116–117, 119, 120, 136, 137
Watson, Rebecca S., 29, 30, 159
Weeks, Kent R., 51
Weeks, Noel K., 57, 59, 67, 79, 81
Weinfeld, Moshe, 156
Wellman, Henry M., 52
Wesselschmidt, Quentin F., 142
Wilson, Deirdre, 5, 9–14, 16–18, 26, 36, 39, 128, 131–33, 136, 150
Wilson, Robert R., 163
Winther-Nielsen, Nicolai, 175
Woodbridge, John D., 120
Woods, Christopher E., 63, 64, 65
Wright, J. Edward, 44, 46, 64, 73, 81
Young, Frances, 87, 88
Young, M. Jane, 56
Younker, Randall W., 57, 78, 81

www.ingramcontent.com/pod-product-compliance
Lightning Source LLC
Chambersburg PA
CBHW022013220426
43663CB00007B/1069